MASH Doctor in Vietnam

A Memoir of the War and After

REUEL S. LONG, M.D.

McFarland & Company, Inc., Publishers
Jefferson, North Carolina

LIBRARY OF CONGRESS CATALOGUING-IN-PUBLICATION DATA

Names: Long, Reuel S., 1942– author.
Title: MASH doctor in Vietnam : a memoir of the war and after /
   Reuel S. Long, M.D.
Description: Jefferson, North Carolina : McFarland & Company, Inc., Publishers,
   2023. | Includes index.
Identifiers: LCCN 2022051218 | ISBN 9781476690483
   (paperback : acid free paper) ∞
   ISBN 9781476648057 (ebook)
Subjects: LCSH: Long, Reuel S., 1942– | Vietnam War, 1961–1975—Medical care—
   United States. | United States. Army. Surgical Hospital, 27th | United States.
   Army—Medical personnel—Biography. | Vietnam War, 1961–1975—Personal
   narratives. | United States. Army. Evacuation Hospital, 95th. | Anesthesiologists—
   Michigan—Biography. | Flint (Mich.)—Biography. | BISAC: HISTORY /
   Wars & Conflicts / Vietnam War
Classification: LCC DS559.44 .L66 2023 | DDC 959.704/37—dc23/eng/20221025
LC record available at https://lccn.loc.gov/2022051218

BRITISH LIBRARY CATALOGUING DATA ARE AVAILABLE

ISBN (print) 978-1-4766-9048-3
ISBN (ebook) 978-1-4766-4805-7

On the cover: *top left to right* photograph of an operating room scene
where Reuel Long is providing anesthesia; Jim Dehlin in his hospital bed
at Camp Zama in Japan in January of 1971; *background* the 95th evacuation
hospital site located beneath Monkey Mountain

Printed in the United States of America

McFarland & Company, Inc., Publishers
   Box 611, Jefferson, North Carolina 28640
   www.mcfarlandpub.com

TABLE OF CONTENTS

Preface 1

The Call 3

The Early Career 6

Basic Training 22

The Respite 28

A Dark Day 32

Off to Nam 40

Getting Acclimated 43

The 27th MASH 47

A Special Triumph 66

A Special Discovery 69

Medevac 73

Unspeakable 76

Fire Support Base Mary Ann 79

R & R 82

Closing the Surg 87

Discovering the 95th Evacuation Hospital 91

TDY Pleiku 96

Okinawa 105

Family Leave 108

TDY Headquarters 113

Winding Down 117

Table of Contents

The Final Six   120

The Residency   127

Return to Flint   136

The Chelsea Years   150

The Bakery Blessing   173

Invincible   178

Closing Thoughts   209

Addendum: The M-16 Debacle: The Untold Story   213

Index   221

PREFACE

Most Vietnam veterans who survived the war went on to lead successful, productive lives, even though their war zone experiences would forever stay with them. Yes, there were some who did not come to grips with it all and succumbed to drugs or alcohol or mental issues and suicide, but that was not the story of the great majority. This memoir looks back at the Vietnam era and the years that followed through the stories of one physician and one casualty that he cared for, a man who survived major injuries from a booby trap but overcame it all and went on to live a remarkable life. I am so grateful for the determination of that casualty, Jim Dehlin, who found me 44 years after our paths had so tragically crossed in Vietnam and was willing to relive his experience for this writing.

There are two people who must be thanked and acknowledged as real gems, Carol and Judy. Carol (Meiklejohn) Dehlin, who got Jim through some rough times after Vietnam and became his life partner, is a real hero. My wife Judy, who cared for our four children while I was away and has always been my devoted partner in life, will always be my hero. Jim and I served in an unpopular war and were disdained by many.

Those who reviled us did not matter, and we needed no homecoming parade. Jim had Carol, whom he had met and married after his Vietnam service, and I had Judy. Life was complete. My thanks to my dear friend, Dan Sebastian, who was willing to share in the addendum what he witnessed regarding the investigation of the M-16 jamming problem at the beginning of his career. A special thanks to my good friend, Dr. Thomas Corbett, for his untiring dedication to the restitution and preservation of my photographs.

THE CALL

The date was July 12, 2014. The early afternoon temperature in Ann Arbor, Michigan, was 84°F, and the sky was clear. There was no breeze to speak of. I was riding my Grasshopper diesel mower near the back of my 30-acre gentleman farm located some 10 miles northwest of Ann Arbor. I had recently purchased the mower at a school auction in Adrian, Michigan. It had cleaned up pretty well. With all new filters, synthetic oil and new blades, it was running like a new one. I was quickly finding out that I could mow a lot more grass with a tank of diesel compared to a tank of gasoline. I was feeling more pleased with my purchase with each swath I cut. I had been retired from my anesthesia practice for about 10 years and enjoyed putting up hay, landscaping the farm and managing the fish in the half-acre pond. I was in the process of converting the pond from bluegill/bass to yellow perch, having stocked 50 yellow perch and a good supply of fathead minnows. I had fallen in love with the property after leaving the Army in 1972. It was the peat bog on the back of the property that had stirred my interest because I knew that it could probably be dredged to make a pond. The property was peaceful and spacious, a good place to raise a family, away from city life.

I was about half done with the mowing around the pond when I noticed my wife, Judy, coming toward me on her John Deere Gator. She waved for me to stop as she got close, and I shut the mower down.

"You need to come in and listen to a phone message," she proclaimed.

I asked who the message was from, and she said, "Somebody you took care of in 1970."

I quickly reminded her that I wasn't even in private practice in 1970, that I was in Vietnam in 1970. She looked at me with what I thought was a very serious expression while simply saying, "I know." I got on the Gator seat next to her, and she drove to the house without either of us

3

saying another word. We went into the house, and I went straight to the phone and punched in the code to listen to the messages. I sat on the edge of my recliner and listened in disbelief:

> "Hello Doctor Long. If this is the Dr. Long of 27 surgical hospital fame. This is a stab from the past. My name is Jim Dehlin. You treated me back in 1970. I just happened to run across your number, and I just wanted to make contact. My phone number is 906_____, Jim Dehlin. Thank you."

I was stunned. I knew exactly who it was. Jim was one of the early casualties I had cared for in December 1970. Only a few months earlier, I had been wondering what had happened to that kid from Flushing, Michigan, who had stepped on a booby trap and lost his legs during that first month I was in Vietnam. I had participated in a program in the spring at Ann Arbor Pioneer High School as part of a panel of Vietnam veterans who spent three hours at the school talking about their experiences in Vietnam and answering the students' questions. At that event, I had described how I had treated a guy from so close to home during my first month in country. After the school event, I had looked through my diary and found my notes about the kid from Flushing. Michigan, but I had not put his name in my diary. I did remember that he had

Reuel Long and Jim Dehlin at the Dexter Bakery in Dexter, Michigan. Reunited 45 years after crossing paths in Vietnam.

graduated from Flushing High School and had been quite an athlete, so I spent a lot of evenings over three months looking around the internet for posts about Flushing High School graduates who had served in Vietnam or any information that could give me a clue about what happened to him. I had no success. Now, he finds me. It had been almost 44 years since our paths had crossed in such tragic circumstances. The good Lord works in mysterious ways.

On September 4, 2015, Jim Dehlin and I met at the Dexter Bakery in Dexter, Michigan, for a 90-minute reunion and a discussion of what we had done since the war. We would stay in close contact after that meeting.

The Early Career

During the summer of 1964, Judy and I made several trips to Ann Arbor to look for a place to live during my medical school years. We found the rental rates to be pretty high, prohibitive for us, and eventually decided that it would be cheaper to buy a small place. We found a little, two-bedroom house on Oakwood, just outside of Pittsfield Village and near the Arborland shopping center. The house was priced at $10,000. We were able to buy it on a land contract with $1,000 down payment and monthly payments of $90.00. We managed to get moved in with our 15-month-old daughter, Lori, and the family dog (a cocker spaniel named Taffy) in time for the start of my freshman year. Judy had managed to land a job with the University Hospital billing department on the evening shift. The first semester was quite a schedule. With Lori in the back seat, Judy would drive me to the East Medical Building and drop me off for the day. Then late in the afternoon, she would load Lori in the car and head into the campus again, where she would pick me up. I would then drive to University Hospital and drop Judy off for her 5 p.m. to 11 p.m. shift and head back home to study and care for Lori. Then about 10:40 p.m. I would load Lori in the car and head back to University Hospital to pick up Judy and head home for the night. It was not an easy time. Funds were pretty tight. A trip to McDonald's was a real treat during those years. The Michigan 1964–65 basketball team generated a lot of excitement on campus with Cazzie Russell generating the most. The team would end up winning the Big Ten Championship and then make it all the way to the NCAA finals in the tournament, only to lose to UCLA.

During my second year of medical school, Judy developed some health problems. She began having abdominal pain and eventually became jaundiced. She was admitted to University Hospital and given a bed on a long surgical floor where the many beds were separated only by curtains hanging from metal rails. There was not much privacy. She began getting mixed messages about her condition from the numerous residents who attended her. After some initial frustrations with Judy's care, a medical school advisor made some phone calls and talked with one of the senior surgeons on staff, the surgeon with the best reputation, about taking over her care. He agreed, and it was a great relief for me to learn who would be taking care of my Judy. I did end up missing some lectures during that time but was able to get the lecture notes. The surgeon who took over Judy's care had her immediately moved to a private room. He quickly determined that Judy's symptoms were the result of gallstones that were small enough to cause some common bile duct obstruction. The surgery was quickly scheduled. It rained all day on the day of surgery. On the day of surgery, I parked my car at a metered spot in front of the hospital entrance, just down the street from the circle drop-off area. I completely forgot about the meter with all the distractions of the day. At the end of the day, I found the rain-soaked parking ticket tucked under my windshield-wiper blade. The surgeon performed a cholecystectomy and common bile duct exploration, placing a T-tube in the common duct. He described the gallbladder as a bag of sand that was spitting bits of sand into the common duct and causing partial obstructions of the duct. The surgery went well, and Judy was feeling pretty good a couple of days after the surgery except for her very limited diet. She was tired of the Jell-O and bland diet and was craving pizza. She begged me to call Domino's and order a pizza. I told her that I didn't think that was a good idea. When I told her that she might get in trouble, she was not concerned about it affecting her health, only about whether she could get a piece of pizza without her doctor finding out. It was about 8:00 p.m., and she assured me that the doctors had already made their rounds and would not be back and that she just wanted a little taste of the bread and cheese and would remove the pepperoni. These were the early years of Domino's Pizza. It had just started to take off a couple of years earlier, but they would deliver anywhere. I called and ordered a pepperoni pizza, and the delivery guy walked right past the nurses' station and brought it right to the room. Judy took a small piece of the pizza, removed the pepperoni, and was nibbling on a bit of the bread and cheese. I was eating a slice with extra pepperoni that had been removed from her piece of pizza. Then, to our great shock and dismay, seven white-clad gentlemen walked into the room. The senior surgical resident with his long, white coat was followed by a junior surgical resident, an intern and four medical students in their short, white coats. The senior resident's face immediately turned red as he looked at Judy and with a raised voice exclaimed, ""Mrs. Long, what are you doing?" Judy sheepishly set her pizza aside. He then looked at me and said, "You should know better." They all then marched out of the room.

After the white-clad crew left, Judy picked up her piece of bread and cheese and took a few more bites. She did express her concern about just how angry the chief staff surgeon might be when he found out what she had done. She was prepared to be scolded by the chief surgeon when he made his next rounds. Judy had a good night with no apparent effects from her failure to follow the prescribed diet. Then, morning came, and the chief surgeon showed up in her room on his morning rounds. He was alone without the residents and medical students. He was pretty easygoing. He smiled and asked her how she was feeling. She said that she felt fine. Then he asked her if she would like to go home. She said that she would love to go home. He smiled and responded with, "Well, if the pizza didn't kill you, you should probably go home." He discharged her to go home with the T-tube still in her common duct and indicated that he would remove her sutures and the T-tube when she came back to his office for a follow-up visit. The sutures and T-tube were removed, and she did very well. She did not have to face the angry senior resident again.

My parents, William and Mildred, along with my siblings, would drive down from Flint occasionally during those first two years of medical school. My dad would usually slip me a little grocery money during those visits. Judy's parents, Ralph and Huldah, would also drive from Flint for a visit occasionally. Our water heater bit the dust at one point, and Ralph bailed us out by buying us a new water heater and installing it. Judy's folks always brought us food.

It got to the point where Judy had to give up her job to care for Lori so I could concentrate on my studies. I got a little financial aid from the school along with a lot of loans. A second child, Amy, was born during my third year of school on March 25, 1967. Judy did some day care in the home to provide a little income. I engaged in a number of different jobs when time permitted. One such job was at the Holsum Bakery Outlet store located between State St. and Industrial Ave. near Stadium Blvd., a short distance from the football stadium. I washed and waxed the floors, cleaned the bathroom and washed the bread-delivery trucks. I even sold some Fuller Brush products for a time. I had a short stint selling sporting goods at a store on Washtenaw Ave. in Ypsilanti. On one of my shifts at the sporting goods store, I became quite impressed with the concentration of medical personnel in the area when a child fell out of a shopping cart and sustained a cut on his forehead. I ran to help the child but was beaten to the scene by a woman who identified herself as a nurse as she offered her help to the child's parent. Then a gentleman stepped up and looked over the shoulder of the nurse while identifying himself as a pediatrician. I immediately felt relief that I had kept my mouth shut as a lowly medical student. During my clinical junior and senior years, I pulled a lot of night shifts working for the nursing department, watching patients who needed someone in the room for observation at all times.

My medical school years were during a period of considerable racial unrest in the country. The summer between my junior and senior years was marked by the bloody Detroit riots which began on July 23, 1967. I was occupied for a time with getting my aunt, Earlene Holifield, my dad's sister, out of the riot area in Detroit, and settled in Swartz Creek, Michigan. She was one tough lady. She had kept her garage from burning down by hosing down the hot coals that had landed on the roof. She had defended herself from an intruder by confronting him with a handgun while saying, "I don't want to shoot you, but I will if you don't get out." He did leave, and no shots were fired. She was tough, but she needed help getting moved. We did get her settled in a small house with a little acreage in Swartz Creek where she had room for raising her Boston terriers. There was some talk about the Vietnam War among the medical students during my senior year with some arguing that everyone should refuse to serve when faced with that decision after graduation. I had not given the war much thought, having my hands full with just surviving and getting through medical school. The Tet offensive in Vietnam began during my last semester of medical school on January 31, 1968. It would continue through the first three months of my internship, ending on September 23, 1968. A third child, Timothy, was born on March 26, 1968. On April 4, 1968, near the end of my senior year, the racial atmosphere deteriorated more when Martin Luther King, Jr., was shot and killed.

During my senior year, my father, William Reuel Long, was teaching history at Flint Northern High School as well as serving as the full-time pastor at the Fenton Road Baptist Church in Flint, Michigan. He had taken the position with the school system to secure health insurance for the family since the church did not provide insurance for him or the family.

The stress load was heavy. He developed abdominal pain but stayed at home and refused to seek medical help right away. He eventually agreed to be taken to the hospital but was in very poor condition and too unstable for any surgery. I heard from my friend, Brent, who was a surgical resident in Flint at the time. He assured me that the surgeon in charge of my dad's care was excellent and that I should not be shaken by the fact that the surgeon had a stuttering problem. Dad was supported with intravenous fluids and antibiotics for almost two months and survived without surgery. At one point near the end of the two months, he was scheduled for drainage of what looked like a subhepatic abscess on the X-ray. Then, on the night before the scheduled surgery, he had a little abdominal pain, and the abscess disappeared, having drained spontaneously into the bowel. The surgeon was clear that Dad had perforated his bowel somewhere, but it was never determined just where in the bowel the problem was located. It was a stressful time during my senior year, and I was not certain my dad would survive, but he did.

Near the end of my senior year, I got another rather unsettling call from my friend, Brent. Brent had been a few years ahead of me at the medical school and was now doing his surgical residency at McLaren Hospital in Flint. He called me to pass on some shocking news. The light had come on at the hospital, indicating that an autopsy was taking place. The system was set up to notify interns and residents in case they wanted to observe. Brent had responded to the notification and gone to the autopsy room. He was shocked to see the occupant of the autopsy table, a 49-year-old science professor that we had both taken classes from at Flint College (now University of Michigan-Flint). He had died of a stroke.

Being married with children, I was not eligible for the draft. That all changed with my graduation from medical school in 1968. The medical degree changed my status and came with new obligations where the government was concerned. Technically speaking, the government declined to acknowledge that a doctor draft existed. Doctors were considered to be "obligated volunteers." So, doctors would be tracked by selective service and then be assigned to reserve units. In what was known as the Berry Plan, some were allowed to continue residency training rather than being called to active duty right away after internship. Others were activated right after internship as general medical officers as the need arose. Some were activated in the middle of their residency training if the need arose. The notice to report for active duty indicated that the recipient was an "obligated volunteer."

After graduation from medical school, I went to McLaren General Hospital in Flint, Michigan, along with three of my medical school classmates, where I did a rotating internship from July 1, 1968, to June 30, 1969. One of the older doctors who had participated in recruiting the four of us to come to McLaren for our internships had promised me, "Son, we will teach you your bread-and-butter medicine here." I had an obligation to return to Flint that my three classmates did not have. The Genesee County Medical Society had seen fit to loan this son of a Baptist minister with no funds for medical school, enough money to cover his tuition. One of the unwritten conditions stated at the time the loan was made was that I return to Flint to practice for at least two years. The strategy seemed to be that if someone came to the area and practiced for two years, there was a good chance that they would stay. The loan still had to be fully repaid.

The internship allowed for two weeks of paid vacation during the year. I used a week of my vacation time to pick up a few extra bucks by substitute teaching at my old junior high school in Flint, McKinley Junior High School. It was an eye-opener! I was assigned to an eighth-grade science class. When the dean of boys showed me to my classroom on my first day, he informed me that I was the third substitute for that class in three days. The other substitutes had refused to return. He showed me to the room and handed me a paddle that looked more like a club. It was almost as long as a baseball bat, and the paddle portion was a good inch thick. There were a lot of names engraved into the wood. As the dean turned and began walking away, he said, "Keep it close, and feel free to use it to defend yourself. If anybody attacks you, hit 'em with it until they don't move any more."

I wasn't sure if the dean of boys was just having a bit of fun with me and being melodramatic or really giving me a serious warning. I had been a student in this pleasant place only 12 years earlier. Well, it didn't take very long for me to discover the truth. I addressed each class regarding my expectations regarding behavior and informed each class that there would be some stability as I would be their teacher for the entire week. The first class period was pretty uneventful. Then the bell rang, and I was confronted with the second hour group of students which brought new challenges. Twenty minutes into the second hour, the students were taking a little written quiz. I noticed that one of the male students had pulled his desk out of the row and pushed it right up next to the girl in front of him where he was now sitting and proceeding to copy her work. The young man who had decided to conduct himself in such a brazen way was an 18-year-old kid who was about 6 feet 2 inches tall. I went to the young man and asked him to stand up. When he got out of the desk, I pushed it back in line and indicated that he needed to do his own work. At that moment, the kid raised both of his clenched fists and announced, "I'm going to kick your ass!" It was immediately clear that the threat was serious and not new to this group, as all the students began quickly moving their desks to the walls. Those parting words of the dean of boys came back to me, and I took a couple of steps backward toward the teacher's desk and grasped the paddle/club that I had laid on the desk. The big, black kid facing me with clenched fists was a pretty imposing figure. He was bigger than me and pretty muscular. He suddenly took a step toward me with his fists still raised and clenched. I brought the paddle around in front of me, grasping the handle firmly with both hands. The adrenaline was flowing. My face felt hot, my heart was pounding, my hands were shaking. I didn't want a fight. I didn't want to hurt anybody, but I was determined that I was not going to take a beating from this punk either. I looked right into his eyes and locked onto them while saying, "If you make any attempt to hit me, I will bash your skull in. The smartest thing you can do if you want to live is walk over to the door, walk through it, and don't come back." As I stood there, ready to defend myself but hoping I would not have to, I noticed that my potential assailant was also shaking. After a minute that seemed like several, the kid took my advice, dropped his arms and walked through the door, and I never saw him again. As he left the room, the students responded with a prolonged "ooooooh," while moving their desks back into the customary rows.

I faced no more physical threats during my week of substitute teaching, but there was one other incident that shed more light on how the school was functioning. During one of the classes on that first day, one young man yelled out and asked if he could throw something across the room to the wastebasket. I told him that he could not. He ignored me and threw the stuff anyway. I then told the smart-ass kid to pick the stuff up and take it down to the dean of boys' office and tell him why I sent him there. The dean of boys soon returned with the kid and informed him in front of the class that he would receive one swat for his conduct. The kid apparently knew what he was in for and began begging not to be swatted. The dean then gave the kid a choice saying, "You can take one swat now, or you can go home and tell your parents about your conduct and get two swats tomorrow. You see, if you delay, there is interest." The kid opted for the one swat. He was taken just outside the classroom door which was left open so the other students could appreciate the extent of the punishment. He was instructed to remove everything from his back pockets, spread his feet and place his hands up against the wall. The dean then laid on an impressive swat to which the entire class responded with a prolonged "ooooooooh!" There were no other discipline problems during my week of substitute teaching. I soon learned that the young man who had physically threatened me had been suspended from school, an action which had destroyed the school's basketball tournament chances, because he was the star of the team. He should have been the star of the ninth-grade team. He was 18 years old. It was good to get back to the hospital and the internship duties.

The rotating internship involved time in surgery, internal medicine, labor and delivery and emergency medicine. I also spent a few weeks working in the office of a general practitioner in Flushing, Michigan. I enjoyed the general practice time the most. The fall of 1968 turned out to be an enjoyable time. There were four of us who had gone to medical school in Ann Arbor and were now doing our internships together. There was another intern who was from Missouri. Well, when the regular baseball season ended, it was the Detroit Tigers facing the St. Louis Cardinals in the World Series. The intern from Missouri made it clear to all that his Cardinals were going to put the big hurt on the Tigers, and he was riding high when his Cardinals defeated the Tigers 4 to 0 in the first game. He was still quite confident even when the Tigers came back in game 2 and won by an 8 to 1 score. He was talking pretty good trash and counting out the Tigers with confidence as the Tigers went down to defeat in games 3 and 4 by 7 to 3 and 10 to 1 scores. He was proclaiming that the fat lady was about to sing every day as the Tigers went on to defeat the high-flying Cardinals over the next three games by scores of 5 to 3, 13 to 1 and 4 to 1. Mickey Lolich came through for the euphoric Michigan interns by pitching three complete game wins, allowing the Tigers to take the Series for the first time since 1945. The intern from Missouri had to put up with a lot of well-deserved trash talk for quite a while.

Early in November 1968, I received a notice from the Army dated 31 October 1968. The letterhead read:

DEPARTMENT OF THE ARMY
HEADQUARTERS FIFTH UNITED STATES ARMY
FORT SHERIDAN, ILLINOIS 60037

The letter was addressed to First Lieutenant Reuel Shannon Long with the appropriate Social Security number. Item 1 on the letter read: "By direction of the President you are appointed Reserve Commissioned officer of the Army, effective upon your acceptance, in the grade and with the service number shown in address above. Your branch and component assignment are shown after A above." Next to A it read Medical Corps, USAR, and next to B were the numbers 3100 which was the MOS number assigned to a general medical officer. The letter went on to instruct that the enclosed Oath of Office-Military Personnel was to be executed and returned which would serve as my acceptance of the appointment. The letter was signed by Virginia L. Piggott, Major, AGC Asst. Adjutant General. I signed the papers and returned them, wondering how long before I would be ordered to active duty.

After completion of my internship, I spent all of July 1969, working in the emergency room at the little hospital at Gaylord, Michigan. I had arranged with the hospital administrator to work 24 hours on and

24 hours off for the whole month of July. I had rented a cabin at a nearby lake where the family was to stay, and I planned to enjoy my off days at the lake with the family. Well, when I reported for my first day in the emergency room at Gaylord, I was greeted by the hospital administrator who told me that he had some good news and some bad news for me. He started by saying that I would have a better income for the month of July than he had promised. He then went on to explain that the other doctor who was supposed to alternate shifts with me had backed out, and he had not been able to find a replacement. It turned out to be a pretty grueling month. I only made it out to the lake for a few short visits. The little emergency department did attract a little major trauma which usually had to be stabilized and sent on to a larger facility. Most of what I had to contend with was fractures, lacerations, superficial infections, and a lot of fish-hook removal. One fish-hook case was quite memorable. A 35-year-old man presented in the emergency room with all three treble hooks of a brand new Rapala plug firmly embedded in his scalp. He looked pretty angry as I inquired as to how this had happened. Without uttering a word, he simply pointed toward the woman standing next to him, never turning to look at her. She dropped her head, looking pretty sheepish. It was all I could do not to laugh. I wanted to congratulate her for the biggest catch of the day but thought better of it and set about the task of removing the unwanted adornment after the administration of some local anesthesia.

It was during that busy month at Gaylord, when I had no access to a television, that Apollo 11 took Neil Armstrong and Buzz Aldrin to the moon where both men would set foot. I had my ear to a radio on July 20, 1969, to hear Armstrong utter those famous words, "One small step for man, one giant leap for mankind." It was a busy month which did result in some much-needed income for the family. Near the end of that July in 1969, police were finally able to identify the serial killer, John Norman Collins, who had terrorized the Ann Arbor/Ypsilanti area for two years, and he was arraigned on murder charges on August 1, 1969, and was eventually sentenced to life in prison, lifting a dark cloud from the Washtenaw County community in Michigan.

After the month in the little emergency room at Gaylord, Michigan, I returned to Flint where I had agreed to work for a four-man general practice group in Swartz Creek, Michigan. I had agreed to work in the office, seeing patients for a flat daily fee. The office was quite busy. It was a friendly staff, and I got along well with all four of the physicians. The one physician who spoke for the group regarding financial matters informed me at the beginning that my workload would be reviewed after a month and that my daily fee would be adjusted up or down based on the income I produced for the group. During my time at the Swartz Creek office, I encountered some abbreviations that were completely foreign to me. On one day, I interviewed a patient, examined her regarding her complaints, then excused myself to seek out one of the other physicians who had previously seen her and written down her chief complaint as "TATT." I was informed that it stood for "tired all the time." On another day, I approached the same physician to inquire about a diagnosis he had abbreviated on a chart simply as "BTHOOM" which I found out stood for "beats the hell out of me." Even though I got a chuckle out of it all, it did cross my mind that I would not want to have to explain such abbreviations in a legal setting.

After a few weeks, I was working some pretty long hours and seeing a lot of patients for my flat daily fee. One of the girls working the desk told me that I was seeing more patients than anybody in the group. I had a little talk with the treasurer of the group and asked if they would be adjusting my pay upward in view of my workload. He responded with a laugh and held up the middle finger of one hand while saying, "Here's your raise." I soon discovered that I was being used to cover the office while the other doctors in the group were covering shifts working in the emergency rooms for twice what they were paying me. I rapidly began cutting back my time at the Swartz Creek office in favor of working the emergency rooms and seeing patients at the small office I had put together at my house.

Knowing that I could receive a notice to report for active duty at any time, I spent the next 10 months working shifts in the emergency rooms at McLaren and St. Joseph Mercy Hospital in Flint, Michigan. I also had a small private practice which I operated out of my house in the residential district where we lived at the south end of Flint. I had converted the basement into a small medical office. There was a side entrance to the house that allowed direct access to the basement office. The year in the war zone of the Flint emergency rooms would serve me well for some of what I would face during my military service, but it could not prepare me for all of it. Knifings, shootings and expressway trauma were plentiful. Emergency room medicine was not a medical specialty at that time. The two Flint emergency rooms were covered by private-practicing physicians who took turns covering the emergency rooms. Most of them preferred to be working in their offices and were eager to offer me their shifts, and I found that I could have all the shifts that I wanted to work. On one night about 2:00 a.m., I got a call from that old doctor who had promised me that I would learn my bread-and-butter medicine if I came to McLaren for my internship. He called to ask me if I could relieve him in the emergency room at St. Joseph Mercy Hospital so he could attend a delivery back at McLaren. I agreed to do it, got dressed and headed to St. Joe. The old doc was waiting at the emergency room door, thanked me as I entered, and quickly headed for his car. Two ambulances arrived before I could change into scrubs. Both ambulances were loaded with expressway trauma and presented me with some challenges. One ambulance crew brought one patient in, completely covered with a sheet, indicating that he was deceased. I felt for a femoral pulse, and to my surprise, there was a faint one. I pulled back the sheet to find a very pale patient with a gaping, open scalp that was not bleeding, and a mouth full of blood and loose teeth. I quickly performed a tracheotomy, and the patient started breathing. I then secured good intravenous lines and started pushing fluids, and the patient started bleeding. I next clamped the open scalp with about a dozen hemostats and started some blood. I managed to get the bleeding controlled and the scalp closed. Surgeons arrived, approved the tracheotomy work, and took over the care of the patient in the ICU. Despite the staff's best efforts, the patient would expire the next day from the brain damage he had sustained in the accident. One of the emergency room nurses told me that the old doctor that I had relieved had not gotten a call from McLaren labor and delivery. He had just heard the call about the trauma on the way to the emergency room. When I checked at McLaren the next day, I was able to confirm that the old boy had not been back to McLaren the previous night. I never said anything to him about it. He really was not comfortable in the emergency rooms and should have declined to work there.

The trauma work was grueling, but the most emotional and gut-wrenching work was dealing with relatives of victims who had been brought in dead on arrival (DOA) from accidents. For me, one of the toughest that will always be with me took place at St. Joseph Mercy in Flint. It was after dark on a Friday evening when two boys, ages 15 and 14, arrived DOA. They had been walking on the shoulder on East Bristol Rd., a two-lane highway. They were en route to a party store to buy some candy and pop. A truck had gone off the road and onto the shoulder and killed both of them. One boy was missing the entire top of his skull at about the hairline. It was wide open and empty of any brain tissue. I had to call the parents to come to the emergency room. I called the number I had been given and found that I had the mother on the phone. I informed her that her boys had been brought to the emergency room at St. Joseph Mercy Hospital and asked her to come to the emergency room. With panic in her voice, she asked how they were. I told her that I was not allowed to discuss anything about a patient's condition over the phone. Her anxiety was increasing as she insisted on knowing their condition, but I just told her that she needed to come to the hospital. With the call concluded, I had to figure out what to do when the parents would, no doubt, need to see the bodies and identify them. The body with the top of the skull missing was too much for any parent to look at. I bunched up enough packing material to fill the empty cranium and then placed a lot of towels around the head to hide the mutilation beneath.

When the parents arrived along with several other relatives, I had the awful task of breaking the bad news that both boys were deceased. The screaming and crying that ensued was gut-wrenching. The mother required some sedation. She eventually insisted on seeing the bodies. As much as I had tried to hide the devastating head trauma, I was worried that the mother might reach up and dislodge the towels and view the empty skull. So, I told her that I would take her to the room to view the bodies, but she had to agree not to touch either of them with the police investigation still ongoing. She agreed, but I still held her arm during the entire viewing to make sure she did not compound her psychological trauma. When the viewing was over, I took the mother back to the room where the rest of the family had gathered. I now had an emergency room that was backing up a bit. I felt drained and sat down in the dictation cubicle. At that point I suddenly realized that my hands had a tremor that I could not control. Ten minutes went by before I started working on the backlog of patients. At the end of the shift, I noticed that the tremor was gone.

The television evening news was always filled with reports on the war in Vietnam. On September 2, 1969, Ho Chi Minh, the man who had become president of North Vietnam in 1945, died of heart failure. His death would not deter the North in their attempt to rid their country of the Americans. He was succeeded by Le Duan, who became the head of the North Vietnamese Communist Party and was more radical and more determined than his predecessor. The war would continue and eventually have a dramatic impact on me and my family. During the month of September 1969, there were 510 United States KIAs (killed in action). While I was facing the trauma cases in the emergency rooms in Flint, Michigan, the United States war casualties kept mounting up each month with 495 KIAs in October, 480 KIAs in November and 474 KIAs in December 1969.

The emergency rooms were always busy on New Year's Eve, the increased workload due in great measure to the increase in the consumption of alcohol during the holidays. December 31, 1969, was no exception. Doctors who had shifts that day were always eager to unload them. I ended up with three shifts between two emergency rooms that day. I covered the 8 a.m. to 5 p.m. shift at McLaren. An ambulance crew then took me across town to the St. Joseph Mercy emergency room where I covered the 5 p.m. to 11 p.m. shift. The same crew then got me back to McLaren for the 11 p.m. to 8 a.m. shift. It was a very busy 24 hours with a lot of trauma cases at both hospitals, but there was one light moment. Near the end of the day shift at McLaren, I walked into a cubicle to see a young man who was complaining about back pain. I recognized him as somebody I had seen before for the same complaints. I had suggested that he see his primary care doctor and had not prescribed any medications for him after the examination. I also noticed his arms had the usual tracks of a drug user. He had clearly assumed that he could come to a busy emergency room and easily get a narcotic prescription from a doctor with a very busy workload. When I made it clear that I would not be prescribing any narcotics for him, he jumped up with no signs of pain, grabbed his belongings, jerked his coat over his shoulder, and stormed out of the emergency room. I documented his behavior on the chart and went on to the next patient. I was about an hour into my evening shift across town at St. Joseph Mercy when I pulled back the curtain on one of the exam cubicles to find the drug seeker I had seen earlier at McLaren. The fellow looked up from the exam table with a look of disgust as I said, "It's just not your lucky day, is it?" Again, the fellow grabbed his belongings and stormed out of the emergency room while muttering obscenities.

Among the alcohol-related cases that night was a fellow who presented at St. Joseph Mercy, smiling and clearly not feeling any pain, as a result of his blood alcohol level. When I pulled back the curtain to see what the challenges would be, I found a man in no acute distress, breathing partially through a hole in his neck and with large contusions on both sides of his neck. It seems that, under the influence of alcohol, the fellow had decided that it was a good idea to ride his snowmobile through the backyards in his neighborhood, the alcohol having erased from his brain the hazard that clotheslines could present. He had indeed encountered that very hazard and had managed to perform a tracheotomy on himself, amazingly without any major bleeding except for that associated with the large bruises over the major vessels in his neck. After examination, I determined that his diminished mental capacities were not the result of any diminished circulation to his head but only the result of his basic IQ and alcohol level, so I turned him over to a general surgeon for monitoring and follow-up care.

On one busy shift at the little emergency room at McLaren, I noticed that there was a loud, painful groan coming from the waiting room every few minutes. I went to the admitting clerk across from the waiting area and inquired, "Who is doing all the groaning over there?"

The clerk pointed out a large, black girl who had arrived with her mother and was complaining of abdominal pain. I instructed the clerk to have her brought back to an exam room right away. The clerk responded by saying that it was not her turn. I told her that I thought it just might be her turn. With the mother waiting in the waiting room, the large girl was taken to an exam cubicle and put in a gown. I took a nurse with me to have a look at her. I put my hand on her abdomen as I interviewed her and asked if there was any chance that she could be pregnant. She answered saying, "Oh no. That's not possible." Before I could ask another question, she began to moan loudly, and I could feel her uterus contracting. I had her promptly transported to labor and delivery. It wasn't long before word came back that she delivered a boy.

On another shift at McLaren, a man about 40 years of age presented to the emergency room with a gash on his forehead and holding a rag pressed against his forehead. I entered the cubicle with the usual question, "Well, what brings you to the emergency room today?" With slurred speech, the fellow answered, "I drove myself." I continued, "OK, what can we do for you?" The fellow then dropped the rag from his forehead saying, "I need to get this fixed," pointing to his forehead. I then asked him how it happened and got a little chuckle with the answer when he replied, "I fell off a stool and hit my head on the stool next to me." I soon learned the location of the bar where the fall had taken place. After making repairs, I asked him who we could call to give him a ride home. He refused to cooperate with us regarding a ride, insisting he could drive himself home and leaving the emergency room for his car over our objections.

One phenomenon that I observed at the McLaren emergency room occurred primarily on Sundays while most churches were in session or shortly after most morning services had concluded. Several times, patients were brought in, having had a seizure or feeling like something was wrong that they didn't understand. They routinely had been brought in from one of the Pentecostal churches. The consistent history was that the congregation had been worked up pretty good with claims of "speaking in tongues." I would administer the usual treatment for hyperventilation by having these patients breathe into a paper bag until they started feeling better. I was quite impressed with the effects of the alkalosis that could be created by hyperventilation.

In addition to the emergency work, I also did a number of deliveries in the spring of 1970 for a general practitioner who had been diagnosed with multiple sclerosis and was unable to continue delivering babies. It was during this time from April 11 to April 17, 1970, that the whole world was on edge and mesmerized by the Apollo 13 space mission and the realization that the chance for survival of the astronauts after an explosion on board the spacecraft was not good. A lot of people were praying for the astronauts and closely following the regular briefings about conditions on the spacecraft. The whole country seemed to take a sigh of relief and celebrate when the three men returned safely to earth, beating the odds. It was certainly a distraction from the Vietnam War news, and President Nixon proclaimed the mission a success even though the planned moon landing had to be aborted.

Nixon's escalation of the Vietnam War, with his approval of the bombing in Cambodia, resulted in a protest at Kent State University in Kent, Ohio, on May 4, 1970. The Ohio National Guard was called out to maintain order at Kent State, but things could not have gone much worse. Shooting erupted during the protest, resulting in four students being killed and nine being wounded with one of them being paralyzed. That event galvanized antiwar sentiment across the country even more. About two weeks later, on May 19, 1970, I delivered my fourth child, Jill Elizabeth, at home. Judy wanted to stay at home for the delivery. One of the ambulance crews that I had gotten pretty close to was nearby in case they were needed, but all went well. That afternoon, Judy was out in the yard, looking for the oldest child, Lori. The lady next door noticed that Judy no longer appeared to be pregnant and inquired, "When did you have your baby?" Judy replied to the astonishment of the neighbor, "This morning. Do you want to come in and see her?" The neighbor did come into the house to get a look at little Jill.

Just a couple of days before Jill was born, I had received the letter that I knew would eventually come. It was dated 15 May 1970. The first line read: "TC112. The above individual is, with his/her consent, ordered to ACTIVE DUTY in the grade held as a reserve officer of the Army. Individual is assigned as indicated and will proceed from his current location in sufficient time to report as indicated on the date specified." The letter indicated that I was to report by 6 July 1970 for a temporary assignment at the U.S. Army Field Service School, Brooke Army Medical Center, Fort Sam Houston, Texas 78234. The letter indicated that the course would be about five weeks' duration and that I would enter active duty with the rank of captain. I smiled as I read the portion of the letter labeled: "Active duty commitment." It read: "Obligated volunteer officer 2 years." The inevitable trip to Vietnam was confirmed in the lower portion of the letter where it read: "Assigned to USARV Transient Detachment. (P5-WOBR-AA) APO SF 96384 for further assignment." It was that APO SF language that caught my attention. It stood for All Points Overseas, San Francisco, through which all mail to and from Vietnam was routed.

I started the process of notifying all the patients that I had been seeing at my home-office practice that I would not be able to continue participating in their care. Only one of my patients found this news to be a problem that resulted in a little panic. It was a fellow who had come to my office after being involved in a little fender bender. His complaints initially were a little neck and back pain. His physical examination had been pretty unremarkable. I had encouraged him to give it a little time and use a heating pad and some over-the-counter pain relievers. He would show up at my office at least once a week, insisting on being examined. After three such visits, I asked him why he kept coming back to the office when there was nothing he really needed to be treated for. The fellow leaned over like he was going to tell me a secret and said, "Look Doc, my lawyer told me that I should come in and see you at least once a week in order to make a record of my complaints. He's going to sue the guy that hit my car. He said I should run up as much of a medical bill as I can." When I told him that it was going to be quite a challenge since I only charged $6.00 for an office call, he admitted that he had been going to the emergency rooms at McLaren and St. Joseph Mercy to run up bills there as well. I told him that I was not interested in seeing him again about anything related to his car accident. When he found out that I was closing my practice and leaving for active military duty, he told his lawyer who then made a phone call to me requesting that I summarize my medical records as well as the emergency room records related to the complaints and treatments of the fender bender case. I was pretty disgusted by the whole matter. The lawyer indicated that he would be happy to pay me for my written report once he received it. I immediately informed the lawyer that the fee for the report would be $100 and that it would have to be paid in advance. He pretended to be shocked and asked if I didn't trust him. I simply responded, "You are a lawyer, right?" He agreed to send the check. I told him that he would get the report after the check cleared. I reviewed the emergency room visits at McLaren and St. Joseph Mercy and summarized them along with my office notes. The final statement in my report to the lawyer declared, "There are no physical findings to support this patient's complaints."

Basic Training

Less than two months after my youngest child was born, I reported for active duty to the U.S. Army Medical Field Service School at Fort Sam Houston, Texas, carrying my papers that indicated my assignment for duty in Vietnam. I had never flown on a commercial airline. While in junior high school, I had been taken on a short flight out of Bishop Airport in a two-seater Taylorcraft plane by one of the church members who was a pilot and a certified inspector. My flight from Bishop Airport in Flint, Michigan, to San Antonio, Texas, for basic training was my first experience with flying on a commercial airline.

I was quite impressed with the military approach for educating and training doctors for functioning in a war zone. When it came to the classroom work, the Army knew how to do it. Unlike too many of the classroom lectures in a university setting where some graduate student or PhD candidate was more interested in demonstrating just how smart they were and how stupid the students were or what their research project was all about, the Army doctor giving the lecture was all about making sure you really learned what you needed. Whether it was about treating malaria or snakebites or some other disease you had not treated or how important it was that there be no deviation from the routine debridement and delayed wound closure of battlefield wounds, the approach was always the same. Every subject was covered three times during a lecture. Every lecturer would start by telling the group what they were going to learn. Then he would present the material. Finally, he would summarize by concluding with, "And now, here is what you have learned today." It was all about repetition of what was important. There were a number of printed handouts. One of the pamphlets dealt entirely with the treatment of snakebites one might encounter in Vietnam.

I felt sorry for the officer who had the assignment of trying to get a bunch of doctors, who really didn't want to be in the Army, to act like officers and form up in ranks and learn to march. It was not

22

a matter of the doctors being untrainable. Most were not sympathetic with the continuation of the Vietnam War and were in the mood to be passive-aggressive. The entire group would never assemble on time. Many would intentionally show up 10 minutes late. The officer in charge would announce that all were to be present at 1400 hours and not 1410, but he was never able to get 100 percent compliance, to his great frustration. These were all doctors with orders for Vietnam, so the general attitude was, "What are they going to do to us if we don't cooperate, send us to Vietnam?" As for me, I did always show up on time and do my part to go through the marching exercises. My dad was a World War II veteran, and I recalled his stories about the long hours of marching in basic training and the marching across France. The marching the doctors were required to engage in was nothing.

The need to train a lot of doctors for the war effort was great enough that the base could not house all of them, so the military reserved rooms at a lot of the motels in the San Antonio area. Judy was able to leave the children in the care of grandparents for a few weeks and fly to San Antonio, where she was able to stay at my motel room, and I could join her after the lectures were all completed for the day. Our time together was interrupted by the three days I spent at Camp Bullis, where the Army tried to give the doctors a taste of what it was like to be a real soldier. Camp Bullis was a military training reservation just northwest of San Antonio. It was about 28,000 acres in size. The doctors were loaded into buses and taken to Camp Bullis for three days of exercises. We all shot M-14s. They ran us through day and night map courses. Then there was the crawling under barbed wire and around explosives with live ammunition flying overhead during the night. The tracers could be seen flying overhead, but it was hard to judge just how far overhead they actually were. They looked close to me. One of the guys crawling next to me yelled to me, "I'll bet you could stand up, and they would still be over your head. They wouldn't dare kill a doctor doing this crap." I yelled back, "I don't think I want to test them." The officers in control of the exercise indicated that the crawling under the live fire would continue until all participants were able to get through the course. With the first attempt, one poor guy didn't make it. They finally turned on the flood lights and went out on the course and cut him out of the barbed wire. There really were not any physical fitness requirements for doctors who were obligated to volunteer for active duty, and the poor guy caught up in the wire weighed about 300 pounds and had a belly that could not get under the wire. Once he was freed from the wire, the announcement came that everybody would have to do the course again because not everybody had made it through on the first try. The announcement was greeted with a loud chorus of booing. We were all marched to the starting line again where we got down on our bellies, the flood lights were turned off, and the firing began again. I crawled through the sand and under all the wire again. It seemed that we had all finished when the flood lights all came on again. We all learned again that the same fat doctor was hung up in the barbed wire again. The powers that be finally decided that we had all had enough and allowed us to hit the showers and turn in on our cots for the night.

The day map course presented another opportunity for some mischief by some of the doctors. During the day map course, a helicopter would occasionally fly over to check on everybody. The pilot was a friendly guy who had pretty good rapport with the doctors. At one point, four of the docs on the map course positioned themselves so that they could moon the helicopter pilot just as he came over a rise. Well, it turned out that the pilot was not alone on that particular flyover but had some of the brass with him. To say that the brass were not amused would be an understatement of undetermined magnitude. It was good to get back to the motel and a soft bed after three nights on a cot at Bullis.

Lectures and marching continued back in town. Lectures were occasionally interrupted by officers who would attempt to entice some of the doctors into joining special units, even units that had to jump out of planes or helicopters. Such sales pitches did not meet with a lot of success. On one fateful day, Colonel Mendenhall came to one of the lectures and identified himself as the Chief of Anesthesia and Operative Services at Brooke Army Hospital in San Antonio. He said that he was there to address general medical officers with orders for deployment to Vietnam. He said, "If there are any general medical officers who have orders for Vietnam who would like to possibly spend at least part of their tour, not out in the field and heat, but working in an operating room that might even have an air conditioner, come and see me over at Brooke Hospital at 1:00 p.m. today." One of my buddies sitting next to me said, "I don't think he said anything about jumping out of an airplane with a good engine, did he?" I indicated that I didn't hear anything about jumping out of an airplane either. As soon as the lecture concluded, my buddy and I headed over to Brooke Hospital to see what Colonel Mendenhall had to offer. My buddy and I were the first to arrive and soon found ourselves at the front of a very long line outside the office of Colonel Mendenhall. I was the first to be interviewed. Colonel Mendenhall, a man who appeared to be about my father's age, introduced himself and offered me a chair in his office. His first question to me was, "Would you be interested in an anesthesiology residency?" I immediately replied, "No, I would not. If that is what I have to do for what you are offering, then I'm not interested." Colonel Mendenhall laughed and quickly replied, "Don't worry. You don't have to agree to get involved with our residency program. What were you doing in civilian life?" My prompt response was, "I was in general practice and working in emergency rooms, and that is what I want to go back to after my time in the Army." Smiling as though he knew something that I was not able to fully appreciate, he went on, "You know, I was in general practice before I got into anesthesia. I think you would love anesthesia. It's like having your own physiology project on the table every day you are in the operating room. What I am offering you is a four-month OJT (on-the-job training) program in anesthesia before going to Vietnam. You will still be going to Vietnam. Are you interested?" I said, "Sure, with no strings attached." "No strings," he replied. He then asked if I preferred any particular part of the country for the OJT training. I told him that it did not matter to me. He then went on, "Well, I think you would enjoy some time at the West Point Military Academy. There is a little hospital on the base where they operate on cadets, mostly for orthopedic injuries, but there are a lot of retirees around the base. So, there is a good variety of cases. There is one anesthesiologist there whose job it will be to train you over the next four months." He got together all my identification essentials and made the arrangements. I went back to the motel and gave Judy the good news that I would not be leaving for Vietnam for at least four months and told her what I had signed on for. There was a total of eight general medical officers selected that day for OJT anesthesia training. Four of us were married guys, and four were single. Only the four married guys ended up being deployed to Vietnam immediately after training.

As basic training began to wind down, the powers that be arranged for photographs to be taken of the various units. I was in the unit that managed to bring out the displeasure of the brass once again. When my group's picture was taken, four of the guys on the back row were standing together and shooting the bird at the unknowing photographer. It was not picked up until the photos were developed. The brass was not happy. Word got around that the four guys ended up with changed deployment orders. Ordinarily, after serving in Vietnam, one would get some choices about where to finish out their time after Vietnam. Not for these dudes. Word was that their orders were changed to Korea after which they would do their Vietnam time.

The marching continued to take place on a large quadrangle of asphalt surrounded by office buildings that were occupied by the brass. On the final day before graduation, some 200 doctors were marching in the heat below these offices. It was a hot summer day, and the office windows were all open. All at once, somebody among the doctor ranks yelled out,

"JODIE, JODIE, DON'T BE BLUE!"

The bulk of the group shouted back, "JODIE, JODIE, DON'T BE BLUE!"

It continued as the prompter shouted, "ONE MORE DAY, AND WE'LL BE THROUGH!"

Now even more participants replied, "ONE MORE DAY, AND WE'LL BE THROUGH!"

A lone voice continued, "ONE MORE DAY, AND THAT'LL BE IT!"

In unison, all now seemed to respond, "ONE MORE DAY, AND THAT'LL BE IT!"

And the final proclamation, "NO MORE OF THIS CHICKEN SHIT!"

Just as the group arrived beneath the general's office, all proclaimed, "NO MORE OF THIS CHICKEN SHIT!"

What were they going to do with 200 doctors that they desperately needed? Send them to Vietnam?

The next morning was supposed to be a formal graduating

Long family photograph in Flint, Michigan, after basic training, just prior to leaving for training at the West Point Military Academy Hospital.

ceremony with pomp and circumstance and speeches from the brass. All the doctors were assembled in a large auditorium. A long row of empty folding chairs was arranged across the stage. There was a single lectern with a microphone and a number of flags behind the chairs, the most prominent being the higher-positioned American flag. The poor MSC officer who had been assigned the task of teaching the doctors how to march was on the stage. As the time approached for the ceremony to begin, one of the doctors presented the MSC officer with a watch which he noted had been set with the time adjusted back ten minutes to commemorate the fact that he was always complaining about the group being ten minutes late for assembly. The officer laughed and expressed his thanks. He then went to the microphone to address the entire group, still with all the chairs on stage empty.

He began with a loud voice, "Gentlemen, the general has asked me to bid you farewell. FAREWELL, AND DISMISSED!"

The general was clearly pissed off and was attempting to show his disgust, but nobody cared. The entire auditorium erupted with cheers and applause as the MSC officer left the stage. The basic training was finished, and we all received our certificates of completion.

Judy and I did manage to make a visit to the San Antonio Zoo as well as to a theater to see the movie *Patton*, starring George C. Scott, during our time in San Antonio. I recalled one of my dad's war stories about almost being run over at an intersection by Patton's jeep which was being recklessly driven. We also managed to visit the Alamo and the River Walk.

THE RESPITE

The months at the West Point Military Academy were pleasant. What a beautiful setting on the Hudson River with such majestic, historic buildings where such famous military giants had set foot. I was able to have Judy and the kids with me the whole time I was at West Point. We were housed a short distance from the West Point campus at Stewart Field. The housing situation was known as "camping out." It was a duplex with minimal furniture and cots, but we were together, and that was all that mattered.

The surgery caseload was made up of a lot of orthopedic injuries from the cadet population who engaged in an extensive intramural sports program along with the regular team sports. These kids were in the age group I would be dealing with in Vietnam. The orthopedic surgeon was a career Army officer and an excellent surgeon. The general surgery and gynecological cases came primarily from the retiree population that lived around the base.

The general surgeon was just in for a two-year hitch and was a very good surgeon. The gynecologist was a Harvard-trained guy who had just finished his training and had a two-year obligation. It took him almost four hours to do a routine total abdominal hysterectomy. The anesthesia staff consisted of one anesthesiologist and one male Army nurse anesthetist. The anesthesiologist, whose job it was to prepare me for doing anesthesia in Vietnam, was a large man who looked like he could have been a football lineman on a professional team. He was from Minnesota and was a great fan of the outdoors. He was an avid hunter and had a number of large animal heads mounted on the walls of his little apartment on the base. He had done enough hunting with firearms that his hearing might have already suffered some ill effects. It was clear to me early on that my mentor was not entirely comfortable in his teaching role. He would induce anesthesia with pentothal and a muscle relaxant and then give me only a few seconds to get the tube in the trachea.

Ten to fifteen seconds was pretty much the limit. If I didn't get the tube in very quickly, I would feel the sharp elbow of my mentor moving me aside so he could do the intubation. Early on, he took me down to the pathology department to see if there was a cadaver on which I could practice intubating. Well, the only cadaver present displayed significant rigor mortis, and neither of us could pry the mouth open. So that idea was abandoned. My mentor routinely used a long, straight, Miller blade for intubating. He was comfortable with the Miller blade and so was starting me out trying to use it. In retrospect, it was not the best blade for me to start with. The straight blade was used to pick up the tip of the epiglottis and expose the vocal cords, through which the tube would be passed. While I did learn to use the straight blade after some initial struggles, it was the nurse anesthetist who introduced me to the curved, MacIntosh blades which I found more to my liking. The curved blade gave a better view while lifting up on the tongue, and I only had to place the tip of the blade at the base of the epiglottis to lift and tilt it up and expose the vocal cords. The induction of anesthesia and intubation process got much smoother for me with the curved blade, and I came to appreciate the nurse anesthetist for his contribution to honing my skills.

During my time at West Point, the time arrived for my mentor's scheduled two-week vacation. For the period of his absence, the military sent an anesthesiologist from Walter Reed to fill in and supervise me. He was a Hungarian fellow who constantly complained that he had to serve in the Hungarian army and then had to serve in the American Army after coming to America. He was impressed with all of the pomp and circumstance and rigidity at the academy. We could look out the hospital windows and watch cadets in full dress uniforms, marching off their demerits in the heat. He found a postcard with three cadets on it in full dress uniforms and holding flags. He sent the card back to a friend at Walter Reed with a note stating, "The original photo had four cadets, but the fourth cadet's catatonic pill wore off." The Hungarian anesthesiologist took up residence in my vacationing mentor's apartment with permission. During my mentor's two-week absence, his replacement managed to drink up the entire liquor supply in the apartment. Near the end of the two-week vacation, my temporary mentor was trying desperately to replenish the liquor supply and trying to acquire enough ration stamps to make the purchases on the base. He was not entirely successful, and my returning mentor was not a happy camper when he discovered what had happened. I soon acquired the skills to do cases without supervision. On October 2, 1970, I was taking a break between cases when the obstetrical department called, asking for help. They had a woman who was about to deliver, and they could not find the OB doctor. I was sent up to labor and delivery. When I arrived, the panicked patient inquired, "What do you do?" I simply responded, "Anesthesia." She then said, "But you're not even an obstetrician." She was pretty scared, and I tried to calm her down as best as I could. I assured her that I had done a lot of deliveries in private practice and that she would be fine. She calmed down with my assurances, and we soon delivered a fine, healthy baby with no problems. I tended to the umbilical cord and got the baby in the hands of the nurses. The placenta delivered easily and was complete. I then headed back to surgery for my next case. It seems that the OB guy was out playing tennis without his beeper. When he returned, he came down to surgery with a pile of papers for me to fill out regarding the delivery. I told him to fill out his own paperwork, saying, "I did the delivery you weren't here for. The baby was headfirst. You figure out the rest." He headed back to labor and delivery, taking his incomplete paperwork with him.

The cadets on the West Point campus saluted everything that moved. If I left the hospital just to go across the street, I would just keep my right hand up to my forehead rather than wear out my arm, constantly returning the salute of a cadet. A large auditorium across from the hospital memorialized the sacrifice of past cadets. Walking into the building, one could turn around and look at the wall where names of graduates who had died in service were inscribed. There were far too many graduates who had already been lost in Vietnam.

My parents drove from Flint, Michigan, to West Point for a visit while I was stationed there. We were able to do some sightseeing. One day, we made a trip into New York City where we took the ferryboat ride around the Statue of Liberty. Dad recalled his return from Germany after the war and what a welcome sight that was.

As we toured the inside of the Roosevelt home at Hyde Park, I noticed an old television that was on display. I recalled that old television that I had watched at my grandmother's house on E. Palmer St. back in Detroit in 1950. I still had that old TV. It was identical to the one on display at the Roosevelt mansion. The TV box was very long, to accommodate all the tubes.

The sight of that old television also triggered my memory of the old icebox in my grandmother's kitchen. I remember seeing the iceman deliver large blocks of ice with large tongs to that old metal box.

My father attended a football game with me at the little stadium on the campus at West Point. The game pitted Syracuse against West Point. The size difference between the players on the two teams was incredible. Just a few minutes into the game, my dad turned to me and said, "This is like men against boys." The much smaller cadets did their best and fought hard, but the big monsters from Syracuse just rolled over them.

During my last week at West Point, I was informed that there were no immunization records in my file even though I had received all of them during basic training. I had them all again. Not a pleasant time. Then I decided to have three wisdom teeth removed while still stateside. After the procedure, I was back in my apartment with Judy, putting up with a mouthful of packing and a bit of pain despite a good dose of codeine. There was a knock on the door. Judy answered the door and was greeted by a sergeant who asked to speak with Captain Long. Hearing the request, I came to the door to be greeted by a smiling sergeant who saluted me and said, "Captain Long, it is the policy that anyone leaving West Point with orders for deployment in Vietnam must qualify with the M-16, and I need to take you to the range to get that done." I responded with, "Doctors only have to be familiarized with the M-14, and I did that during basic training." The sergeant continued and explained that those rules apply only to those who have not been stationed at West Point. I continued to object with my muffled speech as a result of the packing and explained that my vision was very blurred from all of the codeine. In a reassuring voice, the sergeant prodded, "Come on with me, doc. I'm driving, and you will be fine." With my mouth full of packing and blurred vision, I climbed into the sergeant's jeep, and he drove me to the range. He then loaded an M-16 and handed it to me. I told him, "I can't see well enough to handle this thing." He pointed to his right saying, "The targets are right out there. Just shoulder the weapon and point it out that way. I'll tell you when you can pull the trigger." I looked in the direction where he had indicated the targets were located but could not visualize any targets. I shouldered the weapon, pointed it in the direction of the targets and put my finger on the trigger. For several minutes, I would simply pull the trigger when he said fire. After several minutes of this nonsense, he said we were finished. I got back in the jeep, my jaw throbbing a bit, and endured the trip back to my apartment. The sergeant handed me a little card as I left his jeep. My vision was too blurred to read it. I made my way back into my apartment and sank into a chair. I then handed the little card to Judy and asked her what it was. She replied, "It says that you are an expert rifleman." It hurt to laugh, but I could not help myself.

A Dark Day

We checked out at West Point, loaded the kids and our few belongings in the car, and headed back to Flint, Michigan, for some final time together before my scheduled departure for Vietnam on December 1, 1970. The last football game that I watched that fall was the Army vs. Navy game, but I was really not aware of what was going on, distracted by the family separation that was soon to begin. The William Calley trial, related to the My Lai massacre, was regularly reported on the evening news during the last half of November. There were 355 U.S. KIAs (killed in action) during the month of November. When it was time to leave on December 1, the whole family piled into the car, and I got behind the wheel. It would be the worst day of my life up to that point. There was so much that I wanted to say during that drive to Bishop Airport, but I found that I could not say a word for fear of breaking down. My eyes kept welling up, and I had to keep wiping them just to see well enough to drive. I wanted to tell the beautiful woman sitting next to me that I loved her, but I could only bite my lip and keep driving. Everything was racing through my head. I thought back on when I had first set my eyes on my Judy. I was in the eleventh grade at Flint Central High School, and she was in the tenth grade. We had attended the same elementary and junior high school, but I had never noticed her until high school. I began attending Cody Elementary School early in 1951 when my family had moved from Detroit and settled in Flint, Michigan, at a house located at 830 Pettibone. The following year, Judith Holden began attending Cody Elementary School when her family moved from Pepin, Wisconsin, and settled in Flint at a house located at 723 Vermilya, just a couple of blocks from where my family had settled.

While in the sixth grade, I had participated in the safety patrol program and manned one of the crossings near the school. I actually won a trip to Washington, D.C., for my service in that program. I was driven to Washington, D.C., in the spring of 1954 along with patrol students from several other schools. One driver was a representative from AAA. The other driver was Sgt. William LeGree. LeGree was a member of the Flint Police Department who had been tasked with promoting safety programs in the public schools in order to reduce vehicle-related deaths among the student population. He was known as the Singing Cop and promoted safety with many songs which he had written. The two cars that took us to Washington stopped in Ann Arbor at the AAA office on South Main Street, and the group was informed that the structure across from the office was the University of Michigan football stadium, something that did not mean much to me at the time. No football field was visible, just the brick wall along Main Street. During the Washington trip, we participated in a parade during which we carried a large sign about safety. We also got to tour the memorials, the White House and the Congressional chambers. On March 1, 1954, four Puerto Rican Nationalists had shot up the House chambers, and the bullet damage could still be seen and was pointed out to us during the tour. We also paid a visit to the Tomb of the Unknown Soldier and watched the changing of the guard. I was touched more by that than anything else I saw on that trip.

During my time patrolling my intersection while at Cody Elementary, I never knowingly came in contact with Judy. She was a year behind me at McKinley, but nothing brought her to my attention. Then came our time at Central High School. We ended up riding the same city bus home from Central High School, and it was during one of those trips home from school that I first noticed her. She was the most beautiful girl I had ever seen. I could not stop looking at her. She had a complexion without blemish, a beautiful face, wonderful eyes and long dark brown hair that reached her shoulders. I was in love instantly. She wore a long red coat, and some of the kids on the bus would call her Holden Red Stamps when she was standing at the rear door of the bus as her stop approached. She never smiled when they called her Red Stamps. I listened to enough conversations on the bus to learn that her name was Judy Holden. At that time, many of the merchants, especially at gas stations, would give out "Holden Red Stamps" with each purchase. The stamps could be pasted in a booklet and redeemed for a variety of items. So, the last name of "Holden" and the red coat Judy wore prompted the nickname of "Holden Red Stamps" for Judy. There was no opportunity for me to strike up a conversation with her on the bus, but I was desperate for a chance to talk to her. I had noticed that she got off the bus one stop ahead of mine and headed east. Then, one day, I got off the bus one stop ahead of Judy's stop. I crossed Fenton Road and started running east as fast as I could for one full block. I then turned south and began running to the street that lined up with Judy's stop. As I looked back west toward Fenton Road, sure enough, I could see Judy headed my way. I held back and waited for her to get closer. At just the right time, I started walking across the street so that I could pass close enough to her and say hi. As she walked past in front of me, she looked at me, and I looked into those eyes and was mesmerized. As we passed each other, I simply said, "Hi Judy" and kept walking. I heard her say hi as she kept walking. Those were the only words spoken on that first encounter, but I hoped I had at least gotten her attention. Soon after that first encounter, Judy was shopping in downtown Flint with her mother, and I happened to be in the same area by sheer coincidence. We passed on the sidewalk, and I said hi to Judy again, and she responded with another hi. I would learn later that her mother asked her who I was. Judy had responded to her mother's inquiry with, "I don't know his name. Just somebody from school."

I could not get Judy out of my mind, and I was determined to pursue a relationship. I kept getting off the bus one stop ahead of hers and arriving at the critical intersection right on time. Before long, my persistence paid off. We got beyond the "Hi" stage. The conversations got longer. The friendship grew. I began getting off at her bus stop and walking with her. I did not miss all of that running. We fell in love and dated through high school. We got engaged after Judy graduated from high school. After a one-year engagement, we were married on June 9, 1962, just as I finished my second year at Flint Junior College. The ceremony was officiated by my father, William Reuel Long, who was the pastor of Fenton Road Baptist Church located at the south end of Flint. The plan was for Judy to continue to work as a secretary for the two years I would attend Flint College (now University of

Judith Holden's senior high school picture.

Michigan-Flint). Two days after we were married, I started a summer job working at the Chevrolet metal fabricating plant in Flint where I loaded car fenders in box cars. It was a six-day work week, and the shifts were 10 hours long. The job entailed picking fenders up from a conveyor, walking into a railroad box car, and then stacking the fenders in racks. The hands and lower forearms were protected by heavy gloves, but cuts were common at the elbows from the sharp metal on the underside of the fenders. The fenders were covered with a special grease to minimize corrosion, and the grease would always get in the cuts and delay healing. I had my share of cuts. I was exhausted at the end of each workday. I would usually just lie down and fall asleep when I got home. Judy would wake me for supper. I would then very quickly turn in for the night, only to wake up at 5 a.m. to get ready for another 10-hour shift. I was supposed to pitch in a fast-pitch church softball league that summer, but pitching after a 10-hour shift loading fenders was a real challenge. The fastball was just not the same. Fall came, and I was in my first semester of my junior year at Flint College in October 1962 when the whole country was preoccupied with the Cuban Missile Crisis and Kennedy's naval blockade of Cuba. It was an uneasy time with great concern over the possibility of a nuclear war. It was quite a distraction that fall.

Judy delivered our first child, Lori, on June 13, 1963. Then, for the summer of 1963, I made use of the typing skills I had acquired in high school and was hired on at the Flint Police Department. My duties involved typing complaints and warrants and teletype messages. I also did some fingerprinting of prisoners and ran record checks. I even did some of the handgun registrations. On one occasion, an elderly woman presented a rusty handgun to me that she wanted to register. I looked it over and noted the rusty condition and indicated that she should probably get it cleaned up and make sure it was in good working order. Before I could say another word, the old gal picked up the gun, pointed it at my chest and pulled the trigger six times while saying, "It works fine." My heart was pounding hard as I admonished the old gal without raising my voice and told her she should never do something like that again and always assume the gun is loaded. I registered the weapon and sent her on her way.

My upbringing and social life were primarily church centered. I had been spared any contact with the seedy side of parts of the community. This would provide not a little entertainment for many of my colleagues at the police department. On one particular day, I took a telephone call from a woman who indicated that she wished to file a report about a theft of some money and property. I typed the address where the theft had occurred. I then inquired, "Is this where you live? Your home?" The woman replied, "No, it's just a place where I turn tricks." I had no clue what this meant, and I inquired again and got the same answer from a now aggravated woman. I knew that the Shrine circus was in town and wondered if this was someone connected to the circus. I asked the woman, "Do you work for the circus?" She was getting pretty angry by now and expressed her anger with a little profanity. I asked her to hold for a moment. I then turned to the occupant of the desk behind me, a longtime employee with a similar position, and inquired, "Herb, I've got some lady on the phone that I can't quite figure out. I thought she might work for the circus, but she says she doesn't. She says that she wants to file a complaint about stuff getting stolen from a place where she turns tricks." Well, Herb and the whole department got a big laugh out of that one. After Herb finally caught his breath and wiped his eyes, he said, "That's no lady, that's a hooker. I better take this one." Herb took my phone and typed up the report. When he was finished, he expanded my vocabulary as he explained the meaning of the phrase, "turning tricks."

The vice squad was in the habit of recruiting people from my department for assistance with their sting operations. I had declined to get involved in such activities, and that proved to be a smart decision. One of my colleagues showed up one morning with a leg cast and crutches after helping the vice squad the night before, and he was not a happy camper. The plan had been for him to get solicited and taken to a known house of ill repute. Then the detectives were to observe the activity and break in at the appropriate time and arrest the hookers. The detectives were not timely with their break-in, and my poor colleague was getting a lot of pressure from the hookers who were getting suspicious about his failure to promptly engage in sexual activity. When the detectives broke in, they only found the hookers in the second-floor apartment. Noting the open window, one of them looked out just in time to see a white T-shirt fading down the alley. The poor guy made his escape but broke his ankle. He declined any offers for earning extra money with the vice squad after that adventure.

On another day, I took a call from a man who wanted to file a complaint about money being stolen from his wallet while he was at a house of ill repute. I put the fellow on hold and turned to Herb again for assistance, "Herb, this guy says that he paid some woman for sex and that somebody took all the money out of his wallet while he was having sex, and he wants to file a complaint about the theft." The nearby desk sergeant heard what I had said to Herb and immediately yelled across the hall, "I'll take that one." The sergeant walked over to my desk, took the phone from me, and yelled into the phone, "Go back for seconds!" He then slammed down the phone to the cheers of the whole department.

In the fall of 1963, Judy was working as a secretary for six professors at Flint College. The date was November 22. Judy was at work, and I was studying for an organic chemistry exam at our little rental house on Vermilya. It was a little after 1:30 p.m. when I got a phone call from Judy telling me to turn on the television and saying, "The president has been shot." There was no more studying that day and for several more days. It was wall-to-wall coverage. I was watching the coverage when Lee Harvey Oswald was shot while the police were transferring him. For days, there was nothing but wall-to-wall mournful music on the radio. The whole country was in shock. Just 20 days before Kennedy was shot, the unpopular president of South Vietnam, Ngo Dinh Diem, and his brother had been shot and killed after a coup by some of the South Vietnamese generals. The CIA had communicated Kennedy's approval of the coup back in the summer.

I would finish up with my teaching credentials and complete my pre-med requirements at Flint College. The plan Judy and I had discussed was for me to take a high school teaching position after graduation. Early in my junior year, I had gotten together the $50 needed to file an application to the University of Michigan Medical School. To my great surprise, I was invited for an interview. It turned out to be a rather hostile interview, also to my great surprise. There was just a single interviewer. He started out by asking me a few science questions which I quickly answered. He then asked me what medical journals I subscribed to, a question I found to be rather strange. I said, "None." He then asked me if I could name a medical journal. I said, "Not really, there are no medical people in my family." He asked me if I had ever heard of the *Journal of the American Medical Association*, and I said that it sounds like there should be one. He then changed the subject and went on, "I see that your father is a Baptist minister. Do you think the fact that you were raised in such a home by a Baptist minister would be of value to you if you became a doctor?" I said, "Yes, I do." He then seemed to make light of the topic by saying, "You may be right. A minister and a doctor are often the last to deal with a patient before they die." He then inquired, "Tell me, Reuel, what are your plans if you don't get into medical school?" I told him that I would teach for a year and apply again. The same question was asked two more times, and I gave the same answer. The next question would lead to some discomfort as he inquired, "Tell me, Reuel, why do you want to come to the University of Michigan Medical School?" I told him that I liked the town. He seemed a bit irritated with me and asked if I was being facetious with him. I said "Probably," and he repeated the question to which I answered, "Nice campus." Clearly irritated, he demanded, "Just how many other medical school applications have you submitted?" "None," I replied. He responded with, "Are you that confident that you are going to get in here?" I said "No" and found myself looking down at his desk instead of at his eyes. He pressed on, "So, why haven't you applied to other schools?" I continued to look down at his desk and not make eye contact as I explained, "Each application requires a fee of $50, and you got the only $50 I could spare right now." He then demanded to know how I was going to pay for medical school. I told him that my dad would be able to help me some. He pressed on, "So does your Baptist minister father have $10,000 in the bank?" I said that he did not. He continued, "How much do you think he has?" I replied, "Maybe $1,500.00." He would not let up, demanding, "So how are you going to pay for medical school?" I was feeling pretty dejected at this point as I finally had to admit that I would probably have to borrow the money. Rocking back in his big leather chair, the interviewer made his final remarks with a sneer, "So you are going to borrow the money. You really have no money for medical school. I have a little advice for you. Go home and borrow 50 bucks from somebody, and at least apply to Wayne State. If you get in here and I wasted your 50 bucks, you can look me up and tell me I wasted your money." With that, the interview concluded with a handshake. I walked down the steep hill behind the medical school building to the gravel parking lot below, somewhat dazed and nauseated. I was feeling pretty low during my 50-mile drive back to Flint. A few days later, I requested an application from Wayne State Medical School. Before it arrived the following week, I received my acceptance to the University of Michigan Medical School.

I was taking the methods of education course during my senior year when I received the news of my acceptance to medical school. The usual instructor for the course had been replaced by a gentleman who had been serving as the science consultant for the Flint Public Schools. I had done very well with all the projects and papers throughout the class, having received high marks on all graded material. There were only a couple of days of scheduled class meetings with discussion sessions left. We were in the middle of the last scheduled session, and I expressed my opinion on a topic. Then one of my friends chimed in and announced to the whole class, "He's not going into teaching anyway, he just got accepted to medical school." The instructor immediately displayed a red face as he turned to me saying, "I would like to see you after class." At the end of the class, everyone left the room except for the instructor and me. As soon as we were alone, he looked at me and said, "I want you to drop my class!" I pointed out that the class was over as this was the last scheduled day. Again, he looked at me and sternly ordered, "Drop my class!" I was shocked by his behavior and left the room without saying another word to him. I did not drop the class. When I got my grades for the semester, I discovered that the angry methods instructor had retaliated by giving me a C for the course even though I had received an A on every project and presentation I had done in the class. At least the late C would not affect my medical school acceptance. I did take the matter up with the school dean who was quite sympathetic as he listened to my recounting of events. He did acknowledge that there was nothing he could do because of the academic freedom the staff is permitted. I indicated that I understood but thought he should be aware of what happened to inform his future hiring decisions. During the next semester, I was doing my practice teaching at my old Flint Central High School when the old methods teacher showed up to bend the ear of my supervising teacher. He was not able to exert any influence. The University of Michigan professor who had observed my work in the classroom not only gave me an A for the semester but told me that I was the best student teacher he had ever observed, a statement that warmed my heart. I enjoyed the semester of practice teaching at Flint Central where I had spent two of my high school years and met my Judy. I would never forget one incident from my time as a student there. I had missed a week of school with the flu and missed an exam. When I returned to class, the teacher was going over the exam with the class and asked me to wait outside the room in the hall. I went out into the hall and closed the door behind me. After a couple of minutes, two tall male students approached me, pulled out switch blade knives, and proceeded to work on their nails right under my throat. As they worked on their nails, they talked to each other about what they were going to do to the next honkey they encountered. I stood perfectly still, looking straight ahead with sweat breaking out on my forehead. I thought the classroom door would never open. Finally, there was some noise from the other side of the door, and the two dudes closed their knives and scattered, to my great relief.

When I broke the news to Judy about my medical school acceptance, she had mixed emotions about the news. She was looking forward to giving up her job and just raising our new baby. She would have been quite happy with me just taking the teaching job I had been offered with a salary of $4,900.00 a year, but she supported me giving medical school a try. I spent the summer of 1964 working at the Flint Police Department again. At the end of that summer, had I taken the teaching job and forgot about medical school, I would not be facing a year of separation from my family now or the possibility of not making it back.

OFF TO NAM

As we got closer to Bishop Airport, I wanted to talk but still could not. Judy and I did not speak during the trip. The four kids ranging in age from six months to seven years were talkative and really did not realize the significance of what was about to take place. I wondered what their future would hold if I did not make it back. I thought about all those school loans that Judy had cosigned. My parents, sister and two brothers were at the airport to see me off. While we were all waiting for my departure time, my dad, who was a World War II veteran and had served in five major battle campaigns in the infantry, including the Battle of the Bulge and the green hell of the Hurtgen Forest, admonished me not to volunteer for anything. I promised him that I would not. When the time came for my departure, there were hugs and goodbyes. I noticed that there were tears streaming down my mother's face. I treasured every second of that final, long, silent embrace with Judy. Nothing needed to be spoken. Each of us knew the feelings of the other. Her love would sustain me. I went through the big glass doors at the only departure gate at Bishop Airport and climbed the rolling staircase to the airplane entrance. At the top of the ramp, I turned back and waved, even though my eyes had welled up, and my vision was too blurred to see anyone. I would soon be off to see, up close and personal, the war that had been in everyone's living room on the evening news for years.

I left Bishop Airport on December 1, 1970, aboard a United Airlines 727 at 6:35 p.m. The plane stopped briefly at Tri City Airport (now MBS International) and then headed for O'Hare. The plane circled O'Hare for one hour and then finally landed at 8:30 p.m. Central time. I left O'Hare at 9:00 p.m. Central time aboard a United DC 8. I noted that there were a lot of empty seats. The flight did experience some turbulence during the trip to San Francisco but landed safely at midnight local time. I was thinking about the family back in Flint where it was now 3 a.m. I was able to get the last seat on a Greyhound bus headed for Travis. The fare was $3.10. I arrived at Travis at 1:30 a.m. local time and checked in. Then it was just sit and wait. At 9 a.m. local time, I boarded a Seaboard World Airways DC 8 for Anchorage. The flight was full and carrying soldiers of all ranks, all headed for Vietnam. Seaboard World Airways was primarily in the freight hauling business, but they had converted their planes for meeting the demand of hauling troops.

The first leg of the flight to Anchorage took a little over four hours. Everyone was allowed to disembark for a one-hour layover before heading out on the next leg to Japan. There was a large, stuffed polar bear in the waiting area. As we lifted off at Anchorage, our pilot called attention to the wreckage of a plane that had recently crashed. It was another plane that was transporting troops, and all had been lost. The flight course went over the Aleutians, bound for Tokyo. I was impressed with the long hours over nothing but water.

I had a window seat. I mentioned to the guy next to me that there was certainly no place to land out here if there was an emergency with the plane. As I looked down at the water, hour after hour, my mind was occupied with recurring thoughts, "What if this was a one-way trip? What if the plane went down? What if I made it to Vietnam, only to die there? What would the future hold for Judy and the kids?"

There were stewardesses on the plane, but they never smiled and were not very friendly. The fellow next to me noted that there was not a good-looking one in the whole bunch. He also suggested, with a smile, that putting rather homely stewardesses on the flights to Vietnam was by design, as he explained, "They don't want us to think we are missing anything back home."

After all of those miserable hours looking down at nothing but water, the pilot finally announced that he would soon be making his descent into Tokyo and that it would be an instrument landing during a driving rainstorm. Everyone was prepared for a rough landing. The landing was in a driving rain with zero visibility but went without a hitch. The flight had taken about seven and a half hours. After a one-hour layover, the journey continued with the final leg of the flight from Tokyo to Bien Hoa, South Vietnam. It was a five-hour flight. The plane landed at Bien Hoa at 9:50 p.m. local time. Flood lights were trained on the plane, lighting up the long ramp that had been rolled up to the door, down which we were to disembark. As I followed the guys in front of me out onto the ramp, I felt the oppressive heat and the need to get out of my green, stateside uniform that was more appropriate for winter. As we walked down the ramp, we were greeted by a long line of laughing and jeering GIs, many of whom looked pretty ragged, like they had just come out of the jungle. They were waiting to board the plane we were leaving for their trip back to the States. Their tours were over, and they had survived and were jubilant. Their jeering was intense and could clearly be heard by all who were leaving the plane. They were yelling: "SUCKERS!" "IT'S ALL YOURS NOW BABY!" "HAVE A BLAST!" "YOU'RE FUCKED NOW!"

In the distance, I could see flashes of light, not sure if it was caused by explosions or a thunderstorm, but I could not hear any explosions. After a short briefing, I boarded a military bus for the seven-mile trip to Long Binh. The driver was a little on the reckless side. At Long Binh, I processed in, turning in four copies of my orders and exchanging my money for military payment certificates. I was assigned a bunk for the night and was able to clean up and get into cooler clothes. I had a top bunk which had a mattress that was caved in—to the point that it looked like it would swallow any possible occupant. The guy assigned to the lower bunk was processing out and waiting for assignment to a flight back to the States. He really was not interested in any conversation about his tour in Vietnam, only saying that it was the worst year of his life. I noted the time difference between Vietnam and back home and wondered what Judy and the kids were doing. I already missed all of them terribly and prayed that I would eventually make it back to take care of them. When I arrived in Vietnam, the American troop level had been pulled down to about 334,000 and would be down to about 280,000 by the end of the month. Such news would give false hope to those in theater who would soon be dealing with a dramatic escalation of the war by Richard Nixon.

Getting Acclimated

It was Thursday, December 3, 1970. I was briefed about my assignment to the 93rd Evacuation Hospital and informed that I would only be at that assignment for about two weeks before being reassigned. I was provided with some printed materials to introduce me to my new environment.

On December 4, I finished in-processing at headquarters. I was outfitted with the usual jungle fatigues, olive-green underwear and socks and a cap with captain's bars. After a rough night of dealing with the mosquitoes, I managed to secure some repellent. I needed a fairly common size 10 jungle boot, but supply was all out of size 10. The doctor at the 93rd who was helping me settle in said, "I know where we can get you some boots to get you by for now. Come on with me." I followed him to a row of Quonset huts where he told me to wait outside as he entered one of them. After a few minutes, he emerged with a big smile, holding up a pair of size 10 boots that were filthy and covered with a lot of dried blood. As he handed them to me he said, "I knew we could find some in triage. The guy who wore these won't be needing them anymore." I accepted the boots and took them back to my quarters to finally complete my wardrobe. I started my first dose of chloroquine and primaquine tablets to prevent contracting malaria, a weekly ritual that would continue for the rest of my tour. I would experience a little gastrointestinal upset during the first 24 hours after taking the pills each week. I quickly found the PX at the 93rd where I was able to purchase two audio cassette recorders. I packaged one of them up to send home to Judy and got it to the mail room. That was on my early to-do list.

There was no hostile fire at the 93rd during my short stay there. However, I was somewhat taken aback by a loud explosion that seemed quite close during my first visit to the mess hall. When it happened, my first reaction was to duck and consider taking cover under the table.

I was the only one who had reacted in any way. The guy sitting next to me said, "You can always tell who is new in country when that happens. You'll get used to it. They are just blowing up some stuff over at the ammunition dump." I then spent some time getting familiar with the anesthesia equipment and doing a few cases. I did my first case in country on December 5, a skin grafting under general anesthesia. During the case a large explosion knocked several things off the walls of the Quonset hut operating room, a new experience for me. That evening a GI committed suicide by shooting himself.

Regarding the anesthesia equipment, I was introduced to a Fluotec for the first time. I had no idea that such a device existed. The most commonly used general anesthetic at the time was fluothane, and the Fluotec device allowed one to just turn a dial to the percentage of fluothane one wished to deliver with the anesthesia machine. I had never used one. During my training back at West Point, I had to run the liquid fluothane through a vaporizer and then calculate the percentage being delivered, based on the flow through the vaporizer and the total flow through the machine. The Fluotec was flow and temperature compensated and just allowed one to simply dial the percentage of anesthetic to be delivered. It made things much easier. I wondered why they were not using the Fluotec back at West Point. Monitoring patients during anesthesia was pretty basic with a blood pressure cuff, sometimes a precordial stethoscope, a small oscilloscope to track the heart rhythm and a finger on the pulse. My mentor back at West Point had emphasized the practice of keeping a finger on the pulse as much as possible, no matter how else the patient was being monitored, and I would find it to be a valuable habit.

The chief of anesthesia at the 93rd was in charge of anesthesia assignments throughout the country. He had trained at Walter Reed and referred to it as Walter Wonderful. He bragged that he was going to hire a harem of nurse anesthetists to do the anesthesia, and he was just going to supervise them when he got back into civilian life. I could not imagine being responsible for how a case went without being in total control myself. He made a habit of taking the new guys into Saigon during their short stay at the 93rd, just to see the sights and eat at a nice restaurant. He said there was a nice French restaurant that was very good. When my group got to make the trip, we were instructed to take our wallets out of our back pockets and place them in a shirt pocket and maybe put our watch in a front pocket. We were told that if a Vietnamese kid ran or rode by and grabbed your watch or anything else from you, it was not wise to chase them. We were also told that drinking a soda from a bottle or wine poured from a sealed bottle that was opened in front of you was

The streets of Saigon just outside the USO.

One of the many street vendors in Saigon.

fine. However, we were warned not to drink the water or any drink with ice cubes because of the likelihood that the water was contaminated.

I was not that impressed with the food at the French restaurant, not my style. I was impressed with what I saw on the crowded streets of Saigon with all the street vendors selling their produce while under all sorts of makeshift structures to protect them from the sun and frequent rainstorms. The trip was uneventful, and we all returned to the 93rd safely.

At the officers' club and all the social events, I soon noticed that the most popular song that was played and sung with enthusiasm was the song "We Gotta Get Out of This Place" made famous by the rock group known as The Animals. The most popular portion of the lyrics was "We gotta get out of this place … if it's the last thing we ever do … we gotta get out of this place … girl there's a better life for me and you." That song said it all. Even if everyone did not know all the lyrics, everyone chimed in when it got to "We gotta get out of this place."

The two weeks was coming to an end, and the time for my assignment was fast approaching. Along with one of the other OJT anesthesia doctors, I was called to a meeting with a major to discuss our new assignments. We took our seats in front of his desk. He then looked at us and said, "Well, one of you has to go up north, and the other one will go south." The fellow sitting next to me immediately volunteered, "I'll go south! I'll go south!" The major then turned to me and said, "I guess that means you will be going north." I was informed that I would be assigned to the 27th Mobile Army Surgical Hospital (MASH) at Chu Lai.

I did my last cases at the 93rd Evac on Friday, December 11. On Sunday, December 13, I was driven to Bien Hoa at 5:30 p.m. where I spent the night at a location that had received incoming rockets just three nights earlier. The next morning, I boarded a C-130 for a flight to Cam Ranh Bay at 7:40 a.m. The rain was very heavy at Cam Ranh Bay when we arrived. After a three-hour layover, the flight continued on to Da Nang and then on to Chu Lai, arriving at 4:30 p.m.

THE 27TH MASH

The mobile army surgical hospital (MASH) dates its beginnings back to the Korean War and has been part of every military conflict by the U.S. Army from the Korean War through the Vietnam War. On March 25, 1963, the 27th MASH unit was reactivated and attached to the 43rd Medical Group at Fort Lewis, Washington. The unit was alerted for overseas shipment in June, 1967, left for Vietnam on March 4, 1968, and arrived at Chu Lai on March 27. The 27th MASH had been operating in Vietnam for more than two years and eight months when I arrived. The usual tour of duty was one year. So there had been a full turnover of the staff at the unit at least two times since it opened at Chu Lai. The medical staff was not changed over en masse. Each doctor or nurse was replaced as their year was up, and it was rare for

The author just outside the office of Lt. Col. Geer, a general surgeon who was the commanding officer at the 27th MASH at Chu Lai.

two individuals to have their tour end on the same date. Some extended their tours or even signed up for a second tour, but that was rare. I was flown to Chu Lai and reported in at the 27th MASH to Lt. Col. Thomas Geer who was the officer in charge. He was a fully trained general surgeon, a career Army doctor. The facility was not a tent unit when I arrived. It was a series of connected Quonset huts.

The 27th Surgical Hospital was inland a bit, along Highway 1. From the BOQ (Bachelor Officers' Quarters) I could look inland and see nothing but the mountains from which rockets were launched in our direction. The 91st Evacuation Hospital was located on the beach at Chu Lai. The airfield was located between the two medical units and was the prime target. However, incoming that fell short of the airfield risked hitting the 27th. Overshooting the airfield put the 91st at risk of a hit. Patients were usually brought to the 27th by helicopter. A helipad was located just outside the triage Quonset hut. A large fire extinguisher on a dolly sat at the edge of the helipad.

The helipad at the 27th MASH.

A crew would unload the patients at the chopper, putting each stretcher on a gurney, and then push them into the triage area.

Inside the triage Quonset hut, supplies were on shelves all along the walls. There were bottles of intravenous fluids hanging from a rail with tubing hanging down to each set of sawhorses where stretchers could be placed. This is where patients were sorted out. Some casualties were resuscitated and prepared for surgery. Some died in triage when there was nothing that could be done for them. My time was divided between triage and surgery.

Everybody hated working under alert conditions when wearing

a helmet and flak jacket was required. It was exhausting and difficult to maneuver. Between the triage Quonset hut and the surgery hut was another hut that housed the X-ray equipment and another area for a laboratory. There were four operating stalls, all open in the front. There were large surgical lights over each operating table and X-ray boxes on the wall of each room. The little, portable pop-up anesthesia machine was at the head of the table, and large tanks of oxygen and nitrous oxide were against the wall near the anesthesia machine. Large sinks for scrubbing for surgery were in the first area after leaving a small coffee room. There was an area for cleaning instruments near a large autoclave.

The sleeping quarters consisted of two wood-frame structures, two stories high, one for the women, and another for the men. The lower

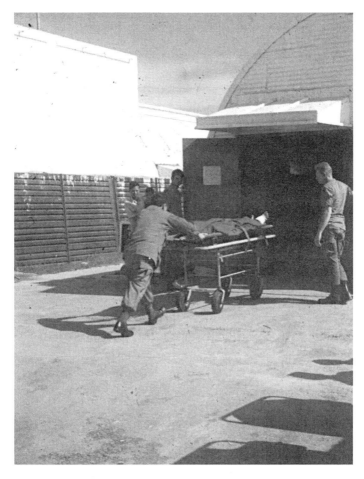

Patient being moved from the helipad into the triage Quonset hut.

The author with portable anesthesia machine.

The author in front of the lower level of the Bachelor Officers' Quarters (BOQ), which was protected by a wall of sandbags.

level of the BOQs was protected by a wall of sandbags. There were also sandbag bunkers near the BOQ.

Just beyond the BOQs was another building occupied by private contractors who maintained some of the equipment on the base, such as the generators and air-conditioner units. Between the BOQs and the contractor building, a volleyball net was set up for use during downtime. There was another Quonset hut that served as a mess hall.

After reporting to Lt. Col. Geer, a man I would come to greatly respect and admire—and against whom all future hospital administrators I would encounter would not measure up—I was assigned to a room on the first floor of the wood-framed BOQ. I took some comfort in the fact that I would be on the ground floor with the wall of sandbags for protection. I soon learned that the nurses' BOQ had burned down just a few weeks earlier on Halloween. Although the official cause of the fire was listed as electrical, it was most likely caused by some burning candles left unattended by one of the nurses. At the time of the fire, the large, water-filled fire extinguishers were completely useless because they had been emptied in a water fight during a raucous party the night

A volleyball game in progress. The building in the background with sandbags on the roof is the contractors' building where contractors who maintained the equipment worked.

before the fire. Occasionally some of the doctors and nurses would blow off some steam during downtime by engaging in water or empty tin can fights. In any event, the BOQ had been completely rebuilt before my arrival.

As I opened the door to my new sleeping quarters, the sunlight sent a wide variety of countless bugs scattering in all directions, seeking the cover of darkness. As I entered the little room, I observed a small bed against the wall to my left and a good deal of trash scattered about the rest of the room. The walking-around space was just a little larger than the space occupied by the twin-size bed. There was room for a very small refrigerator which I would eventually secure, a most valuable acquisition that would house some of the contents of care packages from home. There was a small closet against the wall straight ahead of the door. It was also full of trash. I immediately set about to clean the room. During the cleaning process, I discovered a small plastic bag on the floor of the closet, a bag that contained some water and sand and several dead minnows. I would soon learn that some of the Vietnamese women who worked on the base and did laundry were using the empty room that I was about to occupy to store some of their personal effects along with the dead minnows which they used to spice up their

Vietnamese women whom we hired to do our personal laundry.

rice at lunchtime. For a few bucks, one could have their clothes washed and pressed by these local workers. The clothes would be washed by hand in Styrofoam containers that had been used to deliver blood products to the unit. The clothes were washed and rubbed with a stone and then rinsed, dried and pressed. They could make a new pair of fatigues look 20 years old with one washing, but they were clean and pressed nicely. These women would greet everyone with a broad smile, displaying blackened teeth caused by the betel nut they routinely chewed. Not infrequently, I observed one of them grab a bug that ran by on the ground near where they were doing laundry, pop the bug in their mouth and chew it up like a treat. Protein is protein.

I finished cleaning my room and hanging my clothes in the closet. Then I removed my most prized possession from my duffle bag. I placed my framed, favorite picture of my dear Judy on the little table next to my bed. Then I just sat down on the bed and looked at the picture for several minutes. She was so beautiful. How I missed her. I finally got off the bed and tacked a calendar to the plywood wall and marked off the days that had passed since December 1 with a big X.

Once finished with my room, I decided to take a walk and look over the grounds and the surgery facilities. I made my way over to the surgical hut and discovered that there was some activity in surgery in one of the operating stalls. I stepped into the small room where I saw a coffee pot and a corpsman in scrubs, coffee cup in hand, just sitting alone, staring at the floor. As I entered the coffee room, I greeted the corpsman and told him that I had just arrived at the 27th. He just nodded and didn't seem much interested in conversation. I asked him if he had been in country very long. He quietly responded, "Seven months," without

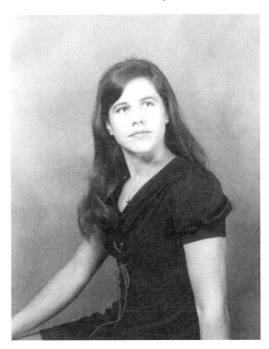

The picture of my Judy that I kept with me during my entire tour.

ever looking up. I pressed on and asked him if he had been on R & R yet. He answered, "Nope. Next week." I then asked him where he planned to go on R & R. Again, he just quietly responded, "Australia." Determined to start a conversation that might produce some information of value eventually, I inquired, "Any big plans?" Well, that question triggered the biggest response as he seemed to have been jarred from his trance. He finally looked up and made eye contact with me. Then, with a serious look on his face, he began, "During the seven months I have been here, I have thought up about 100 new positions for sex. I intend to try every one of them when I get to Australia." I responded, "Very good." I then left the coffee room and resumed my tour of the grounds, leaving the corpsman to his fantasies.

I soon realized that I would have been better prepared for the social structure that I encountered had I seen the movie *M*A*S*H* which was inspired by medical care at mobile army surgical hospitals during the Korean conflict. I soon met the one fully trained anesthesiologist at the 27th MASH, a man whose nickname was taken from *The Wizard of Oz*. He had a short, single-syllable last name that started with an O. So, he had been tagged with the nickname, "The Wizard." I would soon find him to be a skilled anesthesiologist and great mentor. The Wizard had an interesting ritual with which he would begin each morning when he arrived at the surgery area to start cases. He would stretch his arms up and behind his head while reciting a long list of vulgar words that he had memorized. It was always the same words in the same order. He would then dive into the work of the day. I would soon meet many more of my new colleagues and learn their nicknames. One was a big, soft-spoken, black general surgeon who looked like he could be quite successful as a professional football lineman. His nickname was "The Bear." He was in the habit of wearing a large, straw cowboy hat with the word "Sheriff" emblazoned across the front of it. When Christmas arrived, it was The Bear who dressed up as Santa to entertain the Vietnamese kids who were in the hospital. There was one partially trained surgeon who was my age and had actually done his undergraduate work at the University of Michigan and graduated in my class in 1964, but he had not gone to medical school at Michigan. His nickname was "Gross Charlie." Charlie had a little hammer deformity of the middle finger of his right hand from an old rugby injury. So, when Charlie shot the bird at somebody with that bent finger, it gave the gesture special emphasis. Therefore, he became "Gross Charlie." While I was at the 27th, Charlie did something else to bolster his nickname. He sent an audio cassette tape home to his wife that was intended for her ears only. It was somewhat X-rated. As it turned out, there was a big family get together at Charlie's house back home when the tape arrived. Somebody opened the tape and played it for everybody. Charlie admitted to all of us what had happened, and everybody had a good laugh. It didn't seem to really bother Charlie all that much. I met another surgeon whose nickname was "The Rabbit" or "Daddy Rabbit." He had been a track star in college and had some of the fastest hands I had ever seen in the operating room, an excellent surgeon. Another one of the general surgeons was nicknamed "The Lion." His last name started with an L, and he had a full head of hair, but I never learned just how the nickname was assigned for sure. One of the triage guys was called "Black Cloud" because the helicopters seemed to gather over triage like black clouds when he was covering triage. There were other nicknames besides the ones I would deal with most often. Early on, at one point, I was instructed to go to triage where The Lion wanted to orient me to standard operating procedures for triage and demonstrate how I was to insert subclavian lines in the major trauma cases. I reported to triage and was directed to The Lion. I recognized him immediately as he introduced himself. He clearly did not recognize me. The guy who was preparing to orient me to triage was the same guy who had read Judy the riot act for eating pizza two days after her cholecystectomy. I never reminded him of the incident that was now five years in our past. He had finished his surgical residency and now held the rank of major. "What a small world," I thought. The Lion proceeded to demonstrate how a subclavian line was to be placed in all major trauma cases. He called attention to the long, sharp bevel on the large needles that were used, emphasizing that the needle was to be pushed straight in under the clavicle and pulled straight out if one did not hit the subclavian vein. The needle was never to be moved side to side once inserted, an action which could result in a fatal laceration of the subclavian vein. The long, beveled needle tip could do just as much damage as a scalpel. I was also warned that I should never approach a helicopter when the rotation of the blades was slowing down since the blades droop and get closer to the ground as the speed decreases. Drooping helicopter blades can kill you. For that reason, the pilots usually maintained a high speed on the blades when they were unloading casualties. There came a day when I was summoned to triage and asked about what I had been told about approaching a helicopter with slowing blades. They didn't want me to ever forget their instructions. I was then told to go to the end of the triage unit and unzip the body bag. When I unzipped the body bag, I saw a body with the entire front of the chest gone and the heart and lungs gone, just an empty chest cavity with the back ribs in view.

There was one fully trained radiologist and a fully trained internal medicine doctor at the 27th. There was no thoracic surgeon and no neurosurgeon. If a chest had to be cracked, it was the general surgeons who had to do it. There were a few nurse anesthetists at the 27th, some Army trained. There was one lieutenant colonel female nurse anesthetist. The one nurse anesthetist who became a good friend was a guy named Gus. He spoke with a Southern drawl. He would talk to himself during cases, as he was providing anesthesia and pumping fluids and blood, constantly saying aloud to himself, "Now don't get excited Gus, don't be misled." He was an excellent anesthetist. The two of us would often play chess during downtime. Gus was a Seventh Day Adventist, and chess games that were ongoing as sundown approached on a Friday always had to be suspended for 24 hours in observance of his Sabbath. During the chess games, Gus would also talk to himself aloud when contemplating his next move, saying, "Now don't get excited, don't be misled."

Then there was the chaplain. He was on his second tour in Vietnam. Early on, I attended one of his services. The topic was "Our bargain with God." It was immediately clear to me that the chaplain and I had very different views of our relationship with God. When I spoke with Gus about the chaplain's views, Gus simply replied by saying, "He doesn't even believe that Jesus Christ is the Son of God." I soon discovered that his services were usually only attended by a couple of the nurses. As I watched him perform his duties, I was reminded of the old Shakespeare lines, "All the world's a stage, and all the men and women merely players, they have their exits and their entrances, and one man in his time plays many parts." The chaplain was certainly not a typical chaplain. He drank his vodka straight, sometimes from a large glass, sometimes from a new cardboard stool specimen container. His language was also laced with words that one would not think appropriate for a man of the cloth. He liked to party. When called to comfort a dying solder, he did his thing, but I never witnessed what he did. We would occasionally play chess. Whenever he thought he was about to lose, he would yell "MASCAL" (mass casualty) and begin sacrificing pieces in an attempt to destroy my strategy and create a stalemate.

The unit had a dentist who was drunk most of the time and was on his second tour of duty in Vietnam. The rumor was that he was just trying to stay away from his wife who wanted to serve him with some papers related to a divorce. I was not aware of anybody having any dental work done by him. The pharmacist at the 27th was well known for making sure that the punch bowl at DEROS (date of estimated return from overseas) parties had the proper amount of alcohol content.

I did my first cases at the 27th Surgical on December 16, 1970. The two cases were both laparotomies and debridements for multiple frag wounds. On Friday, December 18, I witnessed a quad amputation for the first time. When the surgeons removed both arms and both legs on one patient, they referred to it as "making home plate." I would see too many such cases during my tour. It was so depressing to walk into the recovery room and see a young man with no extremities, suspended between four poles by stockinette taped and glued to each stump.

By the time December 23 rolled around, I was quite comfortable with my duties and had done quite a few cases. I had learned to sleep with a small light on in the corner of my room, a practice which reduced the chances of my sleep being interrupted by small visitors. On my second night at the 27th, I made the mistake of trying to sleep in total darkness. I felt something running across my bare chest and slapped my hand on my chest. When I turned on a light, the bugs scattered off my bed, onto the floor and into the walls. The center of my chest displayed the remains of the large, soft, multi-legged critter that I had smashed. After that, a little light was left on to keep the bugs in hiding.

With the Christmas season approaching, USO shows were scheduled for the Da Nang and Chu Lai regions. Bob Hope was making his customary tour. Several people from the 27th received permission to convoy to one of the USO shows. People who had been in country the longest were prioritized for making the trip. I was part of the group that remained to cover the 27th. It was December 23, when I was faced with caring for a 20-year-old who had stepped on a booby trap. Fortunately, he had no serious head injuries. He did have shrapnel wounds in his neck, chest and abdomen. He had no blood supply left to either of his legs below the knees and would need bilateral above-knee amputations. As we gave him fluids and blood and evaluated his injuries, I tried to distract him and talk with him about home. I learned his name was Jim Dehlin and that he was from Flushing, Michigan, just a few minutes west of Flint where I was from. He was frantic and repeatedly asking us not to take his legs. It somehow seemed appropriate that I was there to take care of somebody from so close to my home. Knowing that this young man would have his life dramatically changed forever on this day really bothered me. We could save his life, but it would be a very different life now. A family near my hometown was going to get some bad news in the next 24 hours.

Jim was frantic as The Rabbit and I moved him to the operating table. Once on the table, Jim wrapped the fingers of his hand around my right forearm as he made eye contact with me while begging, "Please, please, don't take my legs." The surgeon and I both tried to reassure Jim saying simply, "We will do everything we can." Both of us knew full well that Jim's legs could not be saved, but his life could be saved if all the dead and damaged tissue was removed. I continued to reassure Jim as I administered the syringe of sodium thiopental to start the anesthesia. As I was inserting the endotracheal tube, the nurses were already prepping the dead legs for amputation. The monitoring was accomplished with a blood pressure cuff, a precordial stethoscope and EKG leads hooked to a simple oscilloscope. After a satisfactory level of anesthesia was achieved with the anesthesia gases, I signaled to The Rabbit that he could start. He was a very fast surgeon and performed the amputations quickly. There was almost no conversation during the surgery. When the amputations were completed, the shrapnel wounds were also debrided.

When I made my first visit with Jim in the post-surgical ward, I found that he really was not interested in much conversation. He seemed angry, and I didn't blame him. His life had completely changed, and he needed time to take it all in. What a terrible Christmas for Jim. I wanted to do something for him and somehow console him but felt helpless. The next day, Christmas Eve, started out slow. I checked to see if I had any mail and was disappointed to find out that I had none. Then it got busy in the afternoon, starting with a GI who came into triage in critical condition. With blood pumping, he was brought to the operating room where I quickly proceeded with inducing anesthesia and pushing fluids. The kid had multiple frag wounds of the legs, chest and abdomen and a frag wound to the heart. The chest was cracked first to repair the heart. With the heart repaired, the abdomen was opened to repair all of the holes in the bowel. The peritoneum and fascia were closed, leaving the skin open to be closed in a couple of days if there was no sign of infection. Then the debridement of the leg frag wounds was undertaken. It was a long case but with a good outcome. The kid was taken to recovery with his blood volume having been replenished, and his vital signs were good. I left recovery and went back to see if I had any mail and found that six letters, three from Judy, and an audio cassette tape from home had finally caught up with me. Some of the crew was having a little Christmas party and The Bear dressed up as Santa between cases to play Santa for some of the hospitalized Vietnamese kids.

I didn't get a chance to party since I was quickly called back to triage for another casualty that was en route by helicopter. This time it was an ARVN (Vietnamese soldier) who arrived at triage in terrible condition. He had been shot in the abdomen and was shocky. We had to move quickly. A subclavian line was quickly inserted, and we rolled him to the surgery hut with blood pumping. I put him under, and the surgeons had his belly open by the time I had my endotracheal tube taped in place.

There was nothing left of the spleen, and the bowel had been shot to pieces. It was a very lengthy repair. The case wrapped up at 4 a.m. after 15 units of blood had been administered. He was stable when I turned him over to the recovery nurses. I then went back to triage and found it empty and learned that there was nothing else en route. I headed to my room to crash. After a few hours of sleep, I got up, determined to try getting a Christmas call to Judy using the MARS (Military Auxiliary Radio System), which involved ham radio operators back in the States. I didn't have any luck and was soon summoned for another case. It was another South Vietnamese casualty who required a left below-the-knee amputation. Since he had no abdominal or chest wounds, the case did not take very long.

When we finished the case, I was told that the Christmas dinner at the mess hall was pretty good. I checked it out and was pleasantly surprised. There were actually real tablecloths, real plates, and metal eating utensils on the tables. The ham and turkey were good. There was even a little, wrapped Christmas gift at each plate, provided by the Red Cross. Just as I was finishing my meal, I was summoned for another case, another Vietnamese casualty who required a BK (below-the-knee) amputation. As we were finishing up, we learned of another casualty that was en route, a Vietnamese casualty who had been shot in the neck. The entire operating room crew was ready for his arrival, but there was nothing we could do. He was not going to surgery. He had bled out and had no vital signs. The big vessels on one side of the neck had been completely blown away. He had died quickly. It was a very red Christmas, not a happy red.

In the middle of it all, I was still thinking about the kid from Flushing, Michigan, who had lost both legs above the knee. Then, it occurred to me that Jim's family might find some comfort if they could just hear his voice. I had my little cassette recorder that I had purchased for sending tapes home to Judy and the kids, and I had a few blank tapes. I wondered if Jim would be interested in sending a tape home. I also wondered if I would be breaking some Army rules by helping him do something like that from his hospital bed. So, I approached Lt. Col. Geer and told him about Jim and that he was from close to my hometown. I told him what I wanted to do and asked if it would be OK. Without hesitation, he said, "Sure! Go for it!" Relieved that I would not be breaking any rules, I headed to Jim's bedside. I was concerned that he might still be in an angry mood and not wanting to talk. He was still getting narcotics for pain and a little sleepy when I arrived at his bedside. I told him about my cassette recorder and asked if he had any interest in sending a tape home. He indicated that he would like to send a tape to his girlfriend who could share it with his family, and he gave me her address. I went back to my room and gathered up my battery-powered recorder and put in a new blank tape. I then went back to Jim's bed, put the little recorder on his pillow and the microphone on his chest. I told him I would be back later to get the tape and mail it for him. I punched the record button and left to check the mailroom. After about an hour, I went back to Jim's bed and found him sleeping. The microphone was still on his chest, and the tape was still spinning and recording. I did not awaken him. I pushed the stop button on the recorder, picked up the microphone and headed back to my room. I really didn't know if Jim had just fallen asleep after I had left the recorder and never recorded a word, but I really considered it an invasion of privacy for me to listen to the tape. So, I sat down and wrote a letter to Jim's girlfriend, explaining what I had done with the hope that Jim had been able to say something. I wrapped up the tape and letter and took it to the mailroom. After about a week at the 27th, Jim was in shape for the medevac flight to Camp Zama in Tokyo, Japan. His tour of duty was over, but he would have a lot to endure and many challenges ahead.

My tour was just beginning, and I would see many more casualties with injuries identical to Jim Dehlin's and much worse. Christmas evening, I finally had a chance to listen to the audio cassette from home. I sat on the edge of my bed, unwrapped the tape, put it in the recorder and pushed play. It was so great to hear Judy's voice greeting me and letting me know that they were all doing fine. She quickly let me know that Tim, Amy and Lori all wanted to say a few words. She gave the microphone to Tim first. He immediately asked me what I was doing. Then there was a long pause. The next words I heard were Tim saying, "Why doesn't Daddy answer?" Then I could hear Judy explaining to the little guy how the system worked. She explained that the little tape in the machine would record everything he said and that Daddy could put it in a machine just like this one and hear what he said and then send us a tape to play what he said into his machine. Tim seemed to accept the explanation but was not quite comfortable with the system and did not have a lot to say on that first tape. Amy and Lori took their turns talking to me with no problem. Then Judy talked for a while. I listened to the tape several times just to hear their voices. I actually fell asleep that night with the tape playing.

At 5 a.m. I was awakened for another frag case. I turned the power off to my little cassette recorder, the tape having run to the very end, and headed to the surgery hut. When the case was finished, I had the morning off and got a ride to the Americal MARS (Military Auxiliary Radio System) station to try and get a call through to Judy. I sat in line

Photograph of the kids back home that Judy sent to me. From left: Amy, Jill, Lori, and Tim.

all morning but never got to make a call, so I went to the PX and ordered a few things from the PACEX catalog to send home to Judy and the kids. There was time for a little volleyball in the sand between the BOQs that evening. Then I sat down and wrote a letter to Judy.

Tuesday, December 29, was a busy day for me even though I was on third call which meant the third operating stall needed to open. One of the casualties was a Vietnamese soldier with frags to the abdomen and legs. A second lengthy case was a GI with an evisceration, the belly being wide open with bowel hanging out. He did survive. Wednesday the 30th was a full day for me in the operating room that started at 8 a.m. and ended at midnight. There were six long cases. They all survived. I had the day off on New Year's Eve. It rained all day. I finished off my first month in country in my room writing a letter to Judy and reading.

There was a chalkboard just outside the operating room where upcoming cases were listed by the nurse supervisor for the operating rooms after consultation with the surgeons. The patients' names were on a line with a designation of ASAP (as soon as possible) or STASAP (sooner than as soon as possible) which took priority over the ASAP

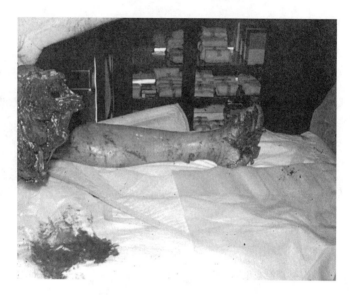

Typical mine injury: ROK (Republic of Korea) Marine has lost right leg at mid-thigh and will need a clean amputation on the right as well as a below-the-knee amputation on the left leg.

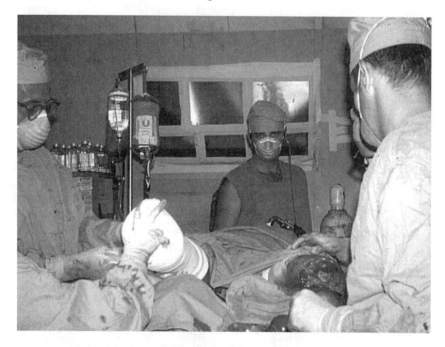

Operating room scene where the author is providing anesthesia for one of the all-too-frequent amputation cases.

cases. Amputation cases were usually ASAP cases. Major vascular cases with ongoing significant blood loss took priority.

I received a lot of letters from Judy, other relatives, church members, friends and acquaintances. There was one letter in particular that I would not fully appreciate until I returned home. It was from my friend, Brent, who was a surgeon in Owosso, Michigan. The letter went on and on about a new television show that had made its first appearance after I left for Vietnam. He said the show was called *All in the Family* with a central character named "Archie Bunker." Brent said that he just couldn't believe the network could get away with broadcasting a show that had a character like Archie Bunker saying the things that he said. I would eventually come to realize that Brent did not fully appreciate the satire of the production.

Sometimes civilians ended up in the military operating rooms with injuries related to the war. Quite often, Caesarian sections were performed on the locals by our general surgeons.

This little girl was sleeping against my flak jacket, holding her brother, while her mother was in surgery. All went well. One of the nurses at the 27th had her heart stolen by a little Montagnard boy who

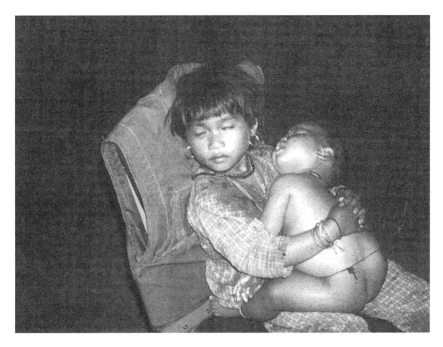

A little Montagnard girl, holding her brother, while her mother was in surgery.

was a patient at the 27th. She adopted him and took him back to the States.

The contents of care packages sent from home, primarily by Judy, were stored on a few shelves that I had attached to the wall of my room just above the bed. Many times, the operating rooms were busy during mess hall hours, and I found myself hitting my private stash just before turning in for some sleep.

The lieutenant colonel who was a career Army nurse anesthetist knew her way around. She knew somebody on the Sanctuary Hospital Ship that was stationed offshore at Chu Lai. She occasionally was able to secure some items that were not available to the 27th MASH. She managed to acquire a fairly new anesthetic agent, ketamine, in exchange for some alcohol that she snuck onto the ship. The ketamine proved quite useful for some of the kids that came to surgery at the 27th. At times she was able to swap alcohol for some nice food items. Only one time did she return with some bad food, some seafood that was not fit to eat. Another 335 U.S. soldiers died in Vietnam during December 1970.

There were a number of volleyball games during my first month at

The author in front of the shelf of goodies that had been sent in care packages from home.

the 27th. Then, one day, a bunch of rockets came flying over us, causing everybody to scramble for the bunkers. The radiologist actually ran over one of the nurses, knocking her to the ground as he scrambled to the sandbagged bunker. When somebody called his attention to what he had done, he simply said, "Everybody out for themselves." I took the advice that I had received early on and dropped flat to the ground, not wanting to get hit by shrapnel while trying to get to a bunker. With no immediate close explosions, I then made my way to the crowded bunker where we all stayed for several minutes. It was more than 10 days before anybody suggested playing volleyball again.

A Special Triumph

As the calendar turned to January in 1971, I found myself assigned to the anesthesia rotation rather than triage at the 27th Mobile Army Surgical Hospital at Chu Lai. Some days were very long and depressing with case after case of unsightly mutilation. Many nights, it just wasn't worth trying to get a little sleep, drifting off for a short period, only to be awakened by the sounds of helicopter blades getting louder and closer with a new load of bloody carnage. As much as we dreaded the sounds of those blades, they must have been such a welcome sound that gave hope for the casualty awaiting rescue. The best chance for rest was when I was on fourth call. To be called to surgery when on fourth call would mean that there were enough casualties requiring surgery to open all four operating stalls.

During the first week of January 1971, President Nixon announced, "The end is in sight." Those of us at the 27th Surgical didn't see any evidence that the end was in sight based on our caseload. The rain was constant from December 30, 1970, through January 3, 1971. I did manage to listen to some of the radio broadcast of the New Year's Day Rose Bowl game in the middle of the night as Stanford beat Ohio State by 10 points. On January 4, I was on first anesthesia call and had a long day and evening in surgery. I had another long day in surgery on January 6 with eight cases. It also rained all day. January was a very busy month with only a little relief provided by the call system. Too often, multiple operating rooms were active. I awoke at 5:30 a.m. on January 18 to hear just the last seven minutes of the Super Bowl V game and learn that the Colts had beaten the Cowboys.

On January 19, the bombing started in Laos and Cambodia, bombings authorized by Nixon in an attempt to interrupt the enemy supply lines from the north. On Saturday, January 30, 1971, I was on first anesthesia call again and would soon encounter a case that I would never forget. I had finished a case at 12:45 a.m. and had gone back to my sleeping quarters. At 3:30 a.m. I was awakened by loud helicopter blades and quickly summoned back to the surgical hut. A GI had been choppered to triage with a single frag wound of his left chest right over his heart. There was no exit wound anywhere on the chest and no wounds anywhere else on his body. An X-ray was quickly done with the portable machine, and there was no evidence of any metal in the chest. A subclavian line was inserted along with an additional line in one arm. His blood pressure was low, and his pulse very fast. The Lion looked him over and immediately concluded that he had cardiac tamponade with blood filling up the pericardial sac and compressing the heart. We had no thoracic surgeon at the 27th, but The Lion had trained at the University of Michigan and spent a good deal of time in thoracic surgery during his residency. We headed to the surgery hut with him. A Michigan man would do the surgery, and another Michigan man would do the anesthesia and push the fluids.

We got the kid on the table, and I induced anesthesia and got him intubated. The Lion did a short scrub while the nurses prepped the chest. The Lion quickly opened the chest and confirmed his diagnosis. The pericardial sac around the heart was engorged with dark, chocolate-colored blood that was compressing the heart and not allowing it to beat effectively. The Lion put his scalpel to the pericardium and filleted it open, removing all the old blood and exposing a beating heart with a pencil-size hole in the left ventricle. The blood pressure improved as soon as the pericardium was opened. With each contraction of the heart, a stream of blood squirted from the hole in the left ventricle. The Lion lifted the heart and examined the back of the left ventricle, finding no exit wound. He then proceeded to attempt a repair of the hole. He couldn't just sew it closed and have no leak. He eventually decided to sew the hole closed using a pledget of material to crimp and close the hole. There was no leak when he finished. With the heart repaired, The Lion closed the chest.

With the chest closed and the dressings applied, it was now time to address what happened to the fragment that had made the hole in the heart. The surgical drapes were pulled away so we could see the entire body. I could immediately see that the right leg did not have the good color that the left leg displayed. The portable X-ray machine was brought to the surgical hut. Sure enough, the lead fragment was now in the femoral artery and limiting the blood flow to the right leg. The area was prepped for surgery, and The Lion removed the metal fragment from the femoral artery. Full blood flow to the leg was established with no ill effects. The fragment had just enough energy to penetrate the chest and front wall of the heart, and then got pumped out into the aorta, lodging in the femoral artery where the passage was too small to go further. We finished the case about 7 a.m., and I took my patient to recovery. It was a very tired but very satisfied crew that could feel good about what had been accomplished. Nobody had lost an arm or a leg or an eye or had their guts ripped apart. We actually had a whole person when we were finished. It was a rare feel-good night and day. The kid did well enough to get on a medevac flight out of the country in one week.

A Special Discovery

Early in my Vietnam tour, I was made aware of a special phenomenon that had been observed during the treatment of casualties several weeks after their initial injuries. Soldiers would survive their initial injuries and their first surgeries at a MASH unit or an evacuation hospital in country. Then they would be evacuated to Camp Zama in Tokyo for follow-up care and more surgery. Some of these casualties were experiencing severe arrhythmias and even cardiac arrest with the induction of anesthesia for these subsequent surgeries. This was discussed in the Navy Medical Newsletter early in 1970 in which it was noted that this phenomenon was seen "in patients with burns, massive tissue injury, hemiplegia and paraplegia." The article went on to point out that such patients seemed to be vulnerable to these arrhythmias if given succinylcholine during induction of anesthesia between 2 and 10 weeks after the initial injuries. When the electrolytes were monitored during the induction of anesthesia for these cases, it was discovered that the potassium levels spiked very high if succinylcholine was administered. Potassium occurs primarily inside cells. The level outside of the cells that is circulating in the bloodstream affects the function of the heart. If the potassium level in the serum gets too high, the heart can beat irregularly or even stop. Very high serum potassium levels also decrease the strength of contraction of the heart. Succinylcholine was used to briefly paralyze the patient after anesthesia was induced so the tube could easily be placed in the trachea for ventilation. When succinylcholine is administered without any other drugs to minimize the effects, it causes generalized contraction of the skeletal muscles throughout the body as it paralyzes the patient. In this special group of patients, especially with neurological injuries or major burns, the succinylcholine was triggering the release of potassium from the cells in the injured areas, causing the potassium level in the bloodstream to dramatically increase and leading to the heart rhythm problems. Since some of these casualties could remain in Vietnam for subsequent surgeries several weeks after their initial injuries, we were all warned about what had been discovered during the treatment of these casualties in Japan so that we would avoid the use of succinylcholine in such patients still in country. This discovery made during the Vietnam era would prove to be valuable information for those who would provide anesthesia in the States for patients with similar injuries.

Most of our casualties were not in country long enough to have the succinylcholine eliminated from the protocol, but there was an occasional one for which we avoided the muscle relaxant. Over the next month, I continued my usual rotation on anesthesia call, doing many cases during which young men had their limbs removed and worse. All of us honed our skills and got very efficient at our tasks, but at a terrible price. February was a very busy month. On February 2, we experienced a bit of a lull in the action late in the day. Somebody yelled out that there was going to be a volleyball game. A number of doctors and nurses promptly showed up at the net between the BOQs. Teams were quickly chosen, and the action was on. A lot of frustration was being vented as that volleyball was smacked, again and again. Then somebody yelled "Incoming!" while pointing to the sky. A bunch of rockets that looked like flying brooms were passing overhead in the direction of the airfield. Everybody scattered to the bunker where we stayed for several minutes until we were sure that nothing seemed to be landing on the hospital compound. Nobody was interested in returning to volleyball. We all headed back to our rooms for the evening, and there was no volleyball between the medical staff for a couple of weeks. That evening, one of my coworkers offered me some pot while saying, "Do you want this shit? It makes me paranoid." I declined the pot offer and suggested to him that the pot may not be making him paranoid since there really are people out there trying to kill us. He acknowledged that I might be right and put the pot back in his pocket.

Then on Tuesday, February 9, the helicopters stopped bringing us casualties for a few hours. The 91st Evacuation Hospital on the beach probably got most the casualties for our area on that day. The USO brought a bunch of professional football players to the 27th Surgical Hospital, including Greg Landry of the Detroit Lions and John Brown of the Pittsburgh Steelers. A volleyball match ensued between the doctors and the football players. It was explained to the football players that the game would be played with "jungle rules." Jungle rules essentially meant that there were no rules. One could reach over, under and through the net to hit the ball and even run under the net and violate the space of a member of the other team to spike the ball to the ground. It was more like a brawl than a volleyball game, the way we usually played, just to vent frustration. During the game with the football players, the chaplain yelled, "Jungle rules!" while jabbing his hand through the net in front of Jim Brown who was trying to hit the ball. The chaplain managed to poke Jim Brown in one eye, and Jim bent over, holding his hands over his eyes. The chaplain turned and starting running at a pretty good clip, trying to get far from Jim Brown. Jim took it pretty well and accepted the apology from the chaplain. The chaplain managed to curb his enthusiasm, and the game continued. A good time was had by all, albeit with the usual disregard for the customary volleyball rules. The NFL players autographed photographs for us and wished us well when they left.

On Tuesday, March 2, I learned that one of the GIs who had been badly wounded with multiple injuries and undergone a hemipelvectomy, had died. I was absolutely disgusted, thinking about the mutilation involved in that case. I sat down on the edge of my bed and wrote letters expressing my disgust and asking, "Why?" I wrote a letter to Richard Nixon. I wrote another to Senator Phil Hart. I wrote one to Senator J. William Fulbright. Fulbright had been a critic of the war for a few years. I described the terrible price being paid by the young men who were engaged in the fight and questioned the whole purpose of the war. I asked all of them why young Americans should lose their lives and limbs and suffer unspeakable mutilation to determine how such primitive people should live and be governed. I challenged Nixon, writing, "When you ran for president in 1968, you suggested that you would bring this war to an end within a year. You have failed to do what you said you would do. The deaths since your inauguration are forever on your ledger now." When Nixon ran for the presidency in 1968, he said he would pull troops out of Vietnam and "pursue a negotiated peace with honor." Instead, he expanded the war, and the doctors and nurses in the war zone had to daily witness the terrible price being paid by a lot of young men.

On Wednesday, March 3, I was taken off the anesthesia rotation and placed in the triage rotation. Some tours had ended, leaving the unit with a shortage of triage doctors. My move to fill the triage shortage made sense because I was the only doctor in the anesthesia rotation with any emergency room experience in civilian life. The triage shifts were 12 hours on, 12 hours off. Most of the casualties could be salvaged, but not without loss of limb or eyesight for many. Some could not be saved. At 4:45 a.m. on March 6, a Vietnamese soldier was brought in from the helipad. He was in shock. I managed to get the usual, big intravenous lines in place and started pumping blood. We got him to surgery where he was opened up. So much of his liver had been blown away that there was nothing to be done except close him up and let him go. On March 10, 1971, China announced its full support for the North Vietnamese in their battles with the United States military. More help soon arrived to cover triage, and I was reassigned to the anesthesia rotation on March 11.

MEDEVAC

The medevac flights were a chance to get out of the country for a few days and experience some sanity, a break from all the depressing mutilation. It was something that we all looked forward to. It represented an opportunity for some sightseeing, shopping and good food in Tokyo. My turn finally came, and on March 12, 1971, I was informed that I would be flying out on Saturday, March 13. I rolled out of bed at 3:30 a.m. on the 13th and left the 27th Surgical by chopper at 6:15 a.m., arriving at Da Nang at 6:45 a.m. The medevac plane was loaded in the front area with the stretchered patients who were attended by nurses. One other physician, an internist, was seated with me near the back of the plane. Ten minutes into the flight, we were informed that we should stay buckled into our seats unless there was an emergency. The pilot informed us that we would not be flying at the planned altitude because the plane could not be pressurized. There was a problem with the rear door which did not latch and seal properly, and it had to be secured with some straps to hold it in place.

The entire flight was at low altitude, but there were no other mechanical problems during the flight. The patients all did well, and we were not summoned to the front by any of the nurses. We landed at Yokota Air Base at 4:30 p.m. local time. After we landed and the plane had come to a stop, an Air Force officer came onto the plane to talk to me and the other physician. He began, "Well gentlemen, I've got some bad news." Both of us immediately concluded that we were going to quickly be put on a flight back to Da Nang. Fortunately, the Air Force guy was just messing with us. He smiled and went on, "It looks like we are not going to be able to get you guys a return flight for about six days." He had a good laugh. We did too, along with a sigh of relief.

My internist colleague and I were then choppered to the hospital. Eventually we made our way via train and subway to the Sanno military hotel in Tokyo. That first evening, I enjoyed a great meal and a big shrimp cocktail at the hotel. I slept well in a very comfortable bed that night, the best sleep I had enjoyed in months. The next day, Sunday the 14th, I was loose in Tokyo with my shopping list. In addition to items I wanted to buy for myself to send home, I had a list of items to find for some of my colleagues back at the 27th Surgical. I had the most success at the PX but had not found everything on my list by the end of the day. Back at the Sanno Hotel, I consumed a really big New York steak for supper. All the rich food was a bit foreign to my stomach, and I did not feel well for a while. At 9:15 p.m. I made a telephone call to Judy. The Sunday rates were a bit cheaper. The cost of the five-minute call was $12. It was worth every penny just to hear her voice.

In the lobby of the hotel, there were a lot of brochures for tours. My internist colleague talked me into signing up for a tour of Nikko. I paid the $20 fee and signed up. The next day, Monday the 15th, I boarded a train with my colleague and headed for Nikko. It was a two-hour, 85-mile trip to Nikko.

The train ride was followed by a bus ride up a winding road to the top of the mountain location. We got to see some snow from the mountaintop location, and I could not resist throwing a snowball down the mountainside.

The return bus and train ride got me back to the Sanno Hotel by 7:30 p.m. where I had a great rice-and-shrimp supper and turned in early. Tuesday was another shopping day in Tokyo. At one of the many camera shops, I found a camera flash attachment that I had been looking for. I also found a little battery-powered train that I sent home for Tim. I bought a kimono for Amy and a silk "Happy Coat" for Judy and mailed them home. I continued to enjoy the civilian food at the hotel while making shopping and sightseeing plans. On Wednesday the 17th, I made my way to the Tachikawa PX for some more shopping. I had not found everything on my list for colleagues back at the 27th. I bought a tripod and a pachinko game and had them shipped back to Chu Lai. I also purchased an electric frying pan, a spatula, plastic clips and an extension cord to complete getting everything on my list. Back at the hotel, I bought a nice silver bracelet for Lori. I mailed Judy a camera bag and a pearl bracelet. For supper, I had a filet mignon steak and a large vanilla shake followed by an evening of watching Japanese sumo wrestling. The next morning, I was up at 6:30 a.m. I got a letter off to Judy. I bought a few wooden dolls and a small Japanese calculator at one of the shops in the hotel. I took a cab and got dropped off near the DIET (the national building where both houses of the Japanese Diet met), the Imperial Palace and Tokyo Tower. I could see several groups of Japanese schoolchildren walking in the streets. The drivers on the streets of Tokyo appeared to be in a state of mass confusion. There was a lot of honking of horns and traffic jams. I was impressed with how many of the Japanese were wearing surgical masks as they moved about on the streets and in the shops. I made my way up to the observation deck in Tokyo Tower where I was able to look out over the city. It was quite a view.

Back at the hotel I continued to take advantage of the availability of great food. I could not resist the ice cream. I ordered a large vanilla malt. My stomach finally ran up the white flag—I could not finish the malt. So, I left the hotel and walked around the Ginza (an upscale shopping area in Tokyo). While walking the streets, I was approached by a young man, holding a small canvas, who offered to do my portrait for a fee. I stood for a few minutes while he quickly sketched my face on his canvas, paid him, and was on my way. After a lot of walking, I made my way back to the hotel and was able to get in another call to Judy a little after 10:00 p.m. During that call, I was able to talk briefly with Lori, Amy and Tim.

Friday the 19th was the scheduled day for my return to Chu Lai. The time in Tokyo had gone by quickly, and I had given no thought to the carnage I had left behind in Vietnam. The nights of uninterrupted sleep after great meals and walking the streets of Tokyo, feeling no risk to my personal safety, were over. I arrived at the Yokota Air Base at 11:15 a.m. Then I was bumped from my flight by an airline stewardess who had priority for the seat. That was fine with me because it meant a few more hours outside of Vietnam. I was then scheduled for another flight leaving at 5 p.m. Then that flight was cancelled over some problem with a CONUS evacuation flight. I finally got a seat on a flight that took off a little after midnight, headed for Clark in the Philippines, arriving at 4 a.m. I then caught an 8 a.m. flight for Da Nang and arrived there at 10 a.m. The final leg of the trip was on a C-123 for the short hop that left Da Nang at 4:15 p.m. and got me to Chu Lai at 5 p.m.

I arrived to find out that I had an accumulation of one week's worth of mail. On the downside, I discovered that the little refrigerator in my room had bitten the dust while I was away. I had some pretty smelly stuff to get rid of and then air out my room. After filing my medevac report, I went through my mail. It was clear that Judy had everything under control back home. In her letters, she said that the kids were all behaving so well. She said that she thought they all felt the need to stick together with their dad being away. She said that when she went shopping with the four of them, little Jill would ride in the grocery cart while the other three would stay very close and hold onto the grocery cart, never running around or misbehaving in any way.

UNSPEAKABLE

After my interlude in Tokyo, I was quickly back in the grind. On Monday, March 22, 1971, I was on first anesthesia call as well as assisting in triage between cases. It was busy all day and into the evening. By 11:30 p.m. I had already done six long cases in surgery. The constant stream of cases could not get my mind off the one casualty that I had been confronted with earlier that evening in triage. The look of terror in his eyes would not leave me. I had always been impressed with how fast the helicopter crews managed to get the casualties to us when time was of the essence if they were to be saved. On this day, they had outdone themselves.

I had been helping out in the very busy triage Quonset hut between cases when a casualty was brought in from the helipad and placed before me, the stretcher being placed on the sawhorses with the patient's head under the line of intravenous bottles with tubing and needles hanging down. The only information passed along to me by one of the stretcher bearers was, "He took a round in the explosive belt he was wearing." The smell of burnt flesh was immediately in the air. The green sheet covered all but the patient's head and neck. He was alert and looking straight up at the ceiling. He did not appear to be in pain. He had no intravenous line in place, and that would be the first thing to address. I noticed that the green sheet seemed to drop down to the stretcher where the legs should be located. I pulled back the sheet, expecting to see that the legs were gone, but what I saw was much worse. I could not believe the poor guy actually got to us alive. There was nothing left below the level of the ball of the hip. Most of the buttocks was gone. There was no major bleeding. Everything was just charred which had temporarily controlled the bleeding. Some peritoneum was trying to bulge through the char with each breath. I had nothing to work with except a head, chest and abdomen. I knew immediately that he would not survive. I went to the head of the stretcher, intending to start an intravenous line in case any medication was needed for pain while he was still with us. As I approached his neck to start an intravenous line, he raised his head and looked down at what was left of his body. He then turned and looked straight into my eyes with a wide-eyed look of terror on his face and firmly asserted, "You let me go!" I did not know what to say to him. If I was going to get a line in place, I needed him to be still and cooperate if we were going to avoid bleeding down below. Contemplating what I would say to him, I took a step back from his head. He dropped his head back onto his pillow and began shaking his head violently from side to side. Assuming I was going to do nothing for the poor guy, the nurse next to me yelled, "You can't do that," as she grabbed one of the needles hanging from a line overhead and went for his neck. He reacted by yelling "No!" very loudly while swinging his right arm, knocking the nurse back a couple of feet. That physical exertion was enough to raise his blood pressure sufficiently to break loose a big vessel down below and grant him his request. There was a splash of blood against the Quonset hut wall. He immediately lost consciousness. He took three more breaths and was gone. The angry nurse turned on me immediately, accusing me of doing something inappropriate by letting him go. I didn't argue with her. I had not let him go. The Good Lord had just taken him. Many of the nurses had been deployed shortly after graduating from nursing school and were confronted with young men, who were their age or younger, being mutilated and killed. The decisions by doctors to let some of them go in triage was hard for them to accept. The young nurses who worked in recovery and ICU had to treat and comfort the terribly injured and were often the first to deal with a young soldier's realization that he had lost his legs or arms or eyes. The nurses working in the operating rooms experienced the emotional rollercoaster with the doctors, the satisfaction of saving a life and the despair of the mutilation. The nurses on the medical floors were greatly impacted by the sick and injured children for whom they rendered excellent care. I could not get the image of that poor guy, blown in half and still talking, out of my mind. The busy caseload would not blur the image. There would never be enough cases to erase or blur his face and the look of terror I saw in his eyes.

I stayed busy with cases in the operating room all night, and the compound was also hit with mortars during the night. The mortars caused no casualties or major damage to the hospital compound. I finished my last case just as dawn was breaking. I headed for my room where I collapsed in my bed, wondering aloud, "How many more have to die or lose their legs or arms or eyes?" I was exhausted and slept all day; nobody bothered me. When I finally awoke, it was dark. I had missed breakfast, lunch and supper, but I was hungry. I dug around in my little stash of goodies Judy had sent from home. It would be Vienna sausages and Ritz crackers that would get me by. I still felt very tired. It had been hunger that woke me up. Hunger relieved, I was back in my bed and asleep within minutes.

Chu Lai is located in Quang Nam Province in Vietnam. The Vietnam Memorial Wall shows only one killed in action for Quang Nam Province for March 22, 1971, a 20-year-old named Clarence Myron Suchon of Stevens Point, Wisconsin. His name is on the Vietnam Memorial Wall on panel 4W, line 69.

Morning came, and I thought about what we were all doing and the carnage we had to witness, wondering if we would all survive without major injury. Would a rocket fall close enough to take out one of us on the medical team? The carnage in the field would certainly continue. I found pen and paper and put down my thoughts:

Vietnam Reflections

CLAP OF THUNDER, CONFLAGRATION,
    FRAGMENTATION, PENETRATION
SULFUR, STOOL, BLOOD, BURNING FLESH
    O'ERWHELM OLFACTION
AGONIZING SCREAMS, LAST REQUESTS,
    PRAYERS TO GOD, PLEAS FOR DEATH
HAND CLENCH WEAKENS, GROANS FALL SILENT,
    A LUCKY ONE TAKES HIS FINAL BREATH
WE WORKED AND SANG TO KEEP OUR SENSES
A FACETIOUS SONG, 'TWEEN PLYWOOD FENCES
"WE LIKE IT HERE" WAS OUR REFRAIN
ON SANER THINGS OUR THOUGHTS TO TRAIN
TOTAL ENUCLEATION, QUAD AMPUTATON,
    HOME PLATE WE DID CREATE
FUTILE TASK TO PAINLESS RENDER,
    OH GOD WHAT BE OUR FATE?

    —Reuel S. Long, M.D., Captain, Army Medical Corp

FIRE SUPPORT BASE
MARY ANN

After spending a long day in the surgical unit doing anesthesia on Friday, March 26, with surgery continuing well into the night, I was assigned to triage at 7 a.m. on the 27th. With no sleep during the night, I reported to triage at 7 a.m. for a 12-hour shift. I was pretty tired when the triage shift ended, but still had the adrenaline flowing pretty good when I was told to go get some sleep. It was even suggested that I should go to the DEROS (date of estimated return from overseas) party for one of the guys whose tour was ending, get a good sample from the punch bowl and sleep all night. The pharmacist was in charge of preparing the punch bowl for DEROS parties and took great pride in the product he produced. I was not used to alcohol, and one glass of punch was all I needed before hitting the sack for what I thought was to be an uninterrupted full night of sleep.

I fell asleep quickly and had only been asleep for about 20 minutes when I heard someone yelling my name and telling me to get up. It was the chaplain, yelling that I was needed in surgery. I told him to go away and informed him that I was off triage and anesthesia call for the night, that I could sleep all night. I turned over in my bed thinking the chaplain would go away and find the person he was actually supposed to summon to surgery. Instead, he grabbed my shoulders and started shaking me saying, "Wake up Reuel, you don't understand, they really do need you in surgery, we've got a MASSCAL on our hands." Hearing "MASSCAL" (mass casualty), I sat up on the side of my bed and rubbed my eyes. I could still feel the effects of the drink I had taken from the punch bowl. Then I said to the chaplain, "I think I might be drunk." The chaplain tossed me my shirt and trousers saying, "Don't worry, I'll get you some coffee. You can start in triage until it's time to open the fourth operating room. By then, you'll be fine."

I quickly got up, got dressed, washed my face and headed to triage with coffee in hand. The strong coffee and the adrenaline surge produced by the triage environment soon obliterated the effects of the single drink from the punch bowl. As I entered triage, which was quickly filling up with casualties, I heard people talking about an attack on LZ Mary Ann. I heard that there were 30 KIAs and 70–80 wounded. The choppers were dividing the casualties between the 27th Surgical and the 91st Evacuation on the beach. Sappers had overrun Fire Base Mary Ann which was almost in a standdown mode. The 91st would get 42 casualties, and the 27th would get 33. Many of the casualties did not have life-threatening injuries. Many had their eardrums blown out. We quickly had 13 casualties sorted out and stabilized for surgery. Just as the chaplain had suggested, I did end up providing anesthesia for the case that opened the fourth operating stall where I continued to do cases all night. That unique smell caused by the evaporation from large amounts of blood hung in the air. The facetious little "We like it here" song could be heard several times during the night and with excellent four-part harmony between the four operating stalls. At times, after hours and hours of dealing with unsightly carnage, the tone of the song became quite angry and loud, followed by long periods of silence, broken only by the sound of instruments being slapped into the open hands of surgeons by nurses who knew exactly what they needed without being asked. I worked in the operating stall all through the night and through the 28th. During the night on the 28th, a sapper was caught coming through our perimeter wire with a mine. I returned to triage at 7 a.m. on the 29th, a day that was marked by rocketing that had started at 2 a.m. The airfield and artillery hill were both hit. We were ordered to wear our helmets and flak jackets for the entire shift. During the night on the 29th, the unit lost power and lights and was placed on red alert at 1:30 a.m. I tried to get some rest with my clothes on and my .45 close at hand, but there would be no rest. I started another 12-hour shift in triage at 7 a.m. on the 30th. When I finally had the opportunity to go to my room after several days and nights with no sleep, my feet did not feel normal as I walked. I sat down to have a look at them and found that they were quite swollen. Below my knees, my legs were quite swollen. They looked like the legs of an old man in heart failure. I crashed into my bed and slept for almost 24 hours straight. The attack on Fire Base Mary Ann was the single deadliest attack on any fire support base during the entire war.

Meanwhile, also on the 29th of March 1971, back in the States, Lieutenant William Calley was found guilty of 22 murders related to the

My Lai massacre of March 16, 1968, after an Army Court Martial trial at Fort Benning, Georgia. Calley had been part of the Americal Division supported by the 27th Surgical Hospital.

There were happy days back home during this time as two of my kids, Amy and Tim, celebrated birthdays on March 25 and 26.

Birthday photograph from March 1971 when Amy and Tim celebrated their birthdays which were just a day apart. I got a chuckle when I saw the Band-Aid on Tim's upper lip.

R & R

The grind of the operating rooms and triage continued as I marked off the days on my calendar, closing in on the date for my R & R. It was Sunday, April 25, 1971, and I was far down on the call list for the operating rooms and not on the triage list at all. I slept in and then played some chess with a couple of the guys. I then did some cleaning on my room and started some packing for my trip that was to begin the next day. I was scheduled to report to the Chu Lai Airport on the 26th at 9:30 a.m. for an 11:30 a.m. flight to Da Nang for the start of my R & R. It had been almost five months since I had last seen my Judy. I would picture her in my dreams every night, but her image seemed less and less real as time passed. I felt like I had already been away for a year. I looked at her picture every day and listened repeatedly to the audio tapes just to hear her voice. Now the time had finally come for my R & R. I was going to meet her in Hawaii for a few days of sanity. I was completely unaware of the protests against the war which had taken place in Washington, D.C., just a few days before I left for R & R.

I got up early on the morning of the 26th, finished my packing, and caught my ride to the airfield at Chu Lai. I boarded a fixed wing C-123, and we lifted off at 12:10 p.m. for the short ride to Da Nang. It was hot and humid, and my khakis were saturated with perspiration when I arrived at Da Nang. At the Da Nang terminal, I caught a bus to Freedom Hill where I checked in my valuables and got a bunk for the night. One of the other guys from the 27th Surgical was there and on his way to Hong Kong for his R & R. We passed the time playing chess quite late that evening. Then I took a shower and turned in, only to find that there was not much sleep to be had. The mosquitoes were clearly the special forces mosquitoes and determined to make sure I got no sleep.

The next morning, I checked out of my quarters at 7:00 a.m. I spent most of the day playing cards. Then I processed out starting at 5 p.m. I checked in my boots and fatigues and went through some kind of fogging procedure. I didn't know what was in the fogging smoke or what they were treating. I was then bused to the air terminal where I boarded a big silver bird that lifted off for the real world at 8:20 p.m. The flight had a lot of empty seats. The stewardesses were just like back in the States on commercial flights. They smiled and were quite friendly. For supper on the flight, I had a filet mignon steak with all the trimmings. It was great. I left nothing on my plate. When the stewardess came to pick up my empty plate and utensils, she smiled and inquired of me, "Would you like another steak? The plane was stocked for a full flight. So we have a lot of extra food." It didn't take me long to accept that offer. I passed on the extra baked potatoes but did eat two more steaks. With a full stomach, I leaned back to sleep it off.

The next day, that big, beautiful, silver bird touched down in Honolulu, and I went through customs. Then, I boarded a military bus with the other passengers, a bus that took us to the area near the Hilton Hawaiian Village. As we approached the hotel area at 4:00 p.m., I looked out the window and saw a number of women waiting for the bus. Then I spotted Judy standing apart from the group. My heart began to pound a little stronger and a little faster as I looked at her, wearing a pair of hot pants and the breeze blowing her hair. She was real again, not just a dream.

Leaving the bus, I quickly made my way to Judy for a big hug. She had arrived a day earlier and checked in at the hotel. She had made all the hotel arrangements and had specified that we were to have an ocean view. When she arrived, they showed her to a room with no view. She demanded the ocean-view room that she had asked for and paid for. They quickly showed her to a nice ocean-view room. I followed her as she took us to our room at the Rainbow Towers of the Hilton Hawaiian Village. It was a beautiful room with a big, double bed and a nice bathroom. The little balcony provided a nice view of Waikiki Beach and Diamond Head. We both experienced some nervousness on arrival at the room. The separation had somewhat made us strangers, but finally we were reunited. I dropped the luggage and wrapped my arms around her for a long hug and a kiss. We enjoyed a steak dinner at the officers' club that first night.

The R & R time was enjoyable and brought back some sanity to my world. Just the use of greenbacks instead of military payment certificates brought back some normalcy. Sleeping with Judy in my arms instead of just dreaming about her was such a joy. The days passed quickly. They were filled with good food, shopping and sightseeing. Just standing on the balcony and watching all the activity on the beach was so relaxing.

Judy and the view of Diamond Head from the balcony of our room.

Judy and Reuel during R & R at the Hilton Hawaiian Village.

We enjoyed two daytrips, one to Ocean Sea Life Park and another to Pearl Harbor. The trip to the Arizona Memorial at Pearl Harbor was moving. The memorial had opened about the time I graduated from Flint Junior College in 1962. It was part of the history of my dad's war. My parents were married just a few weeks after the attack on Pearl Harbor. Dad got his Army draft notice in September 1943. He started basic training on December 20, 1943, at Camp Blanding in Florida. He became a rifleman in the 109th Infantry Regiment, 28th Division. On August 29, 1944, he was among the soldiers marching through Paris after its liberation, having fought through the hedgerows at Normandy. He drove his jeep through Bastogne on a mission just 24 hours before the Germans laid siege to Bastogne. He fought along the Siegfried Line and in the Hurtgen Forest known as the "green hell" and had many close calls. He was at the front during the Battle of the Bulge. He survived. I thought about my dad's brother, Thomas (Pete) Long. He survived 51 missions as a B-17 tail gunner in the European theater. My mother's brother, Reed Owens, was a fighter pilot and was shot down by the Germans and survived months as a POW. Her other brother, Paul Owens, was an engineer in the Army. He was captured by the Germans and died while being held by them. "This is the place where it all started for them," I thought. Yes, what happened right here at Pearl Harbor cemented our entry into World War II and called for such sacrifice by my dad's generation. Standing on the *Arizona,* I could look down at the parts of the ship that could be seen under the water and sticking above the surface. There were oil slicks from the oil that continued to seep from the ship. I thought about the more than 1,100 men that had been entombed in the ship less than a year before I was born. I wondered, "Would the quad amps that we sent home from Vietnam have preferred this fate?"

On Monday, May 3, 1971, the R & R was over. Judy and I awoke at 5:30 a.m. and checked out of the hotel. We took a cab together to the airport. At the airport, we hugged and said our goodbyes. At 10:15 a.m., I boarded the plane that was to take me back to the insanity of Vietnam. Judy had to wait for a later flight back to Michigan. I got settled into my window seat and could see Judy watching my plane. After 30 minutes, the pilot came on the intercom and announced that everyone would be deplaning, and that there would be a delay. The 747 had lost a tire that needed to be removed and replaced, so Judy and I got a couple more hours together at the airport. Then we had to say goodbye all over again when the plane was ready. My plane finally lifted off at 1:30 p.m. I had a window seat over a wing. My last look at Judy that day was out the airplane window. She was standing atop the terminal with the wind blowing her long hair. The flight back to Vietnam seemed much shorter. We had one stop in Okinawa. When I arrived at Da Nang, I encountered another member of the 27th Surgical staff who was heading out on R & R. He told me that the 27th Surgical was going to stop receiving patients and close down in a few days. I spent one night at Da Nang before catching the short flight back to Chu Lai the next day.

Closing the Surg

It was Wednesday, May 5, 1971, and it was announced that the 27th Mobile Army Surgical Hospital would be closing. Everybody would be assigned to new units. Helicopters would stop bringing casualties to the 27th Surgical by the 15th of the month. I continued to work in triage and had the night shift on the 8th. Then on Sunday the 9th, I learned that my next assignment would be at the 95th Evacuation Hospital at Da Nang. I worked the night shift in triage again on the 9th. Then it was like the war stopped. The sounds of helicopter blades were absent. Everyone was packing and preparing to move on. A lot of people were sitting around drinking adult beverages. There was a limit (four bottles) on the amount of alcohol which one could take along to another assignment. Many of the guys had too much alcohol on hand. With no taxes on alcohol purchases at the PX, alcohol was cheap and probably safer than the water. A fifth of vodka could be purchased for 70 cents. A fifth of bourbon cost $1.10. The supply was plentiful. So, with no other responsibilities, the task of consuming the excess stores of alcohol was undertaken with vigor. There were no patients to take care of. The inpatients were being moved to the 91st Evac on the beach. A number of high blood alcohol levels were reached by several staff members during this waiting period. It was a party atmosphere. During these closing festivities, Col. Geer called everybody together with all their booze to make a presentation. He presented the chaplain a special award for doing so much to contribute to the esprit de corps during his service at the 27th Surgical. Later I would learn that the chaplain received a reprimand from his next commanding officer for the same type of conduct for which he had been favorably recognized at the 27th.

It was rather boring for a few days. No choppers, and the patients were moved to other units. I had time to think back on my months at the 27th Surgical. As I sat there in the sun, I removed the little pin we all wore on the lapel of our fatigues. I held it in the palm of my hand and read what was engraved. I read it aloud, "We Care for All." Indeed, the members of the 27th Surgical had cared for all. We had cared for American casualties, the South Vietnamese army regulars, civilian casualties and enemy casualties, with a few Caesarian sections thrown in for variety. I thought about all those hours in the four operating rooms in the surgical Quonset hut.

I thought about the facetious little ditty that, early on, I learned to sing in the operating room. The words were, "We like it here. We like it here. You bet your ass, we like it here." Often somebody would start singing the song after hours and hours and sometimes days of continuous surgery. Then everyone would chime in from all four rooms. Sometimes there was pretty good four-part harmony. The practice was good for keeping a very tired crew awake, but it was actually an act of psychological numbing. There were times when the lyrics were sung over and over again with a lot of anger when there had been a lot of mutilating procedures.

I thought back on one very busy 10-day period during which I gave anesthesia for two quad amps (amputations). One of the poor guys who lost both arms and both legs also lost both eyes. There was nothing satisfying about participating in such procedures even though the patient was still alive when it was over. I recalled the day in triage when three GIs were brought in DOA (dead on arrival) without a mark on any of them. They had all drowned when they waded into a river while carrying heavy loads and stepped in over their heads. No group questioned the war more than the doctors and nurses who had to care for the

Vietnam Song

We like it here We like it here You bet your ass, we like it here

The music and lyrics of the Vietnam numbing song.

casualties. I could not imagine any mission in Vietnam that was worth the cost being paid by thousands of young men.

I smiled as I thought back on what I had discovered carved into the wooden door of one of the latrine stalls during my first week at the 27th. It read, "This is where you make the contribution to this country that you really want to make." After I had been at the 27th for a few months, a career Army nurse anesthetist joined the staff. He claimed that there was a second verse to the "We Like It Here" song. He then went on to sing it to the notes of "Auld Lang Syne," "For all I know, it may be so, but it sounds like shit to me. For all I know, it may be so, but it sounds like shit to me."

Letters, audio tapes and care packages from home had kept hope alive for returning to what was referred to as "the world" back home. Everybody treasured something different. I smiled as I thought back on the day when one of the general surgeons from Florida got his first care package from home. He tore that first care package open with some ferocity and then yelled "YES!" when he saw the contents. He liked his martinis, and there was certainly plenty of cheap alcohol available to make them. There were no olives available. Somebody sent him a jar of olives, and he was ecstatic.

I thought back on that one very serious meeting Col. Geer called for the entire physician staff. One of the new surgeons had exhausted the entire blood supply on one case, and the colonel was furious. He was a man of few words. He called the room to order and began, "Yesterday, one of our surgeons saw fit to completely exhaust our blood supplies on one Vietnamese casualty that was not salvageable. This will not happen again. Dismissed." Nothing more needed to be said. While the motto on our lapels said, "We Care for All," everyone knew that the priority was the American GI. The Vietnamese would never donate blood for the children who were casualties of the war and came to surgery. The American GIs or medical personnel would donate their blood.

I recalled the day The Rabbit brought me a paper from home with an article about antiwar protests at the Capitol with a picture showing a couple of veterans in wheelchairs protesting in Washington, D.C. I just glanced at it. All The Rabbit said was, "I think this is one of our patients," pointing to one of the wheelchair protestors.

As I sat between the BOQs with a cold drink, I had to smile as I thought back on the night I was awakened and informed that I was needed for a medevac flight. I had not yet been on a medevac flight but knew that it usually meant getting out of the country for a few days. Thinking I was headed for Japan, I said, "Let me get a few things packed." The response was, "No need. This will only take a couple of hours. We just need to have you ventilate a kid while he is choppered out to the *Sanctuary* (a hospital ship). He needs dialysis." I made my way to the chopper and took over the Ambu bag and began to ventilate the patient. The chopper headed out over the South China Sea. It wasn't long before I spotted the *Sanctuary*, bobbing up and down in what I thought was rather rough seas. I could see the big circle that marked the landing spot as the chopper began to descend. I wondered how the pilot was going to make a soft landing with the ship going up and down so much. To my great surprise and relief, the pilot did a very smooth job with the landing. As I got off the chopper, somebody took over the ventilation as the patient was carried into sick bay. As I tried to follow along, I began walking off to the right. Did not have my sea legs. Somebody grabbed my arm and helped me into sick bay to give report. It was a different world, like being back in the States. I stood there in my jungle fatigues, giving report to a bunch of Navy doctors who were dressed in stateside tan khaki uniforms. I remembered thinking, "These guys know how to live." I then climbed back on the chopper and was taken back to the 27th Surgical for a short night of sleep.

On Wednesday, May 12, I was able to talk to Judy on a MARS call. The system involved using ham radio operators to make calls home. A ham radio operator in the States would call the home of a service person and patch the call to that number using his radio. The only problem was that each person would have to say "over" so the radio operator could flip the switch to allow the other person to respond.

On the evening of the 14th, I was handed my orders for the 95th Evacuation Hospital assignment. On Sunday, May 16 (Judy's birthday), I got up at 6 a.m. to help load trucks. Then at 11:00 a.m. I climbed aboard a chopper for my trip to Da Nang. Most of the trip was flown at treetop level. The pilot would drop down and skim the water at each river. At each river I was convinced he would never pull up in time to avoid hitting the trees, but he always did. When the chopper got to Da Nang and landed, I wiped the marbles of sweat from my brow as I got out, convinced that the pilot had taken great pleasure in scaring the hell out of me. As I left the chopper, the pilot was laughing loudly and continued to laugh as he lifted off.

DISCOVERING
THE 95TH EVACUATION
HOSPITAL

The beginning of the 95th Evacuation Hospital goes back to 1928, when it was originally constituted by the office of the Surgeon General as the 74th Surgical Hospital, on December 21. It was just an idea on paper for years until it was activated at Fort Warren, Cheyenne, Wyoming, on June 1, 1941. It was reorganized and redesigned as the 95th Evacuation Hospital on August 25, 1942, and landed on the Salerno beachhead on D-Day as the first U.S hospital in Europe in World War II. After the war, the unit returned to the United States and was deactivated at Camp Kilmer, New Jersey, on December 3, 1945. The Vietnam War brought the reactivation of the 95th Evacuation Hospital on March 26, 1963, at Fort Benning, Georgia, and then the alert for overseas assignment. The unit arrived in Vietnam on March 26, 1968. A tent facility was erected on the beach about eight miles south of where the metal Quonset hut facility would eventually be constructed at the base of Monkey Mountain at Da Nang. The movement of the staff to the new site started on July 4, 1968.

I arrived at the 95th Evacuation Hospital on the beach at Da Nang nestled at the base of Monkey Mountain on May 16, 1971. When I arrived, there was a shortage of rooms in the BOQ. The commanding officer for the unit had returned to the States, and no replacement had yet arrived. So I and two other physicians were told that we could bunk in the commanding officer's quarters temporarily. The CO had pretty nice quarters! It was a nice, two-bedroom mobile home with a little kitchen and dining room and bathroom. I and two other physicians were offered the option of staying in the mobile home until rooms became available in the BOQ or until the new CO showed up. The very back of the trailer contained a large bedroom with a double bed. The other bedroom was small with a single bed. The prize was the small bedroom where one could sleep alone. My two colleagues who would be enjoying the trailer with me were both majors. I was just a lowly captain. One of them decided that we should match coins to see who got to sleep alone. I don't know why they didn't just pull rank on me and flip a coin to decide which one of them would get the private room, but they seemed in a big hurry to get the decision made. I got the private room. The two majors would share the big double bed in the back of the trailer. It did not always go well. I did get a few laughs during the night. On one occasion I heard one of them yell, "Get your hand off my ass, and move over." On another night, I heard a bit of yelling when one of them accused the other of silently passing gas. The only time when either of them got the big bed to themselves was when one was off while the other was working.

Most of the nurses were fresh out of nursing school, but there was one who was a little older. She had been an airline stewardess before going to nursing school. She was a British girl, and she had taken a special interest in the unmarried surgeon who was one of my roommates at the trailer. She visited him several times when he had the trailer to himself, no doubt just for an intense game of checkers or chess. He must have been losing the checkers or chess games from pure distraction, based on the risqué attire of his visiting nurse, who had been observed leaving the trailer several times, scantily clad.

The three of us were able to occupy the trailer from May 16 to June 5 when I finally got a room on the second floor of the BOQ. I didn't mind the second floor since the 95th was located on the beach at the base of Monkey Mountain and not in the line of fire. Every time I looked out at the South China Sea, I wondered what was going on at home. I so missed not being able to hug Judy and the kids.

The hospital compound was completely surrounded by a network of barbed wire, including barbed wire that limited access via the beach. Guard towers were also located around the periphery. There was a village beyond the wire just north of the compound, and the villagers utilized the beach as an open toilet. The perimeter was supposedly mined inside the beach wire. My Khe Beach, the site where troops could experience a little in-country R & R and buy snacks and drinks and swim and relax, was located just a short jeep drive south of the hospital. It was nicknamed "China Beach" by the American and Australian soldiers who were able to do a little rest and relaxation there. From China Beach, one could look north and see Monkey Mountain that overshadowed the hospital. The 95th Evacuation Hospital would eventually be used as the

The 95th Evacuation Hospital site located beneath Monkey Mountain. Note the officers' club with sandbags on the roof, fishing boats in the harbor, and an elevated guard tower with a good view of the beach.

Vietnamese shacks all along the entry road to the 95th Evacuation Hospital.

basis for the fictional 510th Evacuation Hospital in the television series *China Beach.*

One of the Army nurse anesthetists, Gus, was reassigned with me to the 95th after the 27th Surgical was closed. The area between the male and female BOQs had some tables and chairs where one could sit and read or play chess or just relax. One afternoon, Gus and I were enjoying a little time off, just sitting in this area and talking. I had my feet propped up and was leaning back with my eyes closed. Suddenly, Gus exclaimed, "Reuel, do you see that?" I opened my eyes and noted that Gus was looking up at the second floor of the male BOQ. Standing near the end of the BOQ closest to the sea was a nurse in a string bikini. Gus persisted, with his gaze fixed on the nurse, "Do you see that?" I replied, "Yes, Gus, I do." Then Gus went on to express his shock and dismay with his usual Southern drawl, "That's just awful. That girl might as well not have anything on at all." I expressed my agreement with my Seventh Day Adventist colleague and then went back to catching some more shut eye.

As Gus neared the end of his tour of duty, he asked me to drive him out to the end of the entrance road so he could take some pictures with the 8mm movie camera he had purchased through the PACEX system. I drove him out to the end of the entrance road where Gus immediately noticed two Vietnamese boys who appeared to be about 8 or 9 years of age. They were playing in the water in the ditch along the main road. He asked me to stop the jeep so he could film them, and I did. Gus stood up in the jeep, held the camera up to his eye, and began filming. The boys looked up and realized that somebody was taking their picture. They both immediately raised an arm, holding up the middle finger on the hand of the raised arm. Without lowering the camera, Gus, with his customary Southern drawl, inquired, "Reuel, are those boys shooting the bird at me?" I replied, "Yes, Gus, they are." Gus continued to film saying, "I thought so." After filming the Vietnamese boys, we drove back to the hospital compound. As Gus neared the end of his tour, his younger brother, who was also a nurse, arrived at the 95th.

Soon after I arrived at the 95th, I noticed that there were a lot of explosions offshore during the day. When I inquired about what was going on, I was assured that it was nothing to be concerned about, that the Vietnamese were just fishing. One of the guys explained that the Vietnamese would steal our concussion grenades and use them to stun the fish which they would then scoop up with nets. No Department of Natural Resources in Vietnam!

The chief of anesthesia at the 95th when I arrived was an Army anesthesiologist named Gene. He was a pleasant, laid-back fellow with a dry sense of humor. He had contracted polio as a youngster, and it had left him with one deformed leg which hampered his mobility. When he was called to the operating room from his quarters, he would make his way, dragging his one bad leg, smiling and saying, "I never wanted to be a missionary." That was his favorite line. It summarized his view of the mission. He wasn't just an administrator. He was always right in the middle of everything and providing anesthesia for cases just like all the other anesthetists under his command. He was a good man.

The 95th was a much larger unit than the 27th Surgical and had all of the medical specialists, including a neurosurgeon. I quickly got exposed to providing anesthesia for some cases with which I had no prior experience, namely craniotomies. There were also a lot of the same kind of cases that we had done at the 27th Surgical. The routine cases continued, the amputations, the debridement of fragmentation wounds, laparotomy for bowel perforations and bleeding. Those that bothered me the most were the cases that resulted in such terrible mutilation that the outlook for any quality of life was bleak. One such case took place just a few days after my arrival at the 95th. It was a five-hour case that started at 7:30 a.m. on May 20. The poor GI underwent a left hip disarticulation, a right femoral artery vein graft and a laparotomy for treatment of bowel and aorta perforations. His right radial and ulnar arteries were also gone. I transfused 48 units of blood for that case. He did survive, albeit with much of his body gone. It was depressing. The next day was taken up with a lengthy craniotomy.

TDY Pleiku

It was Thursday, June 10, 1971, when Gene approached me with a proposal. He began, "Hey Reuel, how would you like to be the chief of anesthesia at a smaller unit?" I pointed out to him that we were not in the line of fire at the 95th and that I could not imagine being in another place that would be better for me. I asked him if he was asking me to volunteer for something. He acknowledged that he was, that he needed somebody to go to Pleiku. Thinking back on what I had promised my dad when we said our goodbyes at the airport back home, I explained to Gene. "I promised my dad that I would not volunteer for anything while I was over here. If I get orders, I will follow them, but I cannot volunteer." Gene said that he understood and headed back to the surgical Quonset. A couple of hours later, he brought me my orders for deployment to Pleiku. It was a TDY (temporary duty) assignment of two weeks' duration. I had no clue about the area where I would be going. I quickly got off a note to Judy, informing her that I was being sent off on a temporary assignment, and that I could not tell her where I was going. I told her that I would not be writing for a couple of weeks, and that the assignment should be over by the time she got my letter.

The next morning, I got up at 6 a.m. and left the 95th Evac a little after 7 a.m. My plane left Da Nang for Phu Cat at 10 a.m. I sat at the Phu Cat terminal from 11:15 a.m. until 4:30 p.m. before getting a dustoff chopper ride to Pleiku. My feet were draped out the side of the open chopper during the ride which was at a high altitude for the most part. My legs and feet had a hollow feeling as I looked down at the space between my feet and the ground and took in the jungle and rice paddies below, wondering if we would encounter any enemy fire during the trip.

When the chopper dropped me off at the helipad at the 14th Medical Detachment at Pleiku, I looked back and snapped a picture of the chopper just before it lifted off. Painted on the front of the chopper in large, white letters just above the red cross was one word, "WHY." That one word, "WHY," pretty well summed up the predominant sentiment.

It was the rainy season, and everything was damp all the time. I was shown around the facilities and quickly noted the frag holes in the various Quonset huts, including the one that housed the surgical facilities. It was clear that, at one time, it had been the home of a much larger medical unit. The only surgeon now assigned to the unit was a fellow whose training consisted of just one year of general surgery residency at an academic

The chopper with the word "WHY" painted on the front, my transportation to Pleiku.

center where he mostly watched. There were a couple of other general medical officers. One was an internist who exclaimed that he was glad to see me because he now wouldn't have to cover the clap clinic every day. I was assigned sleeping quarters in a Quonset hut that was surrounded by sandbags on the outside.

My little room had an elevated bed with sandbags all around it and an opening to allow for getting under the bed. The room reeked with the very strong smell of urine. The male nurse anesthetist, who occupied the room adjoining mine, explained that the strong urine smell was because the sandbags were all polluted with urine from all the wild dogs in the area. He told me that the only way to get rid of the smell was to get rid of the sandbags. When I first arrived, there were no casualties to care for so I spent most of my first day just cleaning my room, but the urine smell persisted.

I had always been impressed by the number of Vietnamese people who could be transported on a single motorcycle at one time. During a jeep ride on my first day at Pleiku, I was very impressed by the courage

Author in front of the sleeping quarters Quonset hut at Pleiku.

displayed by one of the locals who was transporting a ladder across his back on a motorcycle, running the risk of being converted to a primitive helicopter by a passing truck.

During that first evening at Pleiku, I visited with some of my new coworkers and played some cards in the end room of my Quonset hut. There was a lot of artillery noise and small-arms fire all during the card game. At one point, I asked, "What do we do if the enemy comes busting in here?" One of the guys laughed and replied, "Ask them if they want us to deal them in." When I asked how far we were from the Cambodian border, one of the guys indicated that it was more than 20 miles. When I asked about who was providing our security, I was informed that all of our security was the responsibility of a signal battalion. Curious about the emergency that had triggered my TDY assignment, I asked, "What was the big emergency back in the States that got the anesthesiologist out of here for a couple of weeks?" The nurse anesthetist replied, "Oh, his wife was just going to have a routine C-section. So, he applied for an emergency leave to go back and hold her hand, and the leave was granted."

The second morning, June 12, I was occupied with anesthesia duties in the morning and assigned to triage for the evening and night. It was a

A Vietnamese man transporting a ladder on a motorcycle.

fairly slow day. When I did my first cases in the Quonset hut that housed the operating rooms, I noticed all the frag holes in the upper parts of the structure that were highlighted by the beams of sunlight shining through. It was clear that the facility had kept a much bigger staff busy at one time but had been downgraded to a much smaller staff. When I arrived at triage at 7 p.m., I found an empty triage except for one unattended stretcher at the far end, a stretcher occupied by a GI who was not moving but was breathing on his own. I inquired of the doctor I was relieving, "What do you have down there?" He answered, "Frag wound of the head." I asked if there was a medevac on the way and was told that there was no point in a medevac. He suggested that I take a look for myself, so I made my way to the end of the Quonset hut to check the guy out. The patient's breathing was somewhat labored and displayed some stridor. There was a small entrance wound to one temple and no exit wound on the other side of the head. With my thumbs, I pulled open both eyelids, only to observe two unreacting, completely dilated pupils. There was no need to risk a helicopter pilot's life to move him. Somebody back home didn't know how devastated they were going to feel in the next 24 hours. I thought about the word painted on the chopper that had brought me to Pleiku, "WHY."

Back in the States, Richard Nixon was preoccupied with the White House wedding of his daughter, Tricia, on this date and was more concerned about getting re-elected than keeping his promise to end the war. Nixon was laughing and dancing and celebrating while this young man was lying on a stretcher on the other side of the planet, brain-dead but still breathing. It was just a matter of waiting for the damage inside his skull to progress to the point that his breathing would stop, and he could be pronounced dead. Things soon broke loose with several casualties arriving at triage. I was able to treat one of them in triage, cleaning up multiple frag wounds of the legs. I then headed off to the surgical hut to provide anesthesia until 3 a.m. for the other casualties. I returned to triage at 3 a.m. where I found that the brain-dead GI had finally stopped breathing. There would be no bride for him to love and to hold, no children for him to hear say "Daddy," no grandchildren for him to spoil in his old age. No, that was all taken from him because Nixon did not keep his word, and for what? Decades later, I searched for the names on the Vietnam Memorial Wall of those who died on June 13, 1971, at Pleiku. There was just one, a 24-year-old from Salem, Massachusetts, Richard Joseph Gray, wounded on June 12 and died on June 13, 1971. One of the medics on the scene of the attack when Lt. Gray was injured described his last conversation with Lt. Gray. He said that Lt. Gray had taken a frag to the head but was still talking and instructing him to take care of the others who had been injured saying, "I will be all right." Twenty-three of Lt. Gray's men had been injured. Lt. Gray would continue to bleed inside his head and would sustain irreversible brain damage by the time he arrived in triage at Pleiku. His name is on panel W3, line 74 of the memorial wall.

By the third day, it was clear that the internist, who was a short-timer, did not intend to cover sick call or any other duties, and was simply dumping them all on me. I found myself covering sick call and triage on my third day. I had not set my eyes on the internist since I had met him on my first day. The food situation was not good either. Some of the convoys had failed to get through with our food supplies. SOS aka "shit on a shingle" (chipped beef and gravy on a biscuit) was being offered at every meal. My goodies from home were all back at the 95th, so it was SOS or nothing. After a while, a lot of the guys were just meeting at the mess hall for conversation and an adult beverage. On my third day, while meeting at the mess hall, I inquired of the other docs at the table as to the whereabouts of the internist. The question resulted in an eruption of laughter as one of the guys went on to explain, "Nobody has seen him outside of his room for about 48 hours now. There is a nurse keeping him company. Too bad we can't come up with a couple of raw steaks to throw into his room just so they can keep up their strength. We'll see him tonight for his DEROS party. He goes home tomorrow."

Sure enough, the internist showed up for his DEROS party that night. A lot of jokes were told, and there were a number of toasts. Then the internist was asked to make his farewell speech. He started out saying something about "all the new people you get to meet over here," a line that was greeted with a lot of laughter and curious looks by the internist.

By the fourth day, I finally decided that I could not tolerate the smell in my room any longer. Any time I spent more than a few hours sleeping in my room, I awoke with a persistent headache which I attributed to the strong urine smell from the sandbags. I spent a few hours hauling the sandbags out of my room along with some other junk that had been left under the bed. After hours of cleaning, I finally got rid of the urine smell and was quite pleased with my efforts. I enjoyed my sleep time in that room over the next five days and experienced no more headaches. Then came Saturday, June 19, 1971, my ninth day at Pleiku. I had endured a night of constant mortar noise and special forces mosquitoes. I saw a few guys at sick call and then returned to my room for a nap. I was awakened from a sound sleep by a loud explosion and sirens at 11:30 a.m. I rolled off the elevated bed and got down on the floor on my hands and knees but not flat on the floor. My helmet and flak jacket were on the chair right next to me. Rockets usually came one after the other with a steady boom, boom, boom, boom, and it was over. This time, there was just the one explosion and nothing else. After about 15 seconds with no further explosions, I started to push myself up from the floor to get back on my bed when the concussion of another blast flattened me on the floor. My eyes were stinging, and my vision was blurred. My nose burned with a strong sulfur smell. A large, steel light fixture that had hung from the ceiling of the Quonset hut was lying next to my head. I immediately reached for my flak jacket and helmet and dragged them along as I scrambled under my bed for cover, pulling the helmet and flak jacket over my head and neck and praying "Lord, just let me be alive five minutes from now." I laid there under that bed with a prickly feeling in my back, bracing for what I thought would be a direct hit. Fortunately, there were no other explosions, just the two. After several minutes, a voice from the other side of the wall where my nurse anesthetist had been sleeping inquired, "Are you OK, Long?" I said that I was OK. Then the nurse anesthetist, knowing that I had removed all the sandbag protection from my room, could not resist the opportunity and inquired, "How does it smell in your room now?" I responded with, "It doesn't smell like dog piss anymore." We both had a good laugh. I asked him if we should go outside and check things out. He suggested that we should wait until we hear other people outside first, which we did.

As we emerged from our damaged quarters, we could immediately see that a rocket had landed between Quonset huts, almost making a direct hit on the Quonset hut that served as a latrine. There was an impact hole right next to it, and much of the steel had been peeled off one end. Water was spraying in the air from broken pipes. Several porcelain stools were exposed where the steel had been blown off. Looking at the damage, I said to my nurse anesthetist, "It's pretty clear what they are up to now." "Oh?" he replied. I explained, "They are just trying to demoralize us by taking out the latrine." We needed to laugh. We had both survived with no injuries. So I kept going. I pointed out the exposed porcelain stools and asked him, "If somebody had been sitting on one of those stools and survived the blast, would they suffer from diarrhea or constipation for the rest of their life?" He suggested that it might make one nervous about going to the bathroom for a while. A mama-san (slang for older Vietnamese woman) was standing just outside the damaged hut and appeared to be in a trance as she gazed at the damage. She had sustained no injuries. As she stared at the damage, she kept saying, "Numba ten, numba ten.... I go home now ... maybe come back in three days." The "numba ten" phrase was something inspired by the American soldiers. Something good was "number one." Something bad was "number ten." Somebody noted that many of the Vietnamese who worked on the base had not shown up for work and had probably been forced to carry rockets during the night for the enemy. Not all the base workers had gotten the message, a communications failure. There were waist-high frag holes in some of the Quonset huts, but there were no injuries.

My nurse anesthetist and I began the process of putting our rooms back together. The nurse anesthetist did not consider the incident to have been casualty-free because his booze collection had gotten wiped out by the blast. A good breeze had dissipated the sulfur smell in our rooms. Now the prevailing smell was from the evaporation of alcohol with broken bottles littering the floor. As I put my room back in order, I pulled the mattress off the elevated bed and put it on the floor under the bed where I slept for the remainder of my TDY assignment. Then I thought about why I was putting up with all this crap, so a guy can hold his wife's hand during a C-section. It was soon discovered that several dud rounds had landed on the compound which explained the long pause between blasts.

The next morning, I was awakened at 7 a.m. to treat a guy who was experiencing a significant gastrointestinal bleed. He was vomiting

The rocket damage showing the impact hole.

blood. I performed my first blind nasal intubation and then proceeded with administering anesthesia. The young, partially-trained surgeon opened the abdomen with a goal of controlling the bleeding. He was quickly in over his head. The bleeding was out of control. I was pumping blood in two lines, and we were losing ground. He looked up at me and asked, "Can you help me?" I responded, "Do you want me to scrub in?" He quickly said, "Yes!" I sent for my nurse anesthetist, put the patient on the ventilator and pumped up the pressure on the blood bags. I put a nurse at the head of the table to take vital signs until my nurse anesthetist arrived, then I got into gown and gloves. Between the two of us, we managed to get the bleeding under control and had a good outcome. I figured that I had probably done more surgical procedures than my partially-trained surgeon. The time in the Flint emergency rooms had been valuable. I had also watched some very good surgeons at the 27th Surgical. Meanwhile, back in the States, the *New York Times* and *Washington Post* were publishing the leaked, classified Pentagon Papers, and Senator Mike Mansfield, a Democrat from Montana, was making a commencement speech in which he called the U.S. involvement in Vietnam "a tragic mistake."

Two days later, June 22, the anesthesiologist returned from

his emergency leave. Also on that date, the U.S. Senate passed a non-binding resolution that urged the removal of all U.S. troops from Vietnam by the end of the year. The killing and mutilation continued. I never met the returning anesthesiologist. He took over his duties, and I was relieved to arrange for my return to the 95th Evac. Some of the guys got me involved in a little party and card game the night before I was to leave. There was also a little alcohol consumption, something that I should have avoided. The party went until 2:45 a.m.

I turned in for a short night, setting my alarm clock for 6:30 a.m. When the alarm clock went off, I sat up and immediately experienced a wave of nausea and a pounding headache. I immediately assumed the supine position, and the headache and nausea seemed to subside. I sat up again, only to have the nausea and headache immediately return. This happened several times. Finally, I got up and ran for the toilet at the end of the Quonset hut where I proceeded to vomit several times. I thought my head was going to explode. I then went back to my bed to lie down for 20 minutes. I then managed to get my bag into the back of a jeep for my ride to the airfield. The nausea and headache persisted, and I had large beads of sweat on my forehead during the ride to the airfield. At the airfield, I signed up for a fixed-wing flight to Phu Cat. I sat there for an hour just watching the camouflage planes land and take off. Then, suddenly, I was paged and told that I was going to be bumped onto a direct flight to Da Nang, a DC-6 that had just landed. I could see the plane. It stood out because of its silver color and no camouflage. In my tenuous condition, I boarded the plane and took the only empty seat. As I looked around, I saw more brass than I had ever seen in one place in my life. I quickly realized that, as a captain, I was the lowest ranking commissioned officer on the plane, and the only one wearing jungle fatigues. There were lieutenant colonels and bird colonels everywhere, all dressed in stateside uniforms. "Oh Lord," I thought, "Don't let me vomit in the middle of this group." The nausea and headache persisted. As the plane took off and leveled off at altitude, a black sergeant leaned over and whispered into my ear, "Would you like some coffee, Captain?" I wiped the sweat from my forehead and thanked him for the coffee. I sipped the coffee, and it stayed down. I managed to make the trip without embarrassing myself, and I pledged that I would never experience such symptoms again as a result of alcohol consumption. I made it back to Da Nang by noon. It was great to get back to the 95th. I had a lot of mail waiting for me as well as some pearls I had ordered from the PACEX catalog for Judy.

OKINAWA

On June 24, 1971, I was back in the operating room in the anesthesia rotation at the 95th Evac. On June 30, I was far down on the call schedule and would likely see no action. The morning brought news of a major explosion at the ammunition dump at Baxter with several casualties. I made my way over to triage where I found four dead lying at the end of the Quonset hut. We got the news that the Russians had lost three cosmonauts. They had been found dead in their landing craft when it returned to Earth. There was no news about what went wrong. One of the Army nurses, who seemed a bit hardcore to me, laughed and said "Good!" when she heard the news about the cosmonauts. I didn't understand how anyone, especially anyone in the healthcare field, could be happy about the death of anyone. Strange woman.

On Thursday, July 1, 1971, 6,100 American soldiers were pulled out of Vietnam, but it was a very busy day in the operating rooms at the 95th Evacuation Hospital at Da Nang with cases going well into the evening. When I finished my last case in the evening, I was informed that I was assigned to a medevac flight to Okinawa that would be leaving in the morning. I got up the next morning and left the 95th Evac at 6:45 a.m. My patient was suffering from DTs (delirium tremens), malaria, hepatitis and upper gastrointestinal bleeding. He did not have a good chance for survival. My flight left the 15th Aerial Port at 10:20 a.m. and arrived in Okinawa at 3:15 p.m. My patient lived through the trip but later died at the hospital in Okinawa. There was a MARS station at the top of the hospital in Okinawa with all the usual ham radio equipment. I paid a visit to the station in hopes of making some calls to the family. I agreed to hang around and help the guy with his calls, and he offered to help me make a call home to Judy and talk as much as I wanted. I spent five hours at the MARS station from 9 p.m. July 2 to 2 a.m. July 3. When it came time for me to make my call, I provided my home phone number, hoping to talk to Judy. The ham radio operator back in the States called my number. It rang for a long time with no answer. I figured she must be grocery shopping. The ham operator asked if I wanted to call anyone else so I gave him my dad's number. I got an answer this time, and we had a good, long talk. That event sparked an interest in ham radio for my dad, and he would get his ham license a few years later. Finally, at 2:00 a.m., we took another try with my home number and got an answer. It was great to talk with Judy, in spite of constantly saying "over" so the ham operator could flip the switch.

On July 5, I managed to get a flight back to Vietnam with a layover in Taiwan. As my plane was coming into Taiwan for a landing, the flight path went right over a bunch of tall buildings. The tops of the buildings seemed so close that I thought the wheels were going to catch them. Suddenly, the plane dropped down to a runway. When I deplaned, there was some kind of military ceremony taking place at the airfield with a bunch of Taiwanese soldiers marching with rifles on their shoulders. To my great surprise, I encountered a medical school classmate at the airfield. Mike had saved up all his leave time and was taking a terminal leave, just catching military flights around the world and seeing the sights. We both had one night to spend in Taiwan and do some shopping, so we caught a cab to a hotel and booked a room with two huge beds. Each of us threw our gear on a bed and were about to go in search of some food when someone knocked at the open door and entered the room. Our visitor was there to explain the services available at the hotel and went on to tell us about the restaurants and other facilities. Then followed the explanation of the pushbutton console above each bed. Instructions were given regarding which button should be pushed in order to summon a girl to the room. It was also explained to us that all the girls were very healthy. The salesman then went on his or her way. Mike turned to me and said, "Well, I think we just met the hotel pimp. Was the pimp male or female?" I indicated that I didn't know for sure. The two of us then went downstairs to a large dining hall and had a good meal. During the meal, we both noticed that there were finely dressed women stationed against the wall all around the room. They all just stood there smiling. Regarding the women along the walls, Mike opined, "I think those are the hookers." Leaving the restaurant, we set out to shop, not without repeatedly being propositioned on the streets by more hookers. We did manage to find some interesting shops. Copyrights were ignored in Taiwan, and one could buy a $35 medical book for $3.50, albeit on very cheap paper. I could not resist picking up a few books. The next day, I was able to string together enough flights to get back to Da Nang and the 95th Evac, all while having second thoughts about the books I had purchased and now had to lug around.

Back at the 95th Evac, Gene's tour was coming to an end, and I soon had to adjust to a new chief of anesthesia who would occupy Gene's room, right next to mine. There was a large hole in the wall between Gene's room and mine so that I could get the benefit of the air conditioner installed in his room. That hole in the wall became a bit of a problem for me after Gene left. Gene's replacement was a single, Jewish fellow from New York. He was quite distraught about being in Vietnam and complained constantly to me. The complaining was not limited to the downtime during the day. It went on at night as well. Getting a good night's sleep with the new chief in the next room was difficult. He would run his mouth constantly, claiming that he just didn't know how I had stood it for all the months I had been in country. He would say, "I'm not going to be able to do it. I can't stand this." Lying in bed, trying to get some rest, I would try to reassure him and tell him that he would be fine and would get used to it all. Many nights, I would tire of responding in sentences and just say "uh uh" to his constant lamenting until I finally fell asleep. I was starting to find the operating room to be an escape and soon found that I got more rest working at night and sleeping during the day when possible.

Family Leave

In addition to R & R, the Army allowed for a 10-day leave during the Vietnam tour. One could even go home for 10 days on a family leave, but not at government expense, so I paid for a round-trip ticket to go home and see my family in the middle of July. It was worth every cent. I left the 95th Evac on July 15, looking forward to seeing Judy and the kids. The trip home was on a commercial airline, a silver bird with real stewardesses. The route was back through Anchorage, O'Hare and finally to Bishop Airport in Flint. The flight was full, and I spent several hours talking with the general medical officer who occupied the seat next to me. We talked about our Vietnam experiences and how we were looking forward to the visit home. There were a lot of quiet hours as well.

I found myself thinking about my kids and what I wanted for them. I even thought back on my time as a youngster in Detroit where I had lived on the eastside until I was in the third grade. The houses were all very close together with no driveways between them. Family cars were parked on the streets. An alley separated the row of houses on one street from the row on the next street. I thought about that kid who was two years older than me and lived right next door. When I was in the second grade, that kid was always picking on me and hitting me. The problem had come to a sudden halt one day when I came into the house crying and complaining about the kid next door beating up on me. Well, my dad had grown up in Detroit and had been in his share of fights, and he wasn't going to put up with a whining kid who could not defend himself. He angrily turned and threatened me, saying, "If you don't go out there and give that kid a whipping, I'm going to give you a whipping you won't forget for a while." I could see the anger and disgust in my dad's face and hear it in his voice. The fear of my dad and a whipping from him suddenly overcame any fear of a whipping from the big kid next door. Driven by a surge of adrenaline, I charged to the front door, knocking the screen door hard against the wall as I busted through. I jumped

108

from the porch, not making use of any of the five steps leading up to the porch. I ran as fast as I could, crossing the sidewalk and onto the grass strip next to the street where my abuser stood, looking rather surprised by my advance. I charged into him, knocking him to the ground. I then jumped on him and straddled him while pounding my fists into his face and chest. He began crying loudly and screaming for help. His family members came to his rescue and pulled me off him. I went back into my house and just sat down for a while until my heart stopped pounding so hard. My dad's only reaction as he looked out the front door was, "I don't think he will be a problem anymore." He wasn't.

The alley behind the house was where I had learned to ride a two-wheel bike. My dad and some of his friends had gotten me going on a two-wheeler by running alongside me as I peddled and then letting me go. That first try, I stayed up and peddled with no problem after I was let go, but nobody had shown me how to stop. At the end of the alley, I had gone right across the street, hit the curb and flipped over onto the grass. Fortunately, there had been no traffic on the street at the time. As I thought back on those times, I promised myself that my kids would live in a better place.

While my mind wandered during the long flight home, back in Flint, my Judy was up early on the day of my scheduled arrival. She straightened the house that she had been cleaning for a solid month. She started fixing all my favorite dishes—fried chicken, potato salad and chocolate cake. She had spent the past week making cookies and other goodies which she had stored in the freezer so she would not have to spend so much time in the kitchen during the leave. The kids had all gotten up early on arrival day too. They cleaned their rooms and got all dressed up early and went outside to play. Judy could hear them running around the neighborhood chanting, "My daddy's coming home today. My daddy's coming home today." Judy was expecting me to arrive on an afternoon flight. I was supposed to call home when I reached Chicago so Judy and the kids could meet me at Bishop Airport when I arrived.

Judy said that the phone rang more that day than it had in the seven months I had been away. Every time the phone rang, she expected to answer and hear my voice with the news that I was in Chicago. She was repeatedly disappointed by numerous calls from well-meaning people who were calling to see if I was home yet. She repeated the same message to several callers, "I haven't heard from him yet. He is supposed to call me from Chicago. I had better keep the line open in case he tries to call." Evening came, and my parents, sister and brothers came over to my house to have dinner with Judy and the kids. Nobody had much of an appetite. They all mostly just sat around and posed questions like, "Isn't he coming until tomorrow? Did something happen to his flight? Do you suppose he is all right?"

The flight was uneventful until the approach to O'Hare. The plane was in its descent at O'Hare when the pilot came over the intercom saying, "Gentlemen, I just want to update you regarding our landing at O'Hare. When we took off at Anchorage, we heard a loud pop that seemed to come from our nose gear wheel. We will be dropping down low enough to let the tower have a look at our nose gear wheel. Then we will climb again after they look us over." I had a window seat and had a good view of the airport as the plane flew low over the runway. Then the plane climbed and circled for quite a while. Finally, the pilot came back on the intercom, "Gentlemen, this is your pilot again. The tower looked us over, but they were not able to help us regarding the condition of the nose wheel. Before we make our descent for landing, the stewardesses will be coming through the cabin to show you the position we want you to take for landing. Please follow their instructions regarding stowing all materials and bending forward with your head down as we land. There will be emergency vehicles standing by. We have discarded most of our fuel. We have been assigned a long runway, and we will be keeping the nose up as long as possible during the landing."

With that, the plane began its descent, and I said a silent prayer that I would see my wife and kids again. I was looking out the window as the plane was on approach and nearing touchdown and the pilot gave his final instruction to "assume the position." Everyone was bending forward with their heads between their knees and hands clasped over their heads. The guy next to me asked me what I could see out of the window. I told him that I had never seen so many ambulances and fire trucks in one place in my life and that they were lining the runway as far as I could see. He responded with, "Oh shit! This is the crash position you know. I can't believe this. We survive most of our tour in Vietnam, and now they are going to put our heads up our asses right here at O'Hare." That long time circling made sense now. They needed time to get rid of fuel and get all the emergency vehicles in place to put out the fire and haul off the bodies. The nose was up as the main wheels touched down at what seemed like a higher-than-normal speed. For a long time, it seemed like the plane was not going to slow down but just speed down the runway with the nose up. Finally, the plane began to slow down and seemed to be almost at a stop before the nose dropped. All the passengers rose up in thunderous applause, wiping away the sweat. For a while it looked like I was not going to be able to get a flight to Flint, but I finally managed to get the last one. It was time to call home.

Back in Flint, Judy got another call. This time it was my Owosso friend, Brent, who was checking to see if I had made it home yet. She told him that she had not heard anything yet, and he asked to be called when I got in. She turned to my folks and said, "Just another false alarm." Everyone was just sitting around pretending to be interested in whatever television show was on 10 minutes after the Owosso call when the phone rang again. When she answered, I said, "Guess who?" I heard nothing but excited questions, "Where are you? Are you in Flint? When did you get in?" I told her that I was still at O'Hare but was about to board the last flight to Flint in five minutes and should be at Bishop Airport in 35 minutes. Her answer was, "Good, hurry, we will all be waiting for you."

Judy broke the news to everybody at the house. She got baby Jill redressed and straightened the other children's hair and clothes. She welcomed the family's help saying that she felt "all thumbs." The whole group got ready and headed to the airport. Once inside the terminal, they all sat and nervously waited for the arrival of the big jet that would be bringing me home. They watched my plane land and taxi to the unloading ramp. The children were lined up with their noses pressed against the big plate glass window, hoping to be the first to see their father. Judy was standing with baby Jill in her arms, trying to see over the heads of all the other people waiting to greet someone. She said that she was trembling, and her stomach was in knots. The door of the plane opened, and passengers started coming down the ramp. The oldest child, Lori, was the first to spot her dad. "Here he comes," she yelled. When I walked into the terminal, the three children rushed into my arms. Next, I hugged Judy and the baby

The anxious, bewildered look I got from little Jill all during my middle-of-tour visit home.

and planted a big kiss on my Judy. Tears were streaming down my Judy's face, and she whispered, "Welcome home," as we hugged. The children argued over who would carry my baggage, but they finally got everything divided up. We loaded into the car and headed for home. It had been a tense day for everyone. They had dinner again since I had missed out on the earlier dinner. I quickly discovered that my youngest child, 14-month-old Jill, saw me as a complete stranger, a stranger who had imposed himself on her world. When we all first gathered around the dinner table, Jill stood up in her highchair. I was concerned that she might fall and reached out to her to help her sit down. As I took my seat, I noticed that little Jill was looking at me with an expression of fear. Her bottom lip then protruded and began to quiver. Then followed uncontrollable bawling. It took Judy several minutes to calm her down and reassure her. During the entire leave, Jill avoided me as much as possible. If Judy and I were sitting on the sofa in the living room, Jill would make her way into the living room by walking along the wall, hand over hand, and going around the room to get to Judy without having to cross paths with me. She had only known one parent, Judy. It bothered me a great deal that I had not been present for such an important period of her life. All I could do was hug her and hope for the best. The 10 days passed all too quickly, and I made the long flight back to Da Nang, to the relief of my youngest child whose life could now get back to what she considered normal.

TDY Headquarters

I returned to my duties at the 95th Evac and quickly got back into the anesthesia rotation. The war went on and on with more amputations and mutilation of the bodies of young American and Vietnamese men. Then, suddenly, I was pulled out of the bloody operating rooms for another TDY assignment. My general practice and emergency room experience brought me to the attention of the powers that be for a new assignment. A doctor was needed to cover the aid station across town near headquarters in Da Nang. They had been without a doctor for some time. The temporary assignment was supposed to last for two weeks. When I arrived at the aid station, I was greeted by a friendly, black corpsman who seemed very glad to see me. He informed me that he had been without a doctor for two weeks and that he had treated three cardiac arrests all by himself.

The statement about the cardiac arrests piqued my interest, and I had to hear the story. I asked the corpsman to tell me about what was going on when he had to treat the cardiac arrests. He proceeded to tell me that they all happened in the clap clinic when he was giving penicillin shots. On three different occasions, one of the guys he was injecting with penicillin collapsed with what he thought was a cardiac arrest due to a penicillin allergy. I was afraid of what I might hear, but I had to ask. I said to him, "So how did you treat the three cardiac arrests?" Beaming with pride, the corpsman replied, "I gave them all a shot of adrenaline." I felt myself shudder briefly as I continued, "And how did you give the adrenaline?" Again, beaming with pride, the corpsman quickly replied, "I stuck 'em right in the heart with that big cardiac needle." I continued to inquire, "Did they all make it?" The grinning corpsman bragged, "Oh yes. They all came around right away." I smiled at him and said, "I'll bet they did." The thought that crossed my mind at that moment was, "Thank God it's hard to kill an 18-year-old." The corpsman showed me around the aid station and the supply room. We then sat down for a cold drink and a little talk. I told him that I was glad to hear that all three of the guys he treated with adrenaline survived, but he was probably not dealing with a cardiac arrest but simply guys who fainted when they got the penicillin shot. I showed him how to care for someone who faints by simply making sure they have a good airway, pulling the jaw forward until they regain consciousness. I suggested that he forget about giving intracardiac adrenaline to anyone else. I told him that he had over-treated a simple faint, but that would remain just between the two of us. He seemed to appreciate the instructions.

After showing me around the aid station, the corpsman told me that I should never sleep at the aid station. I had to ask why. He went on to explain, "This unit surrounding us is almost completely black. The captain is a white guy that they all hate. There have already been two attempts on his life. He sleeps right outside the aid station door. At night the guys sometimes make a game of trying to roll frag grenades down the hill between the sandbags and into where he is sleeping. So, the aid station gets a few frags once in a while. I'll show you where to sleep up the hill. If I need you at night, I'll come and get you. Otherwise, just stay put. The guys in the guard towers are all smoking shit, and they will shoot at anything that moves. They would feel bad if they shot you, but you would still be dead. Also, if you need to go anywhere while you are here, don't drive yourself. I'll drive you anywhere you need to go." I was beginning to entertain the possibility that my new TDY assignment might actually be more hazardous than the Pleiku assignment, and the risk was not from any enemy action. In 1970, there had already been 200 incidents of fragging, where attempts had been made on officers' lives with frag grenades by men under their command. I soon learned from one of the other guys at the aid station that my new corpsman had taken a two-week leave and had not returned for a couple of months. He faced no consequences for being AWOL for more than two months because of his influence with the black troops. He had been allowed to return to duty with no questions asked.

I did not face a lot of challenges during my two weeks at the aid station, and I took the advice of my corpsman regarding my safety. The Army had instituted an amnesty program for soldiers who had gotten involved with drugs during their tour. It required coming in and admitting to the problem weeks in advance of the DEROS date and starting on a treatment program. I found myself dealing with large numbers of GIs who were drug dependent and wanted to take advantage of the amnesty program.

My black corpsman drove me around Da Nang in a jeep. Whenever we would approach a checkpoint, which was always manned by black

MPs, my corpsman would slow down a little and raise his clenched fist. The black MP would raise his clenched fist and then wave us on through. My corpsman told me that white drivers were always stopped. Every time we went through a checkpoint with him raising his clenched fist, he would turn to me and say, "Don't ever try this without me." I didn't.

Early on, my corpsman took me to see the mess hall where the brass ate their meals. We snuck in while the place was empty. There was a beautiful buffet laid out on a long table with a nice tablecloth. Nice silverware was available. There were no flies. There were no large containers of slop from which somebody could dip a load onto your plate. It was as good as or better than any restaurant back home.

One night the corpsman came to get me to see a neck wound. A GI had sustained a long knife wound to his neck, going down the side of his face and neck all the way to his clavicle. It was a wide, gaping wound. Fortunately, no large vessels had been cut. The wound had been inflicted during a disagreement over a card game. The carving work had been performed by a Mexican-American GI. I had no interest in putting anybody at risk to transport him across town for care, in view of the circumstances that resulted in the injury. I was determined to treat him at the aid station. There was no fine suture at the aid station. It certainly would not be a cosmetic closure. All I could find was heavy silk suture. So that's what I used to close the long wound on his neck. He would have a big scar, but he could always get it revised later. I got the wound closed and dressed and sent him back to his quarters.

On another night at the aid station duty, my corpsman came to me and asked me if I would like some ice cream. I asked him where he was going to get ice cream in such a God-forsaken place. He replied, "Do you want any or not?" I quickly said, "Sure." Twenty minutes later, my corpsman returned with a round, five-gallon tub of vanilla ice cream saying, "We will have to eat it all since we have no way to keep it." I sent him out to find some grunts who wanted some ice cream. He did. Nothing went to waste.

One afternoon at the aid station, a ROK (Republic of Korea) marine came by the clinic asking for some albumin and offered to trade me an AK-47 to keep as a souvenir in exchange for the albumin. I made it clear to him that I could not part with any of my supplies, especially something that I might need to keep somebody alive until blood was available. He kept offering more things in addition to the gun. I finally had to get stern with him and send him on his way. My corpsman showed up a little later, and I told him about the ROK marine. My corpsman explained that the Koreans didn't want the albumin to treat casualties. He said, "They drink it. They think it gives them super strength."

As my time at the aid station was coming to an end, my corpsman said that he wanted to explain some things to me if I would promise not to pass along anything that he told me. I agreed. He began by explaining why he told me never to drive anywhere without him. It seems that the only vehicle assigned to the unit was the ambulance. He had stolen the truck and the jeep. He used the truck and the ambulance to bring prostitutes onto the base at night. His work as a pimp had paid off remarkably well. He also ran a successful gambling enterprise from which he had amassed a tidy sum. He told me that he really wanted to go to medical school some day and now had enough money to pay for it. He suggested that maybe someday I could write him a recommendation for medical school. I asked him if he planned to become a gynecologist based on his Vietnam experience. He replied, "Maybe."

The white captain was still alive when it was time for me to return to the 95th Evac. There were no frag attempts while I was at the aid station. I suspect that my corpsman put the word out that all the mischief needed to wait until after I left. I did not have the opportunity to treat any of the brass stationed near the aid station. It was good to get back to the hospital.

Winding Down

Back at the 95th Evac, the first thing I had to address was my calendar on the wall. I took a pen and marked a big X through all the dates I had spent at the aid station. It was good to get back to my room, no doubt a safer place to sleep than my quarters at the aid station. The crazy aid station assignment was a break from the daily carnage of the 95th Evac, but I was quickly back in the anesthesia rotation and witness to the sacrifices of more young men.

As my DEROS (Date of Estimated Return from Overseas) was approaching, one of the surgeons spoke with me about some surgery that I needed but had been putting off. He said that he could do it for me right there at the 95th and let me recover right there. He then recommended another option. I could go home two weeks early and have the surgery in the States. I chose the second option because it would mean seeing Judy and the kids sooner. I began sending home some hold baggage and sold my little refrigerator for a few bucks, a sale made easier because of all the remaining goodies from home that were still plentiful. I got a letter off to Judy and told her not to send any more goodies, letters or tapes. I told her that I would be home two weeks early for a little surgery, but it was no big deal.

The night before I was to leave, I got the usual plaque from some of my colleagues. There were signatures on the back of it with some one-liners from some of their favorite jokes. The next morning, I got up early and finished packing my bag. I wasn't going to be riding back on a silver bird with great service. I was booked on a medevac military flight back to the States. While waiting for my bus ride to the airfield, I was approached by the chief anesthesiologist who had occupied the room next to mine after Gene had gone home. The poor fellow looked a bit sad and uncomfortable as he began to talk. He began, "Reuel, I wrote you up and recommended you for a Bronze Star for all you have done over here, but the C.O. reduced it to an Army Commendation Medal. He said that too many Bronze Stars have been given out this month." I laughed and tried to put him at ease saying, "Hey, don't let it bother you. The C.O. has no clue about who I am or what I have done. I have been so busy just doing my job that I have never even met him. I think he spends most of his time in his nice trailer. I think I heard that he is a dermatologist by training, but I'm not sure. I'm sure he will get a Bronze Star for sitting in his trailer over here for a year. He is right about one thing though. They do give out too many Bronze Stars which makes them pretty meaningless. I have not seen any doctor or nurse finish their tour and go home without a Bronze Star for service. All that really matters to me is that I survived, and I am going to see my wife and kids pretty soon." We both laughed, and I told him to take care of himself.

It was a short bus ride to the airfield. As I boarded the plane, I noticed that there were very few litters holding war casualties. There were a lot of ambulatory passengers on my flight. I soon learned that my flight would be transporting a lot of guys with drug problems back to the States. These were guys who had taken advantage of the amnesty program and admitted to their drug problem the required number of days before their DEROS date. Once airborne, I was handed a brown paper bag that had been provided by a volunteer organization. Inside, I found a sandwich, an apple and a small bag of potato chips. There would be no hot meals like I would have had on a commercial silver bird. I could not have cared less. If the old, green, Army machine was airworthy and encountered no mechanical problems, I would be hugging Judy and the kids soon. It seemed like a longer flight going home this time, but the plane eventually landed in California. There were several stops and some plane changes as our group traveled across the country, headed for Pennsylvania. At one stop, I ended up on a bus packed with passengers from my flight. I took a seat in the very back of the bus. We were supposed to be taking a short bus ride to board another plane. It was hot, and the bus was packed full. It was a restless bunch. After 15 minutes, the bus had not moved. Many started yelling for the bus to get moving. Then they started rocking the bus from side to side and jumping around like they were crazy. Then I heard one of them yell out that he was going to kill the next officer he saw. I quickly realized that I was the only officer on the bus. I just sat quietly in the back of the bus, thinking about the decision that had brought me to such a precarious situation. I had survived my tour, and now had to worry about surviving a bunch of drug addicts who needed drugs. Fortunately, the bus quickly started to move, and the troops settled down for the trip to the next plane.

As evening approached, my flight arrived at McGuire Air Force

Base in New Jersey where I boarded a bus for the 64-mile trip to Valley Forge Army Hospital. I checked in at the hospital and was assigned a room. The surgeon who was assigned to me gave me the option of going home for a week or two and then coming back for surgery. I opted for having the surgery right away. Judy drove over from Flint and was able to rent a room close by. I had the surgery and stayed until my sutures were removed. When it was time to check out of the hospital, I had to meet with an officer to get my next assignment for my remaining six months. As I was sitting across from the officer who was looking over my file, the officer said, "Well sir, since you served in Vietnam, you get your choice for your next duty assignment." "Great!" I replied. "What's available?" The fellow quickly answered, "Fort Sill in Oklahoma." There was a long pause as I waited to hear the other possibilities. Hearing nothing else, I asked again, "What else is available?" With a smile breaking out on his face, the officer seemed to derive some pleasure out of again saying, "Fort Sill in Oklahoma." I quickly realized that the officer was just messing with me and replied with a smile, "I think I'll pick Fort Sill, in Oklahoma, for my next duty station." The officer closed my file saying, "Very good. It's done." He then handed me an envelope with my orders. I got into the passenger side of the car, and Judy drove us home to Flint for a great reunion with the kids and other family members. Valley Forge Hospital closed on March 31, 1974, and would become the site of Valley Forge Christian College in 1976.

THE FINAL SIX

The reunion with the children was great. The youngest child, Jill, still seemed to regard me as a stranger and intruder. After all, she and her siblings and her mother had not needed somebody like me in their lives during her young life. They had been doing fine. I wondered how much, if any, she remembered of me from my visit home on family leave. If she had any memories of that leave time, they probably were not good ones, because she seemed afraid of me the whole time and cried easily. I wondered about the long-term effects of my absence for Jill. It was clearly going to take some time.

I could have gone to Ft. Sill by myself for my final six months, but the family separation had already been too long. There would be no more family separation. We quickly started preparing for our move to Oklahoma. My sister, Susie, agreed to stay at our house in Flint and look after the house and our dog, Taffy, while we were away. I purchased a new, single-axle, travel trailer for the trip to Oklahoma. There was one bed in the back. The little sofa made into a bed. The dinette converted into a bed. The trailer dealer installed a Reese hitch on my 1970 Chevrolet Impala and installed a brake that connected to the car brake pedal, something that would prove to be a mistake.

Judy and I spent New Year's Eve getting the car and travel trailer packed for the trip to Lawton, Oklahoma. Then early on January 1, 1972, the family loaded into the car and began the two-day trip with a one-night stop in Missouri. We encountered a surprising number of potholes on the Missouri expressway. A stiff crosswind had also kicked up. I quickly discovered that when I was passed by an 18-wheeler, the little travel trailer would get sucked out toward the passing truck, and then swing back in the other direction after the truck completed the pass. The trailer would often fishtail back and forth before I could get it back under control. The wind and the fishtailing trailer were getting to be enough of a problem that I started looking for a place to stop for the night. Before I could find a stopping place, I was passed at a high speed by an 18-wheeler just as I hit a big pothole. The trailer whipped out toward the passing truck and then swung around toward the shoulder of the road and then back toward the driver's side far enough to smash the driver-side rear fender. I managed to get it to a stop without flipping over, to my great relief. The body damage was not enough to interfere with the operation of the rear wheel. We managed to drive down the shoulder to the next exit where we found a place to camp for the night. While talking with some people at the park where we spent the night, I learned that the trailer company should have installed a hand brake for the trailer that would have allowed me to brake the trailer separately from braking the car. That would have allowed me to control the fishtailing. The winds died down during the night, and we got an early start the next morning. It was after dark when we pulled into Lawton, Oklahoma. I found the home of the chief of anesthesia and pulled into his drive with my rig. Keith and his wife offered to have our entire family stay in his house for the night, but we all just camped out in the little trailer in his driveway that first night. The next morning, I officially checked in at Reynolds Army Hospital. Then, during the afternoon, Judy and I went looking for a place to park the trailer. We were able to find a campground where we would live out of the trailer for a few weeks. It was cramped quarters, but we managed. Eventually, we found a place we could rent on a month-to-month basis. Tim turned four and Amy turned five while we were in Lawton, Oklahoma. Their birthdays were just one day apart, but they still had two cakes.

The time at Reynolds Army Hospital proved to be a valuable experience for me. I had applied for the Anesthesiology Residency Program at the University of Michigan while I was in Vietnam, and I was scheduled to start soon after leaving the Army. Keith, the anesthesiologist in charge at Reynolds, told me, "Reuel, you are going to start your residency in six months. So, the operating room is yours. Practice any blocks you want to practice. You can block the whole schedule and let the nurse anesthetists monitor the blocks if you like. The operating room is yours." I never blocked the whole schedule, but I did get to do a lot of blocks. The elective surgery world was certainly much more pleasant than the war zone surgery.

There were a few memorable incidents at Reynolds. One afternoon, I was summoned from the operating room to labor and delivery where the obstetricians were in the habit of giving their own saddle blocks. The caller making the urgent call for help proclaimed that they had a patient with a total spinal who was having trouble breathing. I ran to OB, knowing that they probably did have a patient in distress but not from a total spinal. When I arrived, I found a patient suffering from air hunger from hypotension, quickly administered some intravenous ephedrine and lifted up on the uterus to take the pressure off the vena cava. The patient quickly expressed relief that she could breathe again. Everything settled down, and I quietly explained to the young obstetrician that his patient's inability to breathe was not from a high spinal but from hypotension affecting the respiratory center in the brain. I took a needle and walked it up the patient's abdomen and showed him that he did not have a high spinal. I reminded him that the hypotension was caused by the uterus pressing on the vena cava and the spinal dropping the blood pressure by causing all the peripheral dilatation. After explaining how he should treat similar circumstances in the future, I returned to the operating room. The young obstetrician did express his appreciation for the help and the physiology refresher.

There was one very sad event during my time at Reynolds. It involved the son of one of the career Army nurse anesthetists. Fort Sill was an artillery base, and sometimes there was unexploded ordnance left out on the range. One Saturday afternoon, while I was at home, I got a call asking me to rush to the emergency room at Reynolds to see what I could do for the son of one of the anesthetists who had been injured in an explosion and was being transported to the hospital. Before I could get out the door, the phone rang again, telling me not to bother. He was dead. The anesthetist's son and one other teenager had gone out into the restricted area on the range to gather up unexploded shells and take them apart to recover the powder inside. One of the unexploded shells had exploded while they were trying to take it apart, and the anesthetist's son was killed instantly. When investigators searched the home of the anesthetist, they found enough explosives in the basement to destroy his house and several surrounding houses. The whole neighborhood was roped off, and nobody was allowed in until all the explosives were removed. This all happened while the anesthetist was out of town at a meeting. He returned while the neighborhood was roped off with barricades that did not allow him to get to his house. When he inquired of one of the officers along the barricade as to the nature of the problem, he was told that a bunch of explosives had been found in the basement of a house where a kid lived who had been picking up shells on the artillery range and died when one of them exploded. The anesthetist asked which house and quickly learned that it was his house. It was a rough time.

The family enjoyed driving around the countryside and looking at the wildlife, namely the herds of wild buffalo. For entertainment, we also made several weekend visits to Wichita Falls, Texas, about one hour by car from Lawton, Oklahoma. The visits were made to attend the weekend auctions. I bought several small items. The one item that I purchased and took back to Michigan was an old wind-up Victrola.

The commanding officer at Reynolds Army Hospital was a career Army doctor who held the rank of colonel. He had served during the Korean War. He was a strange one and did not command the respect of the medical staff. He did not seem to concern himself with the medical care being delivered but was obsessed with making sure his medical staff had proper haircuts and properly trimmed mustaches and went through periodic fitness training and gas chamber exercises. Every Friday in the late afternoon, he would convene a meeting of the medical staff at a building across town from the hospital. Then he would make some ridiculous speech littered with clichés. His favorite one was, "We all live in glass houses." The meeting usually convened around 5 p.m. when retreat was being played on the base. It could barely be heard in the distance when approaching the building where the colonel had his Friday meetings. He would often spend a good deal of time yelling at the assembled physicians for not stopping outside the building and looking in the direction of the bugle sound until retreat was finished.

Rumor had it that a lot of the physicians had sent letters of complaint to Washington, D.C., regarding the colonel's leadership or lack thereof. One day we received word that the Surgeon General was going to pay a visit to Reynolds Army Hospital. Our commanding officer sent out the word that there was going to be a formal dinner and reception for the Surgeon General. The medical officers were to attend wearing their dress blue uniforms along with their wives who were to be dressed in formal attire. He could certainly command that all the medical officers must attend and determine which uniforms we were to wear. However, he had no authority to make demands on our wives. He sent out invitations to each of us and our wives with a request that we RSVP. Now he was making his demands on a bunch of doctors who would not be spending their careers in the Army but would soon be returning to a civilian practice. Judy had no formal attire, and I had not even purchased a dress blue uniform, hoping that I would not have to make the purchase with only a few months to go. The colonel did not get a good response to his formal invitation. His MSC officer tried to pressure the medical officers to attend with their wives. He showed up at my office to discuss the matter and began by bringing up the fact that I had requested a weekend pass to attend my sister's wedding. He said that he could get the pass approved if I would agree to attend the formal dinner for the Surgeon General along with my wife. I told him that I would let my sister know that I would not be able to make it to her wedding. He didn't get enough cooperation among the medical officers, and the dinner had to be cancelled in favor of a breakfast with the Surgeon General attended by the medical officers only and with their green uniforms.

The Army liberalized the haircut standards just before I arrived at Fort Sill. The colonel had ordered that pictures demonstrating the new hair standards be posted around the hospital. On two occasions, the colonel's MSC officer summoned me to his office to discuss hair issues. On one occasion, he told me that I needed to trim my mustache, insisting that regulations did not allow it to extend at all beyond the corners of the mouth. On another occasion, I was ushered directly into the colonel's office where I was informed that my haircut did not meet regulations. I told him that my hair looked just like the hair of the guy in the picture that was posted around the hospital as the new standard. The colonel's response was, "The guy in the picture needs a haircut." Rather disgusted at the waste of my time, I returned to the operating room and resumed my cases. I didn't get a haircut right away, and I did not trim my mustache. The surgery schedule was busy and long. I was very soon again approached by the MSC officer about my hair. He left me with a warning. He reminded me that there was a courtesy patrol that traveled around the base looking for violations, including hair length violations. He warned me that if the courtesy patrol picked me up anywhere on the base because of hair length violations, the colonel would fine me one-half of a month's base pay. After that, I made sure to always wear civilian clothes when shopping on the base with Judy.

The colonel's obsession with all things non-medical persisted. With less than a month to go, I received a visit in the operating room from a sergeant who informed me that I had to accompany him on a run as part of the Army fitness program. I told him that I did not have the time because the operating room was too busy. I declined to make the run a couple more times when he returned to the operating room. Then the sergeant showed up in the operating room, insisting that I had to go with him and go through a gas chamber exercise. It was clear that the crazy colonel had singled me out for harassment, and I was getting tired of it. I turned to the sergeant and said, "Look Sarg, I've been gassed by the enemy with better stuff than you've got, and I'm not going to do it again. I've got less than a month to go, and I'm out of here." The sergeant insisted that I had to do it, but I refused. Then I got lucky. The Army decided to do some downsizing, and I qualified for a two-week early out. I seized the opportunity. The out processing was quite interesting. An enlisted man was going through my file during the process of checking out. He kept pulling out papers from my file and throwing them into a wastebasket. Then he said, "The C.O. really had it in for you,

I see. Man, oh man, he was really going to come after you. We'll get this crap cleaned out of here." After tossing everything he thought needed to be tossed, he handed the file to me saying, "I think you are all set for discharge now, Doc. Good luck." We both had a good laugh. Everybody knew the C.O. had a few loose screws.

During our time in Lawton, Oklahoma, Judy fell in love with a couple of horses, and we bought both of them. One was a big pinto mare named "Bubbles." The other one was a yearling palomino quarter horse named "Sunny." We bought a used, two-horse trailer with an open back above the rear doors. Before buying the horses, we made arrangements with Judy's parents, Ralph and Huldah Holden, to drive out and haul the horse trailer home and keep the horses at their property where there was enough acreage. With the approval of my two-week early out, we cleaned and painted the inside of our rental unit and got back our security deposit in the early part of June. Ralph and Huldah left Flint for Lawton, Oklahoma. They spent a few days with us seeing the wildlife. Then we packed the little travel trailer and loaded everybody for the trip back to Michigan. Ralph and Huldah would lead the way, hauling the horses. We would follow, hauling the travel trailer. If either driver wanted to stop for a break, he was supposed to signal by just waving an arm out the window.

The weather was great, sunny and clear, when we left Lawton, Oklahoma. We were on a two-lane road in northern Oklahoma when it began to rain. The traffic was steady in both directions. I noticed a little, red Volkswagen Beetle in my sideview mirror as the driver kept pulling out, trying to pass me several times, only having to pull back behind me because of the oncoming traffic. We were doing the speed limit, but he was determined to pass. The Beetle driver was getting quite frustrated and began honking his horn behind me. It was clear that he was not going to be able to pass Ralph and me in one pass, so I eased back on the gas and allowed some space to develop between myself and the horse trailer ahead of me. After a few minutes, the Beetle driver made it around me and pulled up behind the horse trailer to attempt another pass. He pulled out to pass a couple of times, only having to pull back behind the horse trailer because of oncoming traffic. Then he snuggled right up behind the horse trailer to make another attempt. The rain had stopped. The Beetle was so close to the back trailer doors that there was no way the driver could see the back ends of the horses above the doors in the open back. At that moment, the big, pinto mare, Bubbles, raised her tail and dropped a big, wet load on the windshield of the Beetle. The windshield wipers instantly came on and smeared the load all over the window. The Beetle swerved from side to side as the driver was clearly blinded by Bubbles' message that he was following too close. I slowed up to give the Beetle plenty of room as he finally made it to the shoulder of the road. It took a while for all of us to stop laughing. Ralph had no idea what had happened. We told him about it on our next stop. His response was, "Serves him right!"

We ran into some more rainy, cold weather, and the horses started shaking, so we stopped and bought blankets for them. We stopped for the night when we were about halfway home. We eventually made it back to Flint. Ralph and Huldah got the horses settled in at their place. We got settled back in at our little house in Flint where everybody could finally feel like they were home.

THE RESIDENCY

We got settled back into our familiar house located at 1401 Raspberry Lane, in Flint, Michigan. Hay was plentiful, and we were able to buy a good supply for the horses at 50 cents a bale. Ralph had fixed up a couple of nice stalls for the horses at his place on East Bristol Road. Getting out of the Army a couple of weeks early gave us a little time to start looking for property in the Ann Arbor area. The anesthesiology residency was supposed to start on July 1. It was a two-year program. It was clear that I was going to have to commute from Flint to Ann Arbor for a while. We wanted to find some land where we could have horses and build a house. I really wanted a place where I could have a fishpond.

During our search for property, we met Floyd at the real estate office in Dexter, Michigan. When we described what we were looking for, Floyd told us about some acreage that was being divided up for sale by his in-laws. The property was located on Jennings Road just south of North Territorial. They were selling 20-acre parcels. The parcel that caught my attention was the one furthest from Territorial. It had a half-acre peat bog near the back. At the very back of the parcel, the property dropped off dramatically into a swampy area. From the high ground I could see a lake at the back of the adjoining property and several old cars, lots of bottles, rubbish and some old farm machinery parts that had been dumped from the high ground down the slope toward the swampy area. The area had been used as a dump by the farmers. This parcel had less tillable land and was probably less valuable than the other parcels with the same price, but this was the only parcel that had at least one site and maybe two sites for a pond. The peat bog could certainly be converted to a pond. The low, swampy area at the very back also had pond potential. I thought it would be a good place to raise a family, out of the city with horses and a pond. We bought the 20-acre parcel for $20,000. I arranged for financing at an Ann Arbor bank and

127

contracted with a Dexter builder to construct a house on the property that would be about 1750 square feet. It was going to take seven months to complete the house construction. I planned to park the little travel trailer in the woods on the back of the property and spend the nights there to break up the commute. I had no electricity, but I did have propane for gas lights and heat. The warm months were not bad, listening to the crickets and the frogs as I drifted off to sleep. The winter months were a different story. During that first month of sleeping in the trailer in the woods, I was awakened by the sound of a tractor and voices shortly after dark. I left the trailer and walked toward the tractor lights where I found some fellows in the process of dumping the contents of a large trailer down the slope on the back of my property. They had just begun the process when I yelled out and asked what they were doing. They said they were just dumping an old chicken coop and its contents and explained that they had dumped there for years. It turned out that one of them was the son of the man from whom I had purchased the property. An older gentleman with a limp approached me and apologized and said they would take their junk back with them. He had purchased the old farmhouse from the same seller I had dealt with, and the son of the seller had offered to help him get rid of the chicken coop and other junk. He didn't know the property had been sold to me. Despite the awkward start, the fellow with the limp and I would become great friends and neighbors.

After a short orientation at University Hospital, I found myself doing cases with little or no supervision. In addition to the anesthesiology residency program, there was a nurse anesthetist training program. The operating schedule at the main hospital, women's hospital and Mott Children's Hospital had to be covered, but there were only a handful of residents. A good deal of the schedule had to be covered by nurse anesthetists. It quickly became clear that I had done more anesthesia than any of the senior residents. One of the senior residents actually arranged to have her on-call nights coincide with mine so that I could show her how to do a few things she had not done before. I was shocked to learn that, after a year in the program, she had never done a case with a mask but had intubated every patient she had anesthetized. She had also never inserted a nasotracheal tube, but I was able to demonstrate the technique to her one evening when we were on call together. She asked how we put in big lines in Vietnam, and I showed her how we inserted subclavian lines. I found myself doing a lot of cases over very long hours with very little contact with teaching staff. At least I wasn't watching patients getting their limbs removed.

I did complain a bit about the long hours with no teaching and soon found myself assigned to the open-heart room. The anesthetic technique was one that I had not seen before. Anesthesia was induced with a morphine drip, and 3 mg per kilogram was administered. The patient was intubated and ventilated with 100 percent oxygen and no inhaled anesthetic. I was quite surprised at how well the patients did with this technique. When the surgery was finished, they had to be ventilated until the morphine and muscle relaxant wore off. With that much morphine, none of the patients had any recall of the surgery. The first time I entered that heart room, I took note of the picture that was taped to the little window. It was a picture of Michael DeBakey with a surgical cap on his head and a mask covering his mouth and nose. His steely eyes seemed to be staring right through you. Beneath the picture were the words, "Drive Carefully, This Man Is Waiting for Your Heart." After a full two months in the heart room, I was beginning to think I was never going to get out to do some other cases. So, I took a week of my vacation time, forcing the assignment of somebody else to the heart room. It worked. When I returned, I finally got to do some general surgery cases.

During that first month of anesthesia residency training in July 1972, Jane Fonda made the news by paying a visit to North Vietnam, basically fraternizing with the enemy. She posed for pictures and basically became a propaganda tool for the enemy. I certainly had my questions and concerns about the United States' involvement in South Vietnam, and I had raised my concerns with congressmen, senators and even the president. However, I found the conduct of Jane Fonda to be despicable. How could she demean the sacrifice of those who had given so much—even their lives—when called to serve their country by fraternizing with those who had killed and injured them?

I enjoyed the general surgery cases, especially when I got to work with the old professor who had done Judy's cholecystectomy during my medical school years. I did not remind him of Judy's case, and I don't think he remembered me from that time. He still had the reputation as the best general surgeon on staff. The running joke at the hospital was still that it would be advisable to place a device on the inside of your windshield that would, if you were in an accident, imprint on your forehead that he should be called if you needed a surgeon. He had a great pair of hands and was efficient, and he was an excellent teacher. His face was prematurely wrinkled from his heavy smoking. He would smoke constantly when he was in the surgery lounge between cases. He had a dry sense of humor. One night when I was on call, I was summoned for a case with the old professor. The patient was an elderly woman with a bowel obstruction. The senior resident was a very tall fellow named Rick. It happened to be the night of the Miss America pageant. In the middle of the abdominal exploration, Rick jokingly said to the old professor, "You know we are missing the Miss America pageant for this," to which the old professor replied, "This is your Miss America, doctor." He always came to the hospital after hours to supervise his senior residents.

Not all the surgical teaching staff came to the hospital at night to supervise their residents. On one of my on-call nights, a senior surgical resident undertook an exploratory laparotomy on an elderly patient after consulting with his staff physician by phone. The patient was very distended. The patient was opened, and some adhesions were released. The bowel was very dilated with gas. The surgical resident tried to close the abdomen over the distended bowel, but it was impossible. He looked up at me and said that he was going to need more relaxation to get the belly closed. I told him that I had the patient completely paralyzed with curare, and his belly was as relaxed as possible. He kept insisting that I had to do more, and I told him there was nothing else that could be done with drugs. He got very angry and turned to me saying, "How do you expect me to get this patient closed up if you don't give me some relaxation?" I really didn't want to get involved with giving surgical advice, but this poor resident was in a situation he clearly had not previously encountered, and he had no staff mentor present. I had worked with some of the best surgeons in Vietnam, and I knew what needed to be done. I quietly replied to him, "My suggestion would be that you decompress the bowel by inserting a trochar. Then you could repair the puncture and close the abdomen with no problem." Rather than take my suggestion, he laid his forceps and needle holder on the instrument tray and demanded that the circulating nurse get his staff surgeon on the phone. Once the nurse got the staff surgeon on the phone, she held it to the resident's ear at which point he began to blame me for his problem saying, "I do not have adequate anesthesia and enough relaxation to get the patient closed." The call ended quickly, and the resident folded his arms, awaiting the arrival of his mentor. After about 15 minutes, the staff surgeon arrived. He walked into the room with scrub cap and mask on and glanced at the distended bowel. He then left the room, and I could hear the scrub sink turn on. He next walked into the room and was gowned and gloved. He walked up to the operating table right across from his senior resident. He held out his open hand to the scrub nurse and said, "Trochar." He punctured the bowel with the trochar and proceeded to squeeze out the gas, decompressing the bowel very nicely. He then repaired the puncture hole. With that, he turned toward the door, walked through it and said, "Now close her up." No conversation took place during the remainder of the case as the resident closed the abdomen without ever looking up at me. Over the next few weeks, that surgical resident could not make eye contact with me, diverting his gaze when we passed in the hospital hallway. I doubt he will ever forget how to solve the problem of closing a patient with a distended bowel. The reputation of the surgical program overshadowed the anesthesia program at Michigan. The anesthesia program was rather young by comparison. The chair of anesthesia was a man who had trained at Michigan as a general surgeon and then gone on to Massachusetts General for anesthesia training, returning to Michigan as the first full chair of anesthesia. The surgery program had a longer history and had trained the Mayo brothers.

Late in the fall that first year of the anesthesia residency, I moved the trailer from the woods to a spot closer to the road to make it easier to get out during the winter. When the really cold weather hit, the trailer was not tolerable, so it was back to commuting or finding a room at one of the hospitals. For a short time, I stayed in an empty call room at the veterans' hospital. On one of those nights when I was not on call but just using a room at the veterans' hospital, I was recruited to give anesthesia to an old veteran whom the general surgeons wanted to open. They really were not sure what they were dealing with but opened him up, only to find that they were dealing with an aorta duodenal fistula, which was not survivable. The patient was gone quickly with most of his blood volume quickly filling his bowel, and I informed the surgeon that the patient was gone. The surgeon begged me, "Just give me a few more minutes." I quietly replied, "You're asking the wrong person." It got very quiet. The surgeon realized that there was nothing else to do except close the abdomen.

After seven months, the family was able to move into our new house. It was a better situation for the whole family, not just for me. The house in Flint was a short distance from the General Motors factory on VanSlyke, and heavy paint fumes filled the air many nights. Judy suffered more with her asthma on those long nights with the paint fumes. Little Jill was also having some problems with gastric bleeding that the doctors at Mott Children's Hospital determined to be allergy related. Everybody did better out in the fresh air of the farm. The oldest child, Lori, would finally have some stability regarding school. She had started school in Flint, then to New York, back to Flint, then Oklahoma, back to Flint and finally to Dexter, Michigan. She had not been able to maintain a stable peer group. By the time she found herself at Dexter, she discovered that cliques had formed, cliques that were not receptive to her. Most of the other children were able to experience their K-12 education entirely at Dexter.

My time in the anesthesia department at Mott Children's Hospital provided some new experiences. There were a number of heart defects in children that could not be repaired, even with cardiopulmonary bypass, and the two cardiac surgeons had decided to do some of these desperate cases with profound hypothermia and circulatory arrest. One of these surgeons had a bizarre sense of humor. I was talking with these two cardiac surgeons about how these cases were going to be done with no blood flow for up to an hour. I questioned them saying, "Don't you think we should try this with a chimpanzee first and see if it is still interested in bananas when the procedure is done?" One of the surgeons immediately exclaimed, "Do you have any idea how much a chimpanzee costs?" Both surgeons laughed at the look on my face and then went on to explain that these kids were all going to die soon if we didn't try this. They were confident they could do it with no ill effects. The first such case I did with one of them started with the routine induction of anesthesia followed by initial cooling with bags of ice surrounding the little patient. The chest was opened, and the patient was placed on bypass with continued cooling to the appropriate temperature. Then the pump was stopped for just short of an hour while repairs were made to the heart. The pump was then started again with the patient being warmed. The patient recovered fine. A repair had been accomplished that would not have been possible without stopping all blood flow.

Back on the farm, the colt, Sunny, that had been brought from Lawton, Oklahoma, was maturing and feeling his hormones. He needed to be gelded, and Judy had found a large animal veterinarian who was located on North Territorial just a few miles east of our little farm. He was contacted to perform the procedure. When he arrived, I greeted him and observed the entire procedure. He had a bucket that contained some fluid. He also had a large clamping device. He placed a halter and rope on Sunny. He drew up some fluid from a vial and injected it into Sunny's jugular vein. In just a few seconds he was able to pull Sunny over onto the ground on his side. Sunny was quivering all over and seemed to be gasping for air. The veterinarian moved quickly. He splashed the liquid antiseptic on the scrotum. He quickly made an incision over the scrotum and clamped the vessels supplying one testicle and then removed the testicle with a swift turn of the scalpel. After a minute, he removed the clamp and performed the same procedure on the other testicle. Sunny was still laboring to move air. There was no suturing or cautery. The clamp was removed, and there was just minimal bleeding. The scrotum was not sutured but left open to drain. Sunny soon raised his head and was breathing normally. As the veterinarian gathered up his supplies and returned them to his truck, I asked, "What do you use for anesthesia?" The veterinarian gave a one-word answer, "Sucostrin."

I had never heard of Sucostrin and assumed it was because it was a veterinary term. So, I asked, "What's the generic term for Sucostrin?" The answer was, "succinylcholine." When I asked him how many milligrams he gave Sunny, he said 20 milligrams. I was quite familiar with succinylcholine since I used it regularly in the operating room. It was not an anesthetic at all. It was just a short acting muscle relaxant that caused a brief paralysis. I continued my conversation with the veterinarian saying, "So you don't really use an anesthetic. You just paralyze him, and he feels everything." Looking rather stunned, the veterinarian looked up at me and said, "We just use Sucostrin." There was a long period of silence as the veterinarian prepared his bill. As he handed the bill to me, he asked, "You seem to have some pharmaceutical knowledge. What do you do for a living?" I explained, "Well, I push a little Sucostrin every day to facilitate tracheal intubation of my patients, but I put my patients to sleep with thiopental before I paralyze them. Anesthesia is what I do." We never used that veterinarian again.

The following week, I shared my observations regarding Sunny's procedure with the old anesthesia chairman while we were sitting in the anesthesia/surgery coffee lounge. When I mentioned that I was surprised that it only took 20 milligrams of succinylcholine to paralyze an 1100-pound horse while it takes 100 mg to paralyze a 200-pound man, the old chairman laughed and related how he had learned just how sensitive horses were to succinylcholine. It seems that he had been enlisted to assist in anesthetizing a valuable horse in the past and had to intubate the horse. He had calculated the amount of succinylcholine to give the horse based on his experience with humans. Needless to say, the horse had to be ventilated for an extended period.

The veterinary stories triggered another one on that day when one of the female anesthesia residents shared her encounter with a veterinarian. She shared an apartment with another female physician in a different specialty. They had a small dog that had sustained an injury that left it with a gaping wound on its side. No body cavity had been penetrated, so the two women decided that they could manage the repair. They gathered up some betadine, local anesthetic solution, suture material and a few instruments. They got the little guy comfortable and made a meticulous repair of the wound, a repair that they thought any plastic surgeon would find acceptable. After a few days, the little dog had developed a large swollen area under the sutures and was draining what looked like a little pus, so the two women took the dog to the veterinarian. The veterinarian came into the room, looked at the nicely sutured wound and all the swelling and drainage. He immediately looked up and posed just one question, "OK, which of you is the doctor?" Sheepishly, they both admitted to being physicians. He went on to explain, "Only a medical doctor would close a wound like this. You've got about 15 sutures in a wound that needed about two. You cannot tightly close up wounds in fur-bearing animals. They will all get infected if you don't let them drain." He removed all their stitches, washed out the pus and tacked the wound loosely together with two stitches. The little guy needed some antibiotics but did manage to survive his owners' misadventure.

During that first seven months of my residency while the family remained in Flint, Judy made daily trips to her parents' house to care for her horses. After the end of the first year of residency, we undertook the building of a pole barn so we could get the horses to Ann Arbor. I had no experience with building a pole barn, and neither did my dad. We got some plans, ordered the fabricated rafters and had all of the lumber and steel delivered to the farm. We dug all the post holes by hand. The building was to be 36 feet by 48 feet. We got the holes squared up pretty good and got our posts in. With the side walls up, we took on the task of getting the rafters in place. Only one of them got away from us and needed a little repair. It wasn't perfect, but it was good to get it done and get reunited with the horses.

I was able to find a guy with a dragline and contract the dredging of the peat bog to make a pond. He even offered to make a smaller pond in an area on slightly higher ground for no extra charge just to get the job. The main pond was to be about a half-acre with enough depth to avoid winter fish kill. The small pond would turn out to be more shallow and not able to support fish through the winter without something to keep it open in a small area throughout the winter. The pond project took several weeks longer than I had anticipated. Too often, I would come home after work and find the dragline operator on the back of the property, but not operating his dragline. He was spending a lot of his time looking through the bottles that the previous owners of the property had dumped on the far back of the property for decades. He found a lot of very old bottles in good condition, and I agreed that he could keep them. The pond finally got dug out, leaving a gray clay surface on the bottom that looked like troweled cement. The runoff would fill it quickly. The dragline operator got so distracted with his search for old bottles that I finally gave him a timeline to finish leveling the material that he had removed from the bog. He pulled out his rig without leveling the mounds of material he had removed from the bog. I would eventually get the equipment to do the leveling job myself.

Near the end of my residency, I was invited to the Ann Arbor St. Joseph Mercy Hospital to talk with the anesthesia group about joining their practice. For years, that group had relied on getting graduates from the Michigan program and then working them hard the first year while paying a low salary. They seemed to think such a practice was appropriate. It was like paying your dues to join such a prestigious group, they explained. I decided not to get involved with them and looked at returning to McLaren Hospital in Flint. I spoke with three others in the department at Michigan, including a member of the teaching staff, about going to Flint. The four of us scheduled a meeting with the McLaren group to discuss joining up with them. At that meeting, the teaching staff member surprised everybody by saying that there was something that he needed to tell everybody before they considered him. He acknowledged that, at one time, he had a drug problem that had resulted in him leaving private practice and returning to the University of Michigan anesthesia department. He said that he no longer had the problem, but he would understand if they did not want him to join the group. Speaking for the McLaren group, one of the anesthesiologists stated that the past history would not be a problem, but he was not sure there was enough work for four new people. At that point, I offered to split one position with my teaching staff member until it was determined that there was enough work for four new people. After further discussion, it was decided that all four of us would be welcomed to join the McLaren group.

RETURN TO FLINT

In July 1974, I began my private practice of anesthesia as a member of the anesthesia department at McLaren General Hospital in Flint, Michigan. Two others who had finished their anesthesia residency training at the University Hospital in Ann Arbor joined me along with one of the instructors. The members of the anesthesia group at McLaren were not one corporate unit. Some joined together for billing services, but each physician had the choice of handling his own billing or joining loosely with others for a joint billing arrangement. It was a group primarily for working out a call schedule. Such an arrangement allowed for each physician to determine his own income based on how much he worked without anyone taking part of his income based on how long he had been with the group. The four new additions to the group worked out well with everybody having enough work. A nurse anesthetist was always in the hospital during the on-call hours. Physicians were allowed to take call from home if they lived close by. Since I lived an hour away, I usually stayed at my parents' home in Swartz Creek or in the hospital when I was on call. The instructor, Dr. S, usually stayed in the labor and delivery call room when he was on anesthesia call since he lived more than an hour away in Chelsea, Michigan. The other two new members moved to the Flint area and took call from home.

The first few months were very busy, and I adjusted to the commute between Ann Arbor and Flint. The only complaint that surfaced regarding the new members of the anesthesia group was related to the use of the labor and delivery call room by Dr. S who was a chain smoker and kept the call room full of smoke. The obstetricians began to complain about the heavy smoke, and the problem had to be addressed with Dr. S, who was told he would have to go outside to smoke. It was not long after the smoky call room issue was addressed that another, more serious, crisis arose regarding Dr. S. I was nearing the end of a cholecystectomy case, and the surgeon was about to start his closure. A circulating nurse from the adjoining operating room came into my room and approached me at the head of the table. She got close to my ear and, in a low voice said, "Dr. S is really tired and sleepy next door." I asked her, "Wasn't he on call last night?" She acknowledged that he had been. I said, "He probably had a rough night." She left my room and returned to the adjoining room where Dr. S was giving anesthesia for an abdominal aortic aneurysm case. Within a couple of minutes, she returned to my room and quietly informed me that Dr. S was falling asleep at the head of the table. I suddenly felt my face flush and my pulse quicken as I suddenly realized what might be the real problem in the adjoining room. I instructed the circulating nurse, "Get a nurse anesthetist in here right now to finish my case!" I was quickly relieved and immediately went to the entry door of the adjoining room. As I looked through the glass, I could see Dr. S sitting on a stool at the head of the table. He would nod off, start to lean forward, then catch himself and straighten up. I entered the room and immediately began to check the patient's condition. I made a quick check of the position of the endotracheal tube and found that the balloon near the end of the tube was bulging above the cords. I repositioned the tube. The drowsy Dr. S noticed my presence and responded with, "Oh good. Can you relieve me and let me go wash my face and use the restroom?" I quietly inquired in a whisper, "Your old problem returned?" Dr. S nodded in the affirmative. I instructed him to go and wash his face and just stay in the lounge, and I would finish his case. He pleaded, "Just let me wash my face. I'll be fine." I told him, "No, don't come back. We will talk when the schedule is finished." He left the room and did not return as I had instructed. I checked the patient's pupils and found that they did not look like the pupils of somebody who had received the amount of narcotic that the chart indicated had been administered. Narcotics were always brought to the room by one of the staff who was in charge of keeping track of the drugs. I sent word out to bring some fentanyl to the room. When the aide showed up with the fentanyl, she indicated that she had already brought quite a bit of fentanyl to the room. I finally satisfied myself that the patient was properly anesthetized. One of the vascular surgeons looked up and noticed that Dr. S had not returned and that I had taken over the case. He asked me if Dr. S was sick, and I said that he was and that I was going to finish up for him. The surgeon said that Dr. S didn't say anything about not feeling well. I did not discuss the condition of Dr. S any further during the case. The surgery went well, and I took the patient to the recovery room in good condition. I was concerned about whether the patient had been allowed to become aware or hear anything during the procedure as a result of being insufficiently anesthetized and paralyzed with muscle relaxants. I would have to determine that during post op rounds. It became clear that Dr. S had been abusing fentanyl. After leaving the patient in the recovery room, I went to the restroom attached to the surgery lounge for an inspection. I looked in the two toilet stalls and found broken fentanyl ampules on the floor in one of the stalls.

At the end of the schedule, John, the chief of the anesthesia department, and I went with Dr. S to a restaurant close to the hospital. John and I both ordered a little food, but Dr. S was not interested in eating anything. John informed him that he would not be allowed to work at McLaren anymore and that his conduct would be reported to the state. It had been more than six hours since Dr. S had injected himself with fentanyl, and he was quite capable of driving himself home. It was agreed that he would drive himself home, and John and I would follow him home and speak to his wife. It was an emotional time for both John and me. As we made the one-hour drive, I said to John, "What a mess." Dr. S had a wife and two daughters who were about to get some terrible news. It was almost like having to break the news of a death. In a way, it was a death, the death of a career. His wife was quite depressed and disgusted, but she did not really seem surprised. I suggested that maybe Dr. S could ask to return to the university setting where he seemed to be able to function with supervision.

When I got home that night, I called the anesthesia chairman at Michigan and informed him about the events of the day. I asked if he thought he could do anything for Dr. S. He indicated that he was not sure he could take him back, but eventually he did. The next day, I was dreading post op rounds when I would have to question the patient whose care I had taken on when I relieved Dr. S. Much to my relief, the patient was quite happy with his anesthesia experience and even asked about Dr. S, who he assumed had provided all of his anesthesia care. I did not mention that I had taken over the anesthesia administration in the middle of the case. I simply told the patient that I was making rounds for Dr. S because he was away on vacation.

The remainder of that first year was busy but marked by considerable uncertainty. I had been able to obtain a malpractice insurance policy for that first year at a cost of $4,000 with $1,000,000 of coverage. During the last few months of that first year, insurance companies created a crisis by acting like malpractice claims were out of control, causing them to have to dramatically raise their rates and reduce coverage. A new $1,000,000 policy was going to have a premium that was more than my gross annual income. So that was out of the question. The only policy that was affordable was a policy with only $200,000 of coverage, which was like no coverage as far as I was concerned. There were a lot of meetings of physicians to discuss the insurance cost issue during the months just prior to the end of my first year in practice. Some of the lawyers who represented physicians were giving talks that addressed the problem. At one of the meetings, one physician inquired of the lawyers about the advisability of putting all his assets in his wife's name. The lawyers suggested that the risk of divorce was greater than the risk of a lawsuit that would wipe out one's assets. Some of the lawyers recommended just buying a $100,000 or $200,000 policy instead of trying to get a $1,000,000 policy. They suggested that most lawyers would only go after the policy, not private assets, and that it might be good to just dry up the swamp with smaller policies to go after. The common expression at the time was, "If you find yourself in a swamp full of alligators, the best plan is to dry up the swamp."

I was not comfortable practicing with inadequate coverage. As the last week of my coverage approached, I informed the department that I should be taken off the schedule once my insurance ran out. I had saved enough money to get by for a couple of months and think about what I wanted to do. I spoke with the chairman at Michigan who indicated that I could come back on the staff with a salary that would be about half of what I had earned in private practice. I even considered walking away from anesthesia entirely and returning to general practice or even taking on a high school teaching position. I needed some time.

It was the hay season, so I busied myself with putting up the first hay cutting. Time on the tractor with a nice summer breeze was a welcome experience. Just riding on the tractor, cutting hay, and watching the barn swallows dart all around me and the hay cutter, filling their bellies with the insects the equipment was kicking up from the grass, was so peaceful. I got the hay all up in the barn that summer of 1975, and I had been away from the operating room for several weeks. Then one evening, just a little after dark, the telephone rang. I answered the phone and found myself talking with one of the excellent general surgeons who practiced at McLaren in Flint. He told me that he had an infant with pyloric stenosis that he wanted to operate on as soon as possible, and he was calling to ask for my help. The oldest member of the anesthesia group was not comfortable doing infants, and the family was not comfortable with just the nurse anesthetist. The family had asked for me by name. He also indicated that the infant was the mayor's grandson. I explained that I had not done any anesthesia for several weeks, did not have insurance and was not sure that I even still had privileges at the hospital. The surgeon indicated that he needed to check on a few things and would get back to me. About 15 minutes later, the surgeon called again and indicated that he had spoken with the hospital administrator who indicated that I had the administration's approval to provide the anesthesia for his case. He also indicated that the family did not care that I had no insurance and that they would be grateful if I would come to the hospital and do the case. I indicated that I was not really comfortable working without insurance and that was why I was not working. The surgeon persisted, "Will you do it?" I agreed to make the drive and think about it, knowing that I could not bring myself to say no.

I arrived at the hospital and was greeted by a grateful mother. I changed into scrubs and got my anesthesia equipment organized. I slipped the mask over the little guy's face and breathed him down with the anesthetic mixture. Then I slipped the little tube into his trachea. The abdomen was prepped, and the surgeon went to work. The surgery was over in 15 minutes. I suctioned out the mouth and removed the endotracheal tube. After a couple of breaths, the little guy briefly had a laryngeal spasm which I manage to break, not without producing some large beads of sweat on my forehead. Once the little guy was awake in the recovery room, I headed back home a little before midnight. As I reached the Silver Lake Road bridge near Fenton, a rear tire went flat. I managed to get the car off the road enough to have room to change the tire. I opened the trunk, only to find that the spare tire was flat. I could see a gas station just off the exit ramp, so I hiked to the gas station where I was able to call my brother in Swartz Creek for some help. He was able to get me to a station back in Flint where I got my tires repaired. We then made it back to the Silver Lake Road bridge where I put a good tire on the car and headed for home again, arriving at 3 a.m.

Everything had gone well, but I had exposed myself by doing a case without having any malpractice insurance. I found myself considering going back to work without insurance. At this point in my life, I had not really accumulated any significant assets, just debt. Judy and I talked it over, and she indicated that she would support whatever I wanted to do. Even though joint real estate held by a husband and wife in Michigan is considered to be owned in entireties and not divisible to settle a lawsuit, I took my name off of the real estate, leaving it only in Judy's name. I took my name off all bank accounts and planned to accumulate nothing in my name. I recalled what the lawyers in Flint had said about the risk of divorce being greater than being wiped out by a malpractice claim. My attitude was that it was better that Judy have it rather than the lawyers.

Since I had already done one case without insurance, I asked the administration at McLaren if I would be permitted to practice without insurance if I decided to come back. I was told that I could practice without insurance at McLaren. I ended up practicing several years at McLaren without insurance. My plan was to practice until someone managed to get a major judgment against me, file bankruptcy, and then go back and teach. I had no claims filed against me during my time at McLaren. I actually got quite comfortable practicing without insurance. Nobody liked doing the lawyers, but I found that I relished having patients who were lawyers. When their pre-operative anesthesia interview was done, patients who were lawyers routinely tried to reassure the anesthesiologist who was interviewing them by saying, "I don't do malpractice." I always responded with a smile while saying, "Neither do I." I always informed lawyers that I did not have malpractice insurance in case they wanted to have someone else provide anesthesia services for them. None of them ever asked for someone else. I was very open with patients about my lack of insurance. On one occasion, during a preoperative visit, a patient jokingly stated, "Now don't screw up. I don't want to have to sue you." Some of the anesthesiologists in the department would have cancelled the surgery because of such a statement. I took a different approach. The patient's room had a good view of the doctor's parking lot. I took the patient to the window and asked him to look at the doctor's parking lot. I asked him if he could see all the nice cars in the doctor's parking lot, and he said that he could. Then I called attention to the green Chevrolet Impala with the rust holes in the side and asked if he could see it. He indicated that he saw it. Then I explained, "That's my car. It is really all that I own, and I don't even have malpractice insurance. If you want that old car, I'll give it to you right now." I gave him the option of choosing a different anesthesiologist. The patient went on to apologize for his joke and indicated that he wanted me to do his anesthesia. I agreed to provide his anesthesia and cautioned him not to joke about suing with any of my colleagues because it could get him cancelled.

The anesthesia call time at McLaren was assigned by a method that would eventually prove to be unworkable. Whoever was on call on Friday night also got Saturday and Sunday. If Monday was a holiday, it meant four days of call in a row. If it got very busy, one could end up with four days and nights of cases with no sleep. That is exactly what happened to me. On one stretch of call, I did more than 30 cases over a four-day period with no sleep. I had gone longer than that in Vietnam, I was young and could still do it, but it made no sense in civilian practice. So, the group eventually broke up the call schedule so that nobody covered more than one night at a time.

Having grown up in the Flint area, my time at McLaren General Hospital would produce some interesting encounters. On one particular afternoon, I was finishing my last scheduled case at about 4:30 p.m. when I was approached by the anesthesiologist on call, complaining about the back up of emergency cases for the evening. He asked me if I would consider staying around and doing just one more case before going home. I agreed to help out and do one more case. He offered me the choice of a C-section or a bowel obstruction. Since the bowel obstruction was being set up right across the hall from the room where I was finishing up, I chose the bowel obstruction. As I went into the room with my supplies, the patient was already on the operating table. He was an elderly man with thinning, grey hair. His abdomen was very distended, and he was grunting in pain with each breath. I introduced myself and said that I would be doing his anesthesia. As I looked over his chart, I noticed his name. It was the name of the man who had been the principal at McKinley Junior High School back in the mid-fifties when I attended there. I stepped back and looked again at the face of the old gentleman on my table. Yes, it was him. I asked him, "Were you the principal at McKinley Junior High School back in the fifties?" The old gentleman said yes. I responded with, "You were the principal when I was a student there." He immediately turned his head upward to look at me and inquired with what seemed to be a bit of panic in his voice, "Did we get along?" I assured him that we had gotten along very well and that I would take very good care of him. The case went well, and he recovered nicely. He had Medicare coverage, and I did not bill him for the 20 percent co-pay. His wife got my address and sent me a personal check for the 20 percent co-pay anyway. I destroyed the check but never told them. They just ended up with a little extra money in their checking account.

On another evening, I was doing pre-op rounds and saw a name that I recognized. It turned out to be the wife of the professor at Flint College who had tried to punish me for finishing up my teaching credentials after being accepted to medical school. I had heard that the disturbed fellow had committed suicide. When I interviewed his widow, I told her that I had taken a course that her husband had taught. She told me about her husband's passing and said that she was sure that he would have been proud of what one of his students had accomplished. If she only knew the real story, but I kept it to myself and assigned one of my colleagues to do her anesthesia.

A more enjoyable encounter took place on another day I was assigned to do pre-op rounds. I was surprised to see the name of my McKinley Junior High School homeroom teacher on the surgical schedule. She had contacted me just before I was to leave for my Vietnam tour and insisted on taking Judy and me out to dinner. It had been a most enjoyable visit. Now, years later, here she was on the surgery schedule. She had suffered some vision problems, including retinal detachment, and was almost blind now. I was looking forward to seeing her again. As I entered her hospital room, I did not give my name but simply indicated that I was from the anesthesia department and needed to go over her medical history and discuss the anesthesia for her surgery. It was clear that she could not see well enough to recognize me. As I pulled up a chair next to her bed, she immediately volunteered, "One of my students became an anesthesiologist." I led her on saying, "What's his name?" She quickly replied, "Reuel Long. Do you know him?" I responded with, "I know him very well. He works here." With some excitement in her voice, she sat up straight and said, "He does?" Now, in junior high school, the students all referred to her as Ma ... and her last name. So, I went on, "Yes, he does. As a matter of fact, he will be doing cases here tomorrow, and I can assign him to do your anesthesia if you like." At that she replied, "Oh, could you?" I answered with, "You bet I can, Ma." At that, she sat straight up on the side of her bed and leaned over toward me while inquiring, "Is that you, Reuel Long?" "Yes, it is," I admitted. Hugs ensued and then a lot of good conversation that took much longer than the usual pre-operative visit. The next day, surgery went well, followed by a good recovery. It was such a pleasure to take care of somebody who had been such an excellent teacher and who had taken such an interest in my career.

Back on the farm, the small pond that was located on a little higher ground than the big pond proved to be more trouble than it was worth. It did not have enough depth over a sufficient area to support fish during the winter, so I installed a cylindrical windmill that would spin a blade in the water enough to keep a small area open for oxygenation of the water. Such devices are used on cattle farms out west to water the livestock during the winter. I thought it was worth a try. One cold, January day I walked out to look at the ponds and walked out onto the small pond a short distance from the windmill. I could see that the windmill had only produced a very small hole in the ice right at the windmill shaft. I did not fully appreciate just how much the windmill thinned the ice for quite a distance from the little area of open water at the windmill. The ice seemed quite thick and supported me fine. Then I took one stride toward the windmill, and the ice gave way beneath me as I lunged toward the windmill, hoping to grab part of the T-shaped frame. Not reaching the windmill frame, I quickly found myself completely underwater with my snowmobile suit sucking in the very cold water. I struggled underwater to reach the steel pole that anchored the windmill to the bottom of the pond. I couldn't hold my breath much longer, but I did hold it long enough to reach the anchor pole. My muscles didn't seem to want to work in the very cold water, but I did manage to pull myself up the pole and finally get my head above water and breathe. I was breathing very fast and hanging onto the windmill frame just waiting to catch my breath before trying to get to the shore. I realized that I was not catching my breath in the cold water but was losing ground with every minute that passed. So, I began working my way around to the portion of the windmill frame that was closest to the shore. I finally found some footing and managed to crawl out of the water and get to my feet. I reached a hand to my head and realized that my hair was just a mass of ice chunks. With icicles on my head and an ice-covered snowmobile suit, I made the long walk back to the house. When I walked back into the house, Judy just had one question, "Did you do what I think you did?" What could I say but, "Yes, I did"? I eventually filled the small pond in with material that was removed from the big pond.

In June 1977, I ran successfully for a seat on the Dexter School Board. One of the obstetrician/gynecologists who worked at McLaren and had served on the school board in Flint cautioned me that it would be a thankless job. He said, "The only people who will remember you will be the people who are unhappy with some decision you made while on the school board." I would end up serving a total of 12 years, including as president for four years. When school board meetings went late, even into the early morning hours during teacher contract negotiations, it made for some tiresome trips to Flint the next morning. I was always impressed with the excellent benefit package the teachers had, but they were always pushing for more. On one late night when the board members were sequestered and discussing the benefit package the teacher negotiators were pushing for, I opened the discussion with, "Well, our teachers presently have cradle-to-grave coverage, but they would like to extend it to coverage from erection to resurrection." At 1:00 a.m. a bit of levity was needed. I enjoyed my time with John, the school superintendent who had been the high school principal when I was first elected to the board. At one of the school board meetings, one of the teachers, who was not considered a star, was making a speech to the board during the audience participation part of the meeting. The subject of his remarks was teacher burnout. While the burnout remarks were being made, John leaned over and whispered in my ear, "It's hard to burn out if you've never been on fire." I was presiding over the meeting, and it was hard not to laugh out loud, but I managed to stay composed.

The great majority of the teaching staff at Dexter was made up of good people and good teachers. There were a few bad apples. I had made it clear to all my children that everybody had to be on their best behavior, and I wanted no conflicts with teachers. When my oldest child, Lori, was in high school, a conflict did occur with one of the teachers. A social studies teacher accused Lori of behavior that justified removing her from his class. I was informed by John, the superintendent. I accepted what had been done and agreed to have her change to another class. Then, the following day, I received another call from John who informed me that an injustice had taken place. John had interviewed a number of students, including honor students, who were in the social studies classroom when Lori had been expelled. He informed me that Lori had told the truth, and the teacher had not been honest. I told John to just leave Lori in her new class and that I wanted to observe in the room of the teacher who had expelled her. John said that would be fine. I arranged to take a full day off work and observe the class. I sat in the back of the classroom and, for three full class periods, observed the teacher who had expelled Lori. After the last class, I made my way out the door of the classroom and was confronted by the teacher who inquired about why I wanted to observe his class and what I thought. I told him, "Well, you expelled my daughter from your class, probably without good cause. I just wanted to see for myself if she would be missing out on anything valuable if she did not return to your class, and I have concluded that she would not be missing a single thing of value." I left the building. Lori stayed with her new class.

The superintendent's dry sense of humor revealed itself again about a year later. He called my home and when I answered, John started, "Reuel, this is John. Tell me Reuel, you don't have any orange paint under your fingernails do you?" I assured him that I did not and asked why he wanted to know. Then John went on to explain that one of the high school social studies teachers who was not highly regarded had his classroom vandalized. The windows had been spray painted with orange paint. We both had a good laugh.

On Thursday, January 26, 1978, I was trapped in Flint by a major blizzard (the Blizzard of 1978). It turned out to be the most severe blizzard in Michigan history. A lot of roads were impassable, and many hospital employees could not get to work. I had been on call and staying at the hospital when the storm hit, so I just stayed at the hospital to help cover the operating rooms. The storm raged on into the night. When I called home on Thursday evening, I learned that Judy and the kids had no heat. Nobody could get to them because the roads were completely blocked. The house had a fuel oil furnace, and I was quite familiar with its operation. The authorities announced that everyone should stay off the roads except for emergencies. Well, I considered my family's situation at home to be an emergency. I decided to attempt the trip for home.

U.S. 23 was in terrible condition with cars in the median and off on the shoulder. It was slow going, but I finally made it to North Territorial and headed west for the 2½-mile stretch to Jennings Road. Territorial was covered with a lot of snow, and there were no car tracks marking the location of the road. I slowly made my way west and finally made it to Jennings Road where I found a six-foot drift blocking the entrance to the road. I got my car off to the side of the road as best as I could tell. I got out of my car and headed south on Jennings Road, working my way around the drift blocking the entrance to the road. It was cold, and the wind was biting. I headed south, working my way through and around six-foot drifts. Exhausted, I made it to the first house on the East side of Jennings Road. I knocked on the door and was greeted by a neighbor who agreed to call Judy and let her know where I was and that I was on my way. I then headed for home again. My house was about six tenths of a mile from Territorial. After over an hour, I finally made it to the end of my driveway. I could see the porch light. It was getting hard to just bend my legs as I tried to work my way up the drive. My feet had stopped hurting and were just numb now. I was about 50 feet from the house when I found myself down on all fours with my legs no longer working. Judy had been watching for me and spotted me. She ran out and helped me navigate those last 50 feet. Once in the house, I began the process of thawing out. I removed my gloves and shoes. My feet were numb, and I was concerned about their appearance. I got to the furnace and determined that it needed a new nozzle. I always kept a few spare nozzles in case the furnace malfunctioned. I replaced the nozzle and got the furnace fired up. I had a bad night with very painful feet. Eventually both feet blistered, and the skin peeled off the tops of them. I did miss some work while my feet healed up, but I got some quality time home with the family. My feet healed up nicely. I considered myself fortunate when all the news came out about the storm. About 100,000 cars had been abandoned on the highways, mostly in southeast Michigan. One fatality was reported related to somebody dying of exposure, stranded in their car. There were about 20 deaths from heart attacks and car accidents.

I was in the habit of doing a lot of manual labor on the farm, work that was rough on my hands. I worked on the tractors and the hay equipment. I picked up the hay in the field and stacked it in the barn. This resulted in a humorous event at McLaren Hospital. A patient requested that she have the same anesthesiologist that she had two years earlier for an upcoming surgery. The scheduling clerk asked the patient for the name of the anesthesiologist she had two years ago. The patient could not recall the name. Then the clerk asked if there was anything the patient could remember about the anesthesiologist that would help her figure out who it was. The next statement from the patient left no doubt about the identity of the anesthesiologist. The patient replied, "Yes, he had calluses on his hands, more like a laborer than a doctor." The clerk responded with, "Oh, that's Doctor Long. I'll make sure he gets assigned to your case." The clerk quickly reported the conversation to me in the surgery lounge where everybody had a good laugh.

There was a wide range of surgical talent at McLaren from very good to pretty bad. Everybody who worked in the operating room knew who they would select for themselves or their relatives, and they all knew who to avoid. I was assigned to the mortality/morbidity review committee. The committee met at lunchtime, and the hospital always made a lot of good food available. There were piles of charts to be reviewed. Too often I found the committee work did not appear to be a serious review but just a formality with a free lunch. Charts would be moved from one pile to another like they had been reviewed, but serious discussion was missing. I had some concerns about the mortality rate for the coronary bypass cases being performed at McLaren. The mortality rate was certainly higher than that of the University of Michigan. The cardiac surgeons claimed that they were working on sicker patients than those done at the University of Michigan or patients who had been turned down elsewhere. I wondered if they were operating on patients who should not have surgery. There were a number of death charts of coronary bypass patients for review by the committee. I raised my concerns with the committee and suggested that we do a serious review of the coronary bypass deaths. My statement triggered a quick response from the only pathologist on the committee who immediately expressed some frustration saying, "Now, I don't want to go down this road again if we aren't going to be serious about it. I couldn't get anybody to seriously look at the aortic valve replacement case that I brought to the committee last year. At autopsy, I found that the surgeon had sutured and closed both the right and the left coronary arteries when he sutured the valve in place. How often should something like that happen? Once, twice, never?" There was a brief silence as everyone took in what the pathologist had said. The committee then decided to go ahead with a review of the cardiac surgery cases, a review which would begin in earnest at the next meeting. Shortly after the decision to undertake the cardiac surgery review was made, I was approached by the chief of surgery one morning in the hall just outside the surgery suite. He pulled me aside and quietly asked me, "Hey Reuel, how much money did you make last year?" I was surprised by the question and didn't know what he was up to. I told him approximately what my gross income had been for the prior year. His next question revealed the real issue about which

I was getting attention. He went on, "How much do you think the heart surgeons made last year?" I told him that I suspected that it was a pretty big number that dwarfed my income. "Well then," he went on, "Who do you think can best afford to pay lawyers?" I answered with, "OK. What's your point?" He went on to explain why he stopped to talk with me, "The cardiac surgeon whose death charts are at the review committee right now is going to sue you if you keep making trouble for him. It would probably be best for you if you resigned from the committee and avoid paying a lot of your funds to lawyers. Think it over." He then opened the door and made his way into the surgery coffee room. The surgery chief was a nice guy with whom I had always had a good relationship. I was not sure if he was just trying to look out for me or was trying to protect the hospital's cardiac cash cow. I resigned from the committee, and then several other members resigned as well. The committee was refilled with new members. One of the cardiac surgeons was made chair of the committee. He would be able to review the death charts of the guy with whom he routinely did surgery. I heard nothing more about any review of the cardiac surgery cases. After I resigned from the committee, I declined to do elective cases with the cardiac surgeons.

I asked too many questions to be looked on favorably by the hospital administrator. He could be a real jerk. The hospital required that each doctor register their license plate with the hospital in order to park in the doctor's parking lot. I had the license plate of my old Chevrolet Impala registered with the hospital because that was the car I routinely drove to the hospital. On one Friday, I had some car trouble and had to drive Judy's car to Flint. I was going to be on call all weekend. It was a cold, winter weekend, and the cases went round the clock for three days and nights. I got no sleep. On Monday morning, I bundled up and headed to my car in the doctor's parking lot, only to find that the battery was dead. One of the maintenance people was assigned to assist visitors who needed a jump start. He had a battery pack in the hospital basement that he used to jump start cars, so I found him and asked for some assistance. He immediately asked for the license plate number of my car. I gave him the number. He looked in his file and indicated that my number was not on file. He indicated that he was not allowed to help out with any car in the doctor's lot that was not on file. I explained to him that I had to drive my wife's car after experiencing some trouble with mine on Friday. He refused to help me. I next went up to the hospital administrator's office and asked them to intervene and help me, but I got nowhere. I called AAA and found out that they were swamped. They could not get to me for a few hours. When I finally got help and got the car started, I headed for home. I was fighting to stay awake. I had made it about 20 miles when I fell asleep and was awakened as I went off onto the shoulder of the road. I got out of the car and into the cold air to clear my head. I did that about every 10 miles until I finally made it home in one piece. I really don't like most hospital administrators.

After a few years at McLaren, I was contacted by the anesthesiologist who was running the ambulatory surgery facility at Chelsea Community Hospital. Jim was looking for some anesthesia help and wondered if I might be interested. I learned that Dr. S, who had been kicked out of McLaren because of his drug abuse, was now working with Jim after having spent time back at the Michigan anesthesia department. I told Jim that I would not be comfortable working with Dr. S again. Jim seemed shocked at my attitude. He indicated that Dr. S had put the drug issue behind him and had placed his life in the hands of the Lord. I insisted that I would not consider coming to Chelsea as long as Dr. S was working there. Jim was clearly disappointed in my decision.

A few months later, I received another call from Jim, still looking for help. I asked about Dr. S. All Jim said was, "He doesn't work here anymore." With that news, I agreed to meet with Jim and discuss the possibilities. It would certainly be closer to home for me. After meeting with Jim, I approached the McLaren group about splitting my time between McLaren and Chelsea. The McLaren group insisted that I would have to take call at McLaren as if I were full time even though I would only be working half time. I would eventually make a clean break from McLaren and join Jim at Chelsea full time in 1979. I was still working without insurance at that time. Insurance rates had come back down some, but I was not aware of the latest rates. Jim said he would feel better if I had insurance, at least a $200,000 policy, and even agreed to pay for it for the first year just to get the help.

THE CHELSEA YEARS

Jim employed a couple of nurse anesthetists at Chelsea Hospital on a per diem basis. He had to pay them for a full day even if they were only there for one case. He utilized the hospital physician billing service and billed for his cases and that of the nurse anesthetists. I declined to use the hospital billing service and continued to do my own billing. It was a fast-paced work schedule. There was a busy ear, nose and throat case-load and a good volume of urology and orthopedic arthroscopic proce-dures. The gynecologists from Ann Arbor brought their tubal ligation cases to Chelsea because they could not do them at St. Joseph Mercy Hospital. There were also a lot of podiatry cases. Cataract surgery was sporadic initially. There was a very active infertility practice which resulted in a good volume of laparoscopic procedures. Jim and I worked well together for a few years. Then, suddenly, Jim informed me that he had decided to move to Galesburg, Illinois, and run an operating room there. Jim made the move to Galesburg in April 1982, leaving me to run the ambulatory surgery facility at Chelsea. I took on the responsibil-ity of paying for the nurse anesthetists that were needed on a per diem basis. This was an unusual arrangement. At most hospitals, the nurse anesthetists were hired and paid by the hospital, and the hospital billed for their services. I would have been much better off if I could have just billed for my services, but I took on the expense.

My experience prior to my anesthesia training would continue to serve me well, even at Chelsea. When I first arrived at Chelsea Hospi-tal, there was a small emergency room that was covered primarily by moonlighting residents from the training programs in Ann Arbor. One evening while Judy and I were bowling with friends at the bowling alley in Chelsea, I was paged over the speaker system at the establishment. I went to the desk and learned that there was a telephone call for me. I was surprised to hear a nurse on the line who asked me to come to the emergency room at Chelsea. She explained, "You have a neighbor here who asked us to call you and see if you could come in and look at him. He is having chest pain and trouble breathing." I learned that it was my neighbor, Gene, who lived across the road at the northern border of my property. Gene was a couple of years older than me, a thin fellow who was a heavy smoker. I broke the news to my bowling group and left for the emergency room. When I arrived, I found Gene on a stretcher, looking pale, gasping for air and complaining of chest pain. There was an X-ray film on the wall box that demonstrated an impressive pneumothorax. I inquired of the moonlighting second-year surgical resident from Ann Arbor, "Have you ever put in a chest tube?" The resident replied, "I saw one done once." I quickly responded, "Well, this is a friend of mine, you are going to get to see another one done." I told Gene that he had a big bubble of air that was compressing his left lung and causing his chest pain and shortness of breath and that I was going to put a tube in between the ribs on the left side to let the big bubble of air out so he could breathe. He encouraged me to get on with it. I ordered the nurse to set up for a chest tube with a water seal bottle. I prepped the chest with an antiseptic and selected the intercostal space along the anterior axillary line where I wanted to insert the tube. I injected the area with some local anesthetic, made a small incision and then popped in the chest tube. The pressurized air rushed out, allowing Gene's lung to expand. Gene got immediate relief from his chest pain and began to breathe with no distress. I sutured and taped the tube in place and put the end of the tube into a water seal bottle to maintain the expansion of the lung. I then admitted Gene to the medical floor for observation. The next day, I was approached by the director of medical affairs who informed me that I really didn't have surgical privileges. I pointed out that the hospital really didn't have proper coverage to offer emergency care and that my neighbor was not going to last long if I had not intervened. I reminded him that the moonlighting resident had never inserted a chest tube before. The medical director then suggested that I turn Gene's care over to somebody else who could collect the daily fee for following him. I let him know that I was not charging my friend for any of my services. I then went to the medical floor and arranged to have Gene moved to St. Joseph Mercy Hospital under the care of one of the surgeons who also worked at Chelsea. Gene recovered well.

There was another memorable incident at Chelsea Hospital that I will never forget. It was about 9 p.m., and I was tired and thinking about turning in early when the telephone rang and set off a rather lengthy, emotional roller-coaster experience for me. The nurse informed me that one of the general practitioners wanted to know if I could come in and see what I could do for a patient that he had admitted to the

ICU for oxygen and observation. She indicated that the diagnosis was epiglottitis. She said that he had been getting steadily worse. I told her that he should have never been admitted to Chelsea Hospital with that diagnosis. I told her that I would come to the hospital but that I might not get there in time if the diagnosis was correct. I instructed her to call in a crew for the operating room. I got in my car and headed to the hospital at a pretty good speed for the 25-minute trip, wondering all the time which surgeon had been called in case a tracheotomy was required. There was no 24-hour in-house surgical or anesthesia staff at Chelsea. It was primarily an ambulatory surgery facility. I could not believe any physician would admit a patient for observation when there was nobody at the hospital who could treat the life-threatening complication for which they were being observed, but it just might have happened. When I arrived at the ICU, I discovered that no surgeon had been called. I quickly determined that the diagnosis was probably correct. The patient, who was about 35 years old, was sitting up in an oxygen tent, leaning forward, his tongue protruding, and he was laboring to move air. I told the nurses that we needed a surgeon who could do a tracheotomy if they could find one. The operating room crew had arrived, and I instructed them to set up a room for a tracheotomy. We were going to need a surgeon and soon. I picked up the telephone and called one of the ENT surgeons who did cases at Chelsea Hospital but lived in Ann Arbor. I described the situation to John, and his response was, "Oh fuck! He'll be dead before I get there." He said he didn't even think he had enough gas in his car to make it to Chelsea, but he agreed to give it a try. The patient was still moving air but getting more exhausted, so I sat down with his wife for a heart-to-heart talk. I explained to her that the swelling of the epiglottis above his vocal cords was obstructing his airway and that he would need a tracheotomy. I told her that a surgeon was on the way, but I didn't know if her husband could keep moving air until the surgeon arrived. I explained that if his airway got completely obstructed that I could try to pass a tube down into the trachea but might not be able to do it if the swelling was too great. Then the only option to save him would be a tracheotomy. I told her that I had not done a tracheotomy in years. I explained that he might not survive if I had to do it, but he would die without a tracheotomy if he completely obstructed. She told me to go ahead and do the tracheotomy if he quit breathing before the surgeon arrived. The patient was getting more and more fatigued. I did not want to face trying to do an intubation or a tracheotomy in a poorly lit ICU, so I decided to move him with as little stress as possible to the operating room. I left him sitting up in his ICU bed with the oxygen tent and hooked up portable oxygen tanks to the bed. We then pushed his bed slowly through the ICU doors and across the hall to the operating room. The bed was placed right next to the surgical table. I had my anesthesia equipment at the head of the table. The scrub nurse was standing near the head of the table with a Mayo stand full of instruments. The circulating nurse was standing at the foot of the patient's bed. The general practitioner who was responsible for the admission of this patient to Chelsea Hospital was standing behind the circulating nurse. The minutes dragged on, and I found myself muttering, "Come on John ... come on John." Everybody just stood there quietly waiting for a surgeon to arrive and watching the patient getting steadily worse.

Suddenly, the patient threw himself back and began to turn blue, not moving any air. He was not heavy, and we quickly lifted him onto the operating table. I opened his mouth and inserted my laryngoscope, and the blade was totally engulfed with swollen tissue. I made one quick pass with the tube just in case I might get lucky and find the trachea, but no such luck. I immediately demanded a scalpel which was slapped into my ungloved hand. There was no time to prep the neck in any way. I made a midline, L-shaped incision in the trachea and put a hook on the tissue so I could lift it up and create a hole the patient could move air through. Air and blood began to spray up at me from the hole I had made in the neck. At that moment, John walked into the operating room and exclaimed, "Fuck! He's dead." While pressing sponges around the hole to control the bleeding, I yelled back, "No John, he just quit breathing a minute ago. Get over here!" John came over to the head of the table across from me, and I asked him, "Can you see the hole I've got in the trachea here?" He said that he could, so I told him to put the tube in the hole, which he did. I immediately hooked up my anesthesia equipment to the tracheotomy tube and started to breathe the patient down with the anesthetic agent because he was starting to move around now. At that point, another surgeon showed up, a general surgeon. She scrubbed in, and the two surgeons proceeded to mop up, getting the bleeding controlled and the wound sutured. We all agreed that such a patient should not be at Chelsea Hospital. An ambulance was called to transport him to St. Joseph Mercy Hospital. Once he was awake, I explained to him what had happened and informed him that I was going to ride with him in the ambulance to St. Joe. The trip was uneventful, and we got him settled into the emergency room where I gave report on what had happened. He was admitted and stayed for several days. I managed to get a ride back to Chelsea, made my way to my car, and headed for home. I climbed into my bed and pulled up the covers. As soon as my head hit the pillow, I started shaking and could not stop for several minutes. What had happened in the OR earlier kept going through my head. Then I drifted off briefly, only to find myself back in triage in Vietnam. I sat up, shaking again. I was tired, but I was not going to get any sleep. My eyes were wide open, just looking up at the ceiling. I did not wish to see the scenes that closing my eyes produced. No sleep was to be had that night. John took care of the patient while he was at St. Joe. About two weeks later, John showed up in the surgery lounge at Chelsea. He had a guest with him and walked his guest right over to me and asked, "Do you recognize this guy?" I had no idea who he was. Then John pointed to the man's neck, calling my attention to a vertical tracheotomy scar. I knew immediately who it had to be. I smiled and reached out to shake his hand while saying, "I didn't recognize you since you're not blue." The patient expressed his gratitude for what I had done for him. I was just happy that we had a good outcome. He was alive with no problems from the procedure.

During my time at Chelsea, I would care for patients with health insurance, with no insurance or on Medicaid. Some of the patients could afford to pay for their medical services for which they were not insured. There was one group of patients for whom I thought there should be some accommodation. Some patients could not afford insurance but made just enough to make them ineligible for Medicaid. For some patients in this group, an unexpected surgery could be financially devastating. I had an arrangement with hospital administration that allowed me to do up to 20 free cases a year under certain circumstances. If the hospital was not going to charge, both the surgeon and the anesthesiologist had to agree not to charge. I never had a problem getting the cooperation of the surgeons when I wanted to waive the charges. There were two such cases that gave me great satisfaction. One of the ENT doctors scheduled a 10-minute procedure (a frenulectomy to release the tongue) in a little guy who was the son of a Methodist minister. The minister had a very small church just west of Chelsea. I had the opportunity to interview the family after their visit to the ENT clinic. I learned that the family had no insurance, and they were making monthly payments on their bill at St. Joseph Mercy Hospital where their baby had been delivered. Their story hit home for me. My father had been in the same situation with the church not providing health insurance for our family for years. My dad, a Baptist minister, had always just saved and paid the medical bills. The Methodist minister asked me if it would be possible for him to make monthly payments for the medical services his son needed. I told him that I would have to check and excused myself to seek out the surgeon who was to do the procedure. I found him in the clinic and asked if he would waive his bill as I would so we could eliminate the hospital bill for this family. He agreed without hesitation. I returned to the room with the Methodist minister. I informed him that we would be happy to care for his son and that there would be no bill from the surgeon, the anesthesiologist or the hospital. The minister and his wife were astonished and expressed their gratitude. I made a call to the hospital billing department to give them the information they needed to flag the case for no billing. On the day of the surgical procedure, the mother came with the baby. Her husband did not come into the hospital. I asked about her husband, and she explained to me, "He is a very proud man and is somewhat embarrassed about receiving charity, but he is very grateful." My reply to her was, "Just tell him that it is our pleasure, and that none of us need the money. I'm sure you folks can put the money to better use."

A second memorable case occurred just before Thanksgiving one year. One of the general surgeons had scheduled a cholecystectomy for a 30-year-old lady who was surviving by cleaning homes. She had no health insurance and was just able to support herself. She had already visited the business office and set up a payment plan for the hospital bill when I met her in the pre-op holding area just before surgery. Again, this was somebody who made just enough to disqualify for Medicaid. I found the surgeon in the locker room, and he agreed to waive his fee. I then went to the business office and made sure they tossed the monthly payment agreement and waived the bill. Then it was back to the pre-op holding area. I went to the patient and wished her a Happy Thanksgiving and informed her that there would be no hospital, anesthesia or surgery bills for her gallbladder surgery. I got to see some tears of joy.

Whenever there is such a program and word gets around, there is always the risk that someone will try to abuse it. Indeed, there was one such attempt. The attempted abuse was not initiated by a patient. It was the mischief of a surgeon that I discovered. On one of my very busy days, one of the pre-op desk clerks came back to the desk in the pre-op holding area to inform me that she was checking in a patient for surgery who had no insurance and had been told by the surgeon to ask about having the anesthesia and hospital bills waived. I went out to her office to interview the patient myself. I learned that he was an engineer with an excellent income who could easily afford insurance, I learned that the surgeon had informed him that we had a program where we could waive the anesthesia and hospital bills for people without insurance. I also learned that he had already paid the surgeon for the hernia repair he was scheduled to undergo. I excused myself and went looking for the surgeon. I found him in the changing room and began, "It appears that you led one of your patients to believe that he qualifies for free care for his hernia repair." He quickly replied, "Aren't you doing that program anymore?" I explained, "Yes we are, but it requires that nobody charges, including the surgeon." The surgeon looked up at me and just said, "So?" I was getting a little hot under the collar by now and continued, "So, you've already collected your fee for the surgery from what the patient tells me. Now, this fellow clearly doesn't qualify for our program. He makes an excellent income, but I think we might be able to waive all the charges anyway." The surgeon looked up at me with a surprised expression, and I let him have it. "Here's my proposal. You go with me out to the office where your patient is checking in and write him a check, refunding your surgery fee, and I will waive my fee and get the hospital bill tossed." With a sneer, he replied, "I don't think so." I returned to the clerk's office and informed the patient that he did not qualify for the program which was intended for people in dire circumstances. He got out his check book and wrote two checks, one for the hospital and one for my services.

My time at Chelsea was marked by the filing of a lawsuit against me, a suit that arose from some rather despicable behavior on the part of one of the surgeons. One of the ophthalmologists requested that I perform retrobulbar blocks for his cataract surgery cases. He was an older surgeon who was rapidly being left behind with the advances in ophthalmology and newer surgical techniques. I sedated his first patient on one particular day and proceeded to do a retrobulbar block. When the surgeon sat down at the head of the table to start the surgery, he noticed that the eye still had a very slight movement. Rather than give the anesthetic just a little more time, he decided to supplement the block by injecting above the eye. He drew up the local anesthetic and attached a long needle. He then proceeded to insert the long needle just above the eye. As he began to inject, I noticed that the eye became cloudy, and I told him to stop. When he stopped, the eye cleared. I told him what I saw, and he indicated that the globe of the eye had likely been penetrated. He just froze in place, not speaking or moving for about 30 seconds. Then he announced that the case was cancelled. He taped a patch over the eye, and the patient was taken to the recovery room. About 30 minutes later, one of the nurses who had been circulating the room where the cataract cases were being done approached me, saying, "I overheard the surgeon dictating the operative report for the case that just got cancelled, and I don't think you are going to be happy with what he dictated. You better look at it." I thanked her for the heads up and told her to write up a memo about what she had observed that day, sign and date it and save it in case we needed it. A few days later, when I knew the operative report had likely been typed up, I went to medical records to read the report. Sure enough, the surgeon had dictated the report to make it look like I was the one who penetrated the eye. He started out by stating that a retrobulbar block had been administered by me. He then went on to say that the block was supplemented at which time the globe was penetrated. He never said that he was the one who supplemented the block and penetrated the globe, so it would be natural for the reader to assume that it was me who tried to supplement the block. I had already asked the nurses in the room to make dated, signed notes about what had happened. I did not approach the surgeon about his dictation. The patient eventually lost the vision in the eye that had been penetrated. I soon received a notice from the law firm representing the patient. They were seeking money damages from me for the loss of vision in one eye. I hoped to avoid wasting a lot of time and called the law firm representing the patient. They did not want to talk with me and simply informed me that all communications would take place at the deposition. I contacted my insurance carrier and was assigned an attorney. I explained to the attorney what had happened, and he assured me that there was nothing to worry about. I didn't need his reassurance. I just didn't want to waste a lot of time, but it could not be avoided.

The deposition was scheduled to take place in one of the large conference rooms just off the main cafeteria at Chelsea Hospital. On the day of the deposition, there were a lot of people sitting at the long line of tables that went the full length of the room. I sat next to my attorney at one end of the line of tables. The plaintiff's attorney sat across from me. Attorneys were present who represented Chelsea Hospital as well as a number of other attorneys. The surgeon's attorney was at the far end of the table from me.

The plaintiff's attorney began with all the usual questions about my training and background. He then asked me some anatomical questions about the eye and then asked me to describe how I performed a retrobulbar block. Finally, he got down to the question of the eye puncture and the operative report. He pushed a copy of the operative report across the table to me and asked me to review it. I glanced at it for a moment and then just looked across the table, waiting for his next question. It wasn't supposed to be a pleasant day for me, but I was going to make the most of it by making a fool of the plaintiff's attorney whose goal for the day was to intimidate me. The questions began with me being in the position of defendant:

> PLAINTIFF'S ATTORNEY: "Dr. Long, did you perform the retrobulbar block on the patient listed on that operative report?"
> DEFENDANT: "Yes, I did."
> PLAINTIFF'S ATTORNEY: "Now, the block was inadequate, was it not?"

DEFENDANT: "When the surgeon was ready to begin, the block had not taken full effect."

PLAINTIFF'S ATTORNEY: "Well, in any event, the decision was made to supplement the block, was it not?"

DEFENDANT: "Yes, it was."

PLAINTIFF'S ATTORNEY: "Now, Dr. Long, when you supplemented the block, the globe of the eye was punctured, was it not?"

DEFENDANT: "Well, counselor, I have a problem with your question since you have coupled your question with an inaccurate statement."

PLAINTIFF'S ATTORNEY: "Was the globe of the eye punctured or not?"

DEFENDANT: "Yes, it was."

PLAINTIFF'S ATTORNEY: "So, you punctured the globe when you supplemented the block, right?"

DEFENDANT: "Where in this report does it say that Dr. Long supplemented the block?"

PLAINTIFF'S ATTORNEY: With a touch of anger, "Right here," holding up the report.

The plaintiff's attorney then proceeded to read aloud that part of the operative report that indicated that I had administered the retrobulbar block and that the block had been supplemented. I was starting to enjoy myself because I was able to turn the tables on him and ask him questions. He had made some assumptions and was clueless about what had really happened. He was soon to discover that he was barking up the wrong tree.

DEFENDANT: "I really don't see any place in this report where it indicates exactly who supplemented the block."

PLAINTIFF'S ATTORNEY: "Well, did you supplement the block or not?"

DEFENDANT: "The block was supplemented, but I did not perform the supplemental injection."

PLAINTIFF'S ATTORNEY: "If it wasn't you, then who did it?"

I was having too much fun with the plaintiff's attorney but realized it was all about to come to an end. I leaned forward a bit, looked the plaintiff's attorney directly in the eye and, with a smile, quietly gave my final answer, "The surgeon." A hush fell over the room. The stunned plaintiff's attorney announced that he had no more questions for me. The surgeon was not present at the deposition, but his attorney was sitting at the far end of the row of tables from me. For some reason, he thought he needed to get involved at this point. He spoke up and said that he had just one question for me and went on to ask, "Dr. Long, do you think the surgeon dictated the operative report with the intent of making it look like you had done the supplemental injection and penetrated the eye?" I was surprised by the question and didn't see how the question would help the surgeon, but I quickly answered, "Yes, I do." The conference room quickly emptied. I soon heard that the claim against me had been dropped. The surgeon's malpractice carrier quickly settled the case. I declined to provide anesthesia services for that surgeon's cases after that deposition. Another anesthesiologist had joined me at Chelsea prior to that case, and he decided to continue providing anesthesia for his cases. The hospital administrator at Chelsea informed me that I could not decline to provide anesthesia services for this surgeon since his privileges were in good standing. I told the administrator that not only did the surgeon in question no longer possess the skills to continue practicing, but he had also demonstrated a lack of ethics that disqualified him from booking cases with me. The administrator was not happy with my decision, but I never did another case with that surgeon.

I would have a number of disagreements with the hospital administrator at Chelsea during my time there. In an attempt to add to the bottom line of the hospital, the administrator began pushing for the establishment of a birthing center at the little hospital. My position was that all the deliveries should continue to be done in the Ann Arbor/ Ypsilanti area at the University of Michigan Women's Hospital or at St. Joseph Mercy Hospital where there were physicians who could handle any complications that might arise. I also pointed out that the quickest way to destroy an ambulatory surgery facility would be to expose the schedule to interruptions by emergency C-sections. I listened in disbelief as the administrator explained that only normal deliveries would be done at Chelsea, so there would be no C-sections to interfere with the surgery schedule. I laughed and told him, "Well, if you can figure out ahead of time which deliveries are going to be normal deliveries and never have a complication, you have a skill that no physician on the planet possesses." The administrator was a bit dull and was convinced that a birthing center would work at Chelsea, but his dream of a birthing center never materialized while I was there.

I also did not see eye to eye with the hospital administrator regarding his fundraising efforts. He created a full-time position and hired a guy as a fundraiser. It was a substantial salary. The usual tree was put on the wall in the lobby where names could be engraved on silver or gold leaves depending on the amount of the gift to the hospital. A lot of pressure was put on the doctors to donate to the hospital. When I was approached by the administrator, I was told that it was important for the doctors to donate because it would make it easier to get money from the local businessmen. He also suggested that the doctors had an obligation to donate to the hospital to help cover the cost of uncompensated care for the hospital. I pointed out to him that the doctors were providing their services without compensation whenever the hospital was not being paid. I also pointed out that one of the reasons hospitals enjoy not-for-profit status and pay no taxes is because they end up with some uncompensated care. I told him that he should concentrate on running the hospital and keeping costs down and stop trying to fleece everybody for donations. I also suggested that he terminate the position of fund-raiser to save some money. Eventually the position was eliminated, but not because I suggested it. The guy was a miserable failure.

In the fall of 1981, Judy and I were faced with a new challenge. Our son, Tim, was attending the middle school in Dexter. He was halfway through the fall semester and seemed to be doing well. With no prodding, he always concentrated on doing his schoolwork when he got home prior to any recreation. He was participating in intramural basketball at the school as well as playing saxophone in the middle school band. Judy had always been an avid reader and had exposed all the children to the pleasure of reading, and Tim was no exception. There was no hint of any of the children having problems at school. Then suddenly, we were contacted by Tim's middle school teacher who asked us to call and schedule a meeting with her about some concerns she had regarding Tim. We scheduled the meeting right away. As the meeting began, she admitted right away that she did not know what to do about Tim and hoped we had some ideas. I responded by saying that we had no idea he was having any problems with his schoolwork. She smiled and reassured us that he was having no trouble with his schoolwork. She went on to indicate that the problem was that the schoolwork presented no challenge to Tim at all, and that she didn't know what to do with him. She pointed to the textbook and a stack of papers on her desk, saying, "You see, Tim has already read through the entire textbook, done the exercises at the end of each chapter, presented them to me, and wants to know what's next. He belongs in a program for the gifted, but we don't have anything like that here. I was hoping you might have some ideas about what can be done to keep him interested and challenged." I replied with, "So, we need to find something to challenge him and keep him busy for the rest of the semester?" The teacher shook her head from side to side and saying, "No, for the rest of the school year. He has finished everything we usually cover during the entire school year." I assured the teacher that we appreciated the information and that I would see what I could do. We did not share anything about that meeting with Tim. Then one evening, shortly after that meeting, I asked Tim if he would be interested in learning to play the piano. He said that he would like that. We purchased a piano and found a piano teacher in Ann Arbor. There were many trips for piano lessons that followed. Both Tim and his younger sister, Jill, took piano lessons. All the children were also heavily involved in 4-H with ponies or horses. Judy established a 4-H club named The Tumbleweed 4-H Club and, for 13 years, would spend Mother's Day at the Washtenaw County Farm Council Grounds in Saline as the children showed their horses at the Spring Roundup, followed by the 4-H fair in July.

Tim's high school years began just as computers were coming onto the scene and getting introduced into the schools. While Tim was in high school, the school purchased the first computers for use in the classrooms, the Apple IIe. I purchased a couple of the Apple IIe computers for the home. Tim was captivated by the computer. He played some games on it but quickly became curious about how the machines were designed. He wanted to know how they were programmed to do all that they did. I took him to a bookstore where he purchased some books on computer programming. He pored through them and quickly learned how to write programs. He took to it like a duck to water. Soon, a couple of Dexter teachers were visiting at our house so Tim could teach them how to use the new computers that had been purchased for the school. Tim would go on to finish all of his high school classes early. There was an open final semester that needed to be filled with something. Tim spent that time designing several computer programs which he gave to the school. One was a program for keeping statistics, another for learning German. He was not a nerd, though. He played on the high school basketball team, and we so enjoyed going to those games. During his senior year, Dexter defeated their archrival, Chelsea, three times, twice during the regular season and once in the playoffs. During those games with Chelsea, he was often guarding one of his good friends from 4-H who was an excellent guard on the Chelsea team. On one Friday night game, Tim had a spectacular last few minutes that secured the win. The next morning, Judy and I were surprised when we opened the sports section of the *Ann Arbor News*. There was a big picture of Tim and another Dexter guard, holding their fists in the air, and the headline read, "DEXTER'S LONG ON LATE GAME HEROICS." I bought several extra papers that day. Tim played saxophone in the high school band and took a leadership role with the band as the student director and drum major. Tim also developed an interest in building and flying model airplanes. Other kids would often bring their crashed planes to Tim for repair. On one Saturday afternoon, Tim's friend, Paul, brought his plane over to the house. He and Tim went out to the front pasture where Paul wanted to fly his plane. After a while, Tim came back into the house and approached me and said, "Hey Dad, you know that one post you have out in the front pasture?" I answered, "Yeah." Tim went on, barely holding back the laughter, "Well, Paul found it." Holding out his hand which held just a model airplane engine, Tim said, "He wants to know if I can rebuild it." Tim then lost control and began laughing. Paul knew that Tim could fix anything. It was not the first time Paul had crashed his model plane. Later in life, Paul would get his pilot's license, but Tim has never flown with him.

Tim would go on to attend the University of Michigan on a pre-med course while playing saxophone in the marching band. During his time with the Michigan marching band, he would make three trips to the Rose Bowl and one to the Gator Bowl. Judy and I made one trip to Pasadena to see one of those games. In the fall of 1989, Tim began applying to medical schools. Tim had become a die-hard Michigan Wolverine. He really wanted to pursue his education at the University of Michigan Medical School, but he had also applied to Wayne State. He went through the interview process at Michigan and was delighted to receive the letter from Michigan welcoming him to the next medical school class. About a week after Tim got his acceptance letter from Michigan, I was approached at Chelsea Hospital by one of the surgeons who had maintained a relationship with the medical school and was somewhat involved in the screening of applicants. He was aware that Tim had applied to the University of Michigan Medical School even though I had never discussed it with him. At that time, I had been elected by my peers to be the chief of the medical staff, and I served on the committee that reviewed applications for privileges at Chelsea Hospital. The surgeon indicated that he was aware that another young surgeon in his specialty was coming to the Chelsea area and had applied for privileges at Chelsea Hospital. He made it clear that he had talked with the new surgeon about selling him his practice. He then told me that he did not want the new surgeon to be given privileges at Chelsea Hospital unless he purchased his established practice. I reminded him that Chelsea Hospital was an open staff hospital, that the new surgeon was well qualified, and that his credentials were all in order. The surgeon then told me that I needed to make sure the new surgeon did not get privileges without buying his practice. I assured him that I would not get involved with trying to block the new surgeon's privileges. The surgeon then locked his eyes on mine, not hiding his anger, and said, "Maybe I'm going to have to check on the status of Tim's medical school application." He then turned and walked away. I felt my face flush with anger while thinking, "What a dirt bag." I did not know what he was capable of doing, but I had to let Tim know what had happened in case the dirt bag had enough influence to mess things up for Tim. That evening, I sat down with Tim and explained the circumstances and all that had happened. I told him that I didn't know what the surgeon would be able to do. I really didn't need to ask, but I did ask Tim what he thought I should do. His response was, "Don't worry about it, Dad. Just do the right thing. I've been accepted to Wayne State too." Another week went by before another letter from the University of Michigan Medical School arrived for Tim. The letter informed him that there had been an error regarding the previous acceptance letter, and they wanted to schedule another interview with him. He went for the second interview. At that interview, he was asked if he had been accepted anywhere else, and he let them know that he had been accepted to Wayne State. Then they asked him what he thought he would be doing, and he told them that it looked like he would be going to Wayne State. I told Tim that it would be Michigan's loss and that he should make his mark and make them regret they didn't get him. Tim rented a second-floor apartment from a nice Polish lady in Hamtramck and had already finished his first week of medical school at Wayne State when he received another letter from the University of Michigan Medical School indicating that they had a spot that had opened up, and they were offering it to him. He tossed the letter and never replied.

Tim graduated from the Wayne State Medical School and was well into his internship, considering where he might do his anesthesiology residency. He looked at a lot of programs around the country. Then, just for fun, he scheduled an interview at Michigan. The interview was conducted by one old professor. Tim entered the office and took a seat. The old professor began looking through Tim's file. After a few minutes, he looked up at Tim and inquired, "Are you aware of what took place here?" Tim replied, "I think so." The professor went on, "I sure hope you don't hold this against us." Tim assured him saying, "It's water over the dam." The interview concluded with the old professor indicating that he sure hoped Tim would match with Michigan and join the program. I really think Tim took some pleasure out of making sure he matched with the Mayo Clinic, leaving Michigan with an unfilled position that year. He was amazed that the surgeon who had screwed him over had evidently left some tracks in the record that were obvious to someone who did not know the whole story.

Lori, Amy and Jill were all very active with their horses in 4-H and did very well. Tim, Amy and Jill were all active with the Dexter High School equestrian team. They were all very competitive and rode their horses a lot on the farm getting ready for competition. Amy competed in track at school and was part of the flag corps in the marching band. Tim played the saxophone and became the drum major. Little Jill was a dynamite, fast-dribbling guard on the girls' basketball team in Dexter. All the girls were real beauties, and I have the evidence. When Amy was a senior, she was elected homecoming queen. Jill was in the ninth grade at the time and was selected to be part of the queen's court. At the football game, when the queen and the girls in the court were to walk out onto the field, they were to be walked out on their father's arm. I had two girls in the ceremony. Amy walked out on my arm while Jill walked out on my dad's arm. He was one proud grandpa!

In the fall of 1988, I got a call from one of my medical school classmates. Bob had some bad news about our mutual friend, Brent, the general surgeon who practiced in Owosso. He said that Brent had developed a bowel obstruction and had undergone surgery the Sunday before Thanksgiving. At surgery, he was found to have metastatic colon cancer. When Brent was an undergraduate and taking classes at Flint College, he met my dad who was also taking some classes there. They had become great friends, and Brent had kept me updated on my dad's serious illness when I was in medical school. Brent had written to me during my Vietnam tour. After Brent recovered from surgery, he decided that he did not want to have any chemotherapy. However, he did want to meet with my dad and me. Dad and I met with Brent at his home in Owosso at which time Brent acknowledged his faith and the hope he had in Christ. Brent asked my dad to officiate his funeral services when the time came, and Dad said that he would be honored to do so. Brent had never married but had simply cared for his parents and his brother, David, who lived with the disabilities of cerebral palsy. David lived with Brent and his aging father at the time of Brent's cancer diagnosis, and Brent was concerned about David's care after he and his father both died. David had a deformity of one hand and one leg but was able to get around pretty well and could actually engage in bowling at the local bowling alley. Brent told me that he had set up a trust fund for David that could be used to supplement his Social Security disability income. David was not in a position to manage his own financial affairs, so Brent asked me if I would be willing to look out for David and act as his conservator and guardian after Brent and his father were both gone. He even offered to pay me for my services. I agreed to take on the responsibility but declined any payment. I told him that I was certain that he would do the same for me if the situation were reversed. Brent said that he knew he could trust me saying, "You and I are cut from the same cloth." Brent went home to be with the Lord on June 21, 1989, at the age of 49. My dad conducted the funeral service and assured those gathered of the hope in Christ that had sustained Brent and had provided him comfort to the end of his time on earth. Over the years, the guardianship provided some challenges for me after the passing of Brent's father. At one point, a relative petitioned the court regarding the guardianship and argued that I should not be allowed sole responsibility for David's financial affairs. At the hearing, the judge asked David, "David, are you happy with the way Dr. Long is taking care of you?" David replied, "Very happy." Then the judge questioned me as he looked through some of the annual reports, "Dr. Long, I don't see in any of the reports where it lists your fees or your reimbursable expenses." My answer was, "That's because I do not charge anything." The judge responded with, "I see. The guardianship will continue with no changes." It has been 32 years since Brent's passing, and David is still living independently in Owosso in a house that he now owns free and clear, and all his needs are being met with the funds left in trust for him by his brother, Brent.

There was one lighthearted, memorable moment over the years regarding David. David regularly attended his church in Owosso. He would sometimes ride his bike to a fishing spot at the edge of town. He loves to fish. He loves to play video games at home where I have him set up with a nice console and a lot of games with a large TV. Early on, he loved to bowl at the only bowling alley in Owosso. Over the years, David has called me every Friday evening around 8 p.m. to report on what was going on in his life. He would often call on other evenings as well, but Friday evening was always our time to talk. If anybody died that David knew at all, he would call to tell me about it. David does weigh a bit more than he should, and he rarely missed any of the dinners that took place related to the passing of anyone that he knew. One Friday evening, I answered the phone for the expected call from David. David was very distraught and saying that he didn't know what he was going to do. He went on and on saying, "You are never going to believe what happened." Assuming somebody very close to David had died, I urged him to calm down and tell me what had happened. When David finally got calmed down, he gave me the horrible news that the bowling alley had burned down, and he just didn't know what he was going to do. I realized that the loss of the bowling alley was going to leave a void in his life, but I did have a little trouble not laughing. I assured him that they would likely rebuild it, and they did.

My position as the chief of staff at Chelsea Hospital gave me a seat at the board meetings. It quickly became clear to me that the hospital administrator had managed to maintain operative control of the board by controlling who got on the board. The whole board was not even privy to the details of the administrator's contract and salary package. A compensation committee took care of his contract. A hospital junior administrator, who was a good friend of the administrator and answered to him, assembled a bunch of material regarding the compensation of various heads of industry, and that material was used by the compensation committee to justify the salary they set for the hospital administrator. The administrator was constantly looking for a way to get another bigger, institution to take over Chelsea Hospital, and I was suspicious that there was a golden parachute in his contract that would pay him off handsomely if he managed to peddle the hospital. I would eventually learn that there was such a golden parachute. I pushed for more transparency and asked too many questions which made the administrator quite uncomfortable. He controlled enough of the board to write his own contract. He set out to undermine me and my ability to practice at Chelsea. He announced to the board that the hospital administration had decided to "go in a different direction" regarding anesthesia services. He contracted with the anesthesia group at St. Joseph Mercy Hospital in Ypsilanti to be the exclusive provider of anesthesia services at Chelsea beginning March 1, 1991. Our children were all pursuing their own careers. Lori had her own business as a cosmetologist. Amy received her BA from Eastern Michigan University and would eventually go to work for a CPA firm. Tim was pursuing a medical career. Jill would get her BSN from the University of Michigan Nursing School and eventually get her master's and become a nurse practitioner at the Ann Arbor Veterans Hospital. So, Judy decided to go back to school and get her nursing degree. She would get her BSN from the University of Michigan Nursing School and work for a time at the Ann Arbor Veterans Hospital and the Saline Evangelical Home.

After leaving Chelsea, I started providing locum tenens coverage. For a time, I provided coverage with my old group at McLaren Hospital in Flint. On one of those days, I made contact with an old high school classmate. I was giving anesthesia to a woman for a cholecystectomy, and I glanced at the general information on the front of the chart. I noticed the name of the patient's husband which was the same name of someone I had gone to school with from elementary through high school, and the patient was about my age. In the middle of the case, I told the surgeon that the husband of the patient might be somebody with whom I had attended high school. The surgeon suggested that I go with him when he went to talk to the husband after the surgery was finished. When the two of us went to talk with the husband, I recognized him right away. My old classmate did not recognize me. The surgeon's first words to him were, "I think you might know this guy," as he pointed to me. Irv looked at me, shaking his head, indicating that he didn't recognize me. So, I told him who his girlfriend was in elementary school. Irv nodded and smiled but still didn't know who I was. I identified myself, and we shook hands and had a good laugh. He invited me to his house for dinner, and one week after the surgery, I had dinner with Irv and his wife and met the rest of his wonderful family.

I also provided some anesthesia coverage at War Memorial Hospital in the Upper Peninsula at Sault Ste. Marie. It was in the middle of winter, a good time for the guy I was covering to get out of town for a meeting. I stayed at the Ojibway Hotel, overlooking the Soo Locks. Ojibway was an appropriate name for a hotel in its location since the Ojibway Indians, also known as Chippewa, at one time occupied most of the Upper Peninsula. At the time, the hotel was owned by the town's only orthopedic surgeon. The hospital was just a few blocks away from the hotel. The bar across the street from my hotel room kept the bright, colored lights flashing all night long. On one cold night, I got called out at 3:00 a.m. for an emergency. As I walked past the desk clerk, I inquired as to the outside temperature. The clerk responded, "Twenty below." I then said, "Not the wind chill, the actual temperature." The clerk responded, "Like I said, twenty below." It was not a good time to be in the Upper Peninsula. When I arrived at the hospital and said something to the surgeon about how cold it was, the surgeon pointed north with a smile while saying, "The tundra is not that far away." The next morning, I made my way to the Grand Traverse Bay Store to buy a warm hat and some warm gloves. I did enjoy the restaurants and the plentiful whitefish with the all-you-can-eat specials. On one cold morning, I got a call to standby for the arrival of an Indian who had gone through the ice. After a few hours of waiting, I was finally informed that the poor fellow was never recovered. Occasionally, a few inmates were brought over from one of the state prisons for elective surgery. On one occasion, I was summoned from the operating room to labor and delivery because a baby needed to be resuscitated. I intubated the baby and got it quickly pinked up. The staff seemed surprised. I learned that the guy for whom I was covering was not good with kids. Word got around and back to the administrator who approached me about my resuscitation of the baby and offered me the job of the guy I was temporarily replacing. I declined the offer.

On one of my stints at War Memorial, I arranged for Judy to fly up and spend a few days and be with me during the drive home. She found the flight to be an adventure that she did not wish to repeat. When I greeted her on her arrival at the airport and inquired about the flight, she only had a one-word reply which she gave through clenched teeth, "Rough." As we walked to the car, she described her flight experience, "There was just one seat on each side of the aisle. We bounced around all over the place. There was just a curtain separating the pilot and copilot from the cabin. The pilots looked like high school kids, and you don't even get peanuts." I had to chuckle a bit as I assured her that she would not have to experience such a thing again.

I was back home in Ann Arbor on Labor Day weekend in 1992 and caught the news report that President George H.W. Bush stayed at the old Ojibway Hotel with his Secret Service team for one night before participating in the Mackinac Bridge Walk to close out the Labor Day weekend. Then in May 1993, I did my last stint of coverage in the Upper Peninsula. A stint in the spring was certainly more pleasant than during the middle of winter. I opted to stay at a different hotel across town just to get away from the lights and noise of the establishments across the street from the Ojibway. I soon discovered that I was staying at a hotel that had more than a 100 percent occupancy rate. The room next to mine had been rented to a pimp who was determined to get his money's worth. The thin wall between the rooms did not deaden any of the sounds, and it was clear what was going on. I turned up the television sound pretty loud at times to drown out the noise. When the work schedule permitted it, I enjoyed watching the big ships go through the locks and navigate the St. Mary's River. I also went over to the dam and watched the Indian kids catch undersized trout with impunity since the DNR rules did not apply to them. I was impressed with just how many Canadians came down to Sault Ste. Marie to have elective orthopedic surgery at War Memorial and pay out of pocket rather than stay on the long waiting lists in Canada. Most of the cases I did at War Memorial were orthopedic cases. I also gave anesthesia for a fair number of C-sections. The patients were usually unmarried teenagers from Paradise, Michigan. They were consistently on Medicaid and accompanied by their very young mothers and sometimes rather young appearing grandmothers. The surgeon explained to me that nearby Paradise, Michigan, had gotten its name from the miners who went there for entertainment and sought out the women of ill repute. He said that Paradise had become a town with multiple generations of unmarried women with children, living off of the state.

It was during that last stint in the Upper Peninsula that I got a call from home, informing me that my cousin and fishing buddy, Dave, had died in an automobile accident. I was supposed to meet up with Dave for some fishing in Manistee where he had a cabin when my locum tenens stint was finished. Dave's pickup truck was no match for the 18-wheeler that he encountered in a head-on crash at night on a two-lane highway not far from his cabin. He was only 58. The news was a real gut shot for me. It didn't seem possible that Dave was really gone. It was a long, sad drive home. My dad officiated the funeral. I helped carry Dave's casket to his final resting place. Dave loved to fish, but he did take too many chances and lived on the edge. His favorite line was, "God doesn't count the days against your time on earth that you spend fishing." He should have been fishing instead of driving that fateful night.

My good friend, Tom, had been on the anesthesia teaching staff at Michigan when I was a resident. He had joined the anesthesia group at St. Luke's Hospital in Maumee, Ohio, and practiced anesthesia for years. He then went back and completed a residency program in occupational medicine. He had not been doing anesthesia for a few years, but I talked him into getting back into anesthesia and doing some locum tenens coverage with me at McLaren Hospital in Flint. For several months we shared a ride to and from Flint to do locum tenens coverage. Then we got the word that Tom's old group in Maumee, Ohio, needed some help, and the two of us started doing some locums coverage for them. Tom and I were both still working in Maumee as my son, Tim, was nearing the end of his anesthesia residency at the Mayo Clinic in Rochester, Minnesota. Since the Maumee group was looking for new members, I asked Tim if he or any of his fellow graduates would be interested in coming to Ohio. There was some interest. The leadership at Mayo wanted Tim to stay as part of the teaching staff. When he indicated that he was thinking of trying private practice, they pressed him by telling him that they usually did not take people back on the staff if they leave for private practice. Tim and one of his colleagues ultimately decided to give the group at St. Luke's a try, so I was able to work at St. Luke's along with my son for two years, and I enjoyed it. It was early in Tim's second year at St. Luke's when I was approached by Tom who inquired of me, "Do you realize what a special guy your son is?" I replied, "He's my son, so I might be a bit partial, but I've always thought he was special." Tom went on, "No, I think you are too close to him to realize just how special he is. I don't know if you have noticed, but whenever any doctor has a medical question, they go to Tim with it. I've heard a lot of the interactions, and he is impressive. I think he is wasting his talents here in private practice. He should really be training other doctors." I thanked Tom for his input and told him that my talking Tim into leaving the Mayo Clinic may have been a mistake. Then, near the end of Tim's second year at St. Luke's, Tim became concerned about how some of the care was being delivered at St. Luke's and approached the head of the anesthesia group with some suggestions. The head of the group was not receptive to Tim's suggestions and even suggested that maybe he should leave if he didn't like the way things were being done at St. Luke's. At this point, I can only say that the Lord does, indeed, work in mysterious ways. Just a few days after Tim's suggestions to the head of the anesthesia group were rebuffed and coupled with an invitation to leave, he got a call from the anesthesia leadership at the Mayo Clinic asking him if he would consider coming back. When he indicated that he might, he was asked if he would have the upcoming weekend available to come out for a talk. He indicated that he was not on call for the upcoming weekend and would have time for a talk. There was one other call to inform Tim of his flight time and notify him that the tickets for him and his wife, Lynn, would be waiting for him at Detroit Metro Airport. After Tim's trip back to the Mayo Clinic, he told me what he had been offered. I encouraged him to take it, and he did. When word got around that Tim would be returning to the Mayo Clinic, one of the surgeons at St. Luke's, who needed a major procedure, scheduled his procedure so that Tim could provide his anesthesia before he left. All went well. Tim would ultimately be recognized as a teacher of the year at Mayo. At this writing, he holds the rank of professor and is the program director for the anesthesia department at the Mayo Clinic in Rochester, Minnesota, and is extensively published.

I continued providing some coverage at St. Luke's for a short time after Tim returned to the Mayo Clinic. Then I stopped working at St. Luke's altogether and just worked at a free-standing plastic surgery facility for a few years. Then, in late 2004, I received notice that my malpractice insurance carrier was going to stop providing coverage in Ohio at the end of the year. I was also having frequent nosebleeds that were hard to control and discovered that my blood pressure was very high. I decided that God was sending me a message and made the decision to retire and get my blood pressure under control. There would be no more early trips to the operating room. It was time to enjoy the farm.

Over the years, we had a variety of horses, including quarter horses, Arabians and Morgans. We ended up with just the little ones, the miniature horses. We raised a number of miniatures. I encountered more challenges with equine deliveries than I ever did in human medicine. A placental abruption in a horse will result in a dead foal almost 100 percent of the time. One afternoon while I was doing some work in the horse barn after the miniatures had been put in their stalls for the night, I heard one of the mares, who was not due to deliver for a couple of weeks, grunting. When I looked into the stall, I saw a big, red bag of blood protruding from the rear of the mare. I went into the stall and quickly broke the sack and reached inside for the foal's feet. I grabbed the feet and pulled the little premature foal out and dried it off, rubbing it vigorously. The little filly started breathing. I dried it off and got it warmed up. The mare quickly expressed the separated placenta. The little filly got to her feet fairly soon and was able to nurse. Mare and foal did well. Just lucky to be there at the right time.

There were a number of odd positions that I had to deal with over the years. The one that I dreaded the most was when the back legs and nose presented together. It was one giant cone that could not be delivered without reaching in and bending the rear legs back. The process would usually result in enough compression of the cord to doom the foal. My goal with such a presentation was just to save the mare. Fortunately, I only had to deal with this presentation a couple of times. The miniatures were fun to watch and great company over the years. We also got plenty of exercise putting up hay and cleaning stalls.

In the spring of 2009, I got a call from my good friend, Dan, who had moved to Logansport, Indiana, to run a spring company. He had a history of hypertension. In 2007, he had undergone a cardiac stinting.

Judy and Reuel Long.

He had recently undergone another cardiac catheterization which had been followed by a CAT scan. The CAT scan had revealed the presence of an adrenal tumor. Further testing had revealed that the tumor was a pheochromocytoma. Dan had been referred to a local general surgeon to have the tumor removed. I talked with Dan about just how rare pheochromocytoma is and emphasized to him that this would not be a routine surgery. I suggested to Dan that he talk with the surgeon and ask him if he and his team had ever operated on a pheochromocytoma before. It turned out that the surgeon had never operated on one of these rare tumors. I suggested that it would be wise to have the procedure done at a place that did it routinely, like the Mayo Clinic. Dan agreed. I called Tim and asked him to make the arrangements for Dan to be evaluated at the Mayo Clinic. Dan and I flew out to Rochester, Minnesota, for his evaluation and surgery. The meeting with the endocrinologist was interesting. A general surgeon might not see a single patient with a pheochromocytoma even once during a career. The endocrinologist at Mayo who saw Dan stated that Dan was the fourth pheochromocytoma patient he had seen that week. He said that the Mayo Clinic received such patients from all over the world. During the discussion, he mentioned that President Eisenhower had a pheochromocytoma, but it was not found until the autopsy was performed. I recalled how I had often noticed Eisenhower's face flushing when he was speaking. He was a sitting duck for all those heart attacks and strokes with an undiagnosed pheochromocytoma. During that meeting with the endocrinologist, I couldn't help but think back on my old professor at Flint College. He died at age 49 from a stroke. His face would often flush for no apparent reason. We could be talking casually about all the earthworms he had collected around the country for his research, and his face would flush suddenly. He must have had a pheochromocytoma. On August 4, 2009, Dan underwent successful surgery for his pheochromocytoma at the Mayo Clinic in Rochester, Minnesota, and recovered with no complications.

THE BAKERY BLESSING

Jim Dehlin had found the old audio tape and tracked down my phone number, making that fateful call to me on July 12, 2014. The following month, on August 21, 2014, my father, William Reuel Long, died at the age of 94. He was a World War II veteran, and I had his letters from the war as well as his handwritten battle descriptions. I eulogized him at a service with an overflow crowd and accepted the flag and expressions of gratitude from the military when he was laid to rest at the Great Lakes National Cemetery. As his oldest child, I was in the best position to write about his life. I was occupied for several months with writing his biography which I published in early 2015 under the title of "Friend of God ... homeward bound." On December 23, 2014, the 44th anniversary of when our paths first crossed, I called Jim Dehlin. We stayed in touch during 2015 but did not manage to meet up until September. The meeting was scheduled to take place at the Dexter Bakery in Dexter, Michigan, at 8:30 a.m. on September 4, 2015. It was a day that Jim was scheduled to drive down from Higgins Lake for a medical appointment. I got to the bakery ahead of Jim and was waiting outside when Jim arrived, right at 8:30 a.m. As I looked west, I could see a man, perched on an electric wheelchair, moving at a pretty good clip toward me. I extended my arm, pointing in his direction, and then greeted him with a warm handshake. As we shook hands, Jim exclaimed, "You haven't changed a bit." I laughed and told him that he didn't lie well. We went inside the bakery where I was able to purchase coffee and some pastries for our visit. We then went outside where the weather permitted us to visit at one of the outside tables and enjoy the mild temperature and light breeze. Jim had pictures from his time in Vietnam as well as some family pictures. He told me that he had a pilot's license and showed me a picture of his airplane. I could only imagine what feeling of freedom a bilateral amputee must feel while flying his own airplane. The expression on his face when he talked about flying said it all. I asked him how he managed to find me. He said that his sister had found the old audio cassette tape that I had helped him make and send home from the 27th Mobile Army Surgical Hospital after his surgery. The tape had my name and identification on it. The rest was easy with the internet. I learned that Jim had a few rough years before getting his life together. He then pursued all of his passions in education and taught at Northern Michigan University before retiring. His teaching field was Aviation Maintenance Technology. I expressed some frustration about what had happened to so-called higher education with kids majoring in fields like gender studies that had no future. Jim just smiled and replied, "My students all get jobs." Jim told me that he was married to a wonderful woman and had been blessed with two great children. He also said he had a grandson, and his face beamed when he mentioned him. I asked him if he would change anything that happened to him if he could. Without hesitation, he replied, "Not a thing. If you change one thing, you change everything. I met and married a wonderful woman, have wonderful children and a wonderful grandson."

Jim recalled the moments on the operating table at Chu Lai just before I started his anesthesia. He said that he knew his legs were gone even though he was begging us not to take them. He said that he was comforted by my words just before falling asleep with the anesthesia. I was touched by his gratitude. We visited for more than 90 minutes. John, the former superintendent of schools in Dexter, was walking by so I stopped him and asked him to take a picture of us with my cell phone. As our visit was coming to an end, Jim expressed his thanks for all that I had done for him. His parting words were, "You saved my life." I was caught off guard by Jim's expression of gratitude and found that I could not respond to his parting comment. I had just been the recipient of gratitude from a veteran that I had cared for as part of a fabulous team of caregivers. I could only wish that they could all know about Jim. Jim and I would have many more meetings.

I thought a lot about the reunion with Jim Dehlin and how it had happened, totally out of my control. The story of Jim's life after Vietnam and his expressions of gratitude had touched me and had been therapeutic. Most of the time, the long work hours during my career had allowed me to push the Vietnam blood and mutilation somewhere deep in solitary confinement in my brain. Retirement had allowed much of it to escape that solitary confinement. The most troubling memories involved keeping people alive with such unspeakable injuries that they had no future quality of life. Some had no extremities. I often recall one unfortunate kid who lost all four extremities and both eyes. There were those nights when I found myself back in Vietnam dealing with the carnage. It was all so real. I would awaken in the middle of the night to find the fitted sheet off the top of the bed, one of the pillows on the floor, the blankets either off the bed or in a big ball, and my Judy having sought refuge in another room where she could get some rest. Sometimes I would have to wipe the sweat from my forehead before lying down to try to get some sleep. Usually, there was no sleep to be had on such nights. I would close my eyes, unable to go back to sleep, then open my eyes every 30 or 40 minutes to check the time until the hours passed, bringing the morning daylight. On some nights, when sleep was not to be had, I would turn on the television just to hear the news that I had already heard in order to get my mind occupied with something else. Sometimes it worked, and I would eventually fall asleep for a few hours. Any febrile illness increased the risk of a return to Vietnam during the night.

Now comes Jim Dehlin back into my life to remind me that my efforts were not totally in vain. Maybe there are many more veterans with success stories like Jim Dehlin, Vietnam veterans who served their country with honor, overcame their injuries, and then went on to make the most of their lives. I felt blessed by Jim's call and was grateful to the Good Lord for that call. A call takes place between us every December 23.

The decision to go to war is never made by those who have to go in harm's way to wage war. Presidents make such decisions, and such a decision may even be a big mistake. It could be argued that the war in Vietnam was a big mistake. That in no way detracts from the honor of those who

The Vietnam Veterans Memorial wall.

served this country in that war. Some gave all, and their names are on that black, granite wall in Washington D.C. Their service was honorable, and their sacrifice is sacred. Others gave some, if not all, with sacrifice of sight or limb or unspeakable mutilation or disfigurement or mental anguish. Their service, likewise, was honorable, and their sacrifice is sacred. Those who served and were spared physical or psychological trauma also provided honorable service, and their service is sacred. May God bless all those who answered the call to serve.

When Jim and I met in March 2019, Jim brought the tape that I had sent home for him along with the letter that I had enclosed with it. The letter was addressed to Jim's girlfriend at the time and read as follows:

Miss ....
Flushing, Michigan 48433

Dear Miss ....

This note is being written to accompany the tape recorded by James Dehlin. I am from Flint, Michigan, and was in general practice there for one

year before entering the Army. I am presently doing anesthesiology at the 27th Surgical Hospital at Chu Lai. I was on duty the night Jim was brought in. It is against regulations for me to discuss his condition with you, but there are no regulations against Jim sending you a tape. So he recorded this one Christmas evening. He got tired out pretty fast but managed to record half the tape on one side. May God bless you and Jim's folks. Pray for peace.

Reuel S. Long, Cpt MC

27th Surgical Hospital
Chu Lai
APO SF 96325

I had never listened to the tape, but Jim brought it with him on one of his

The cassette and letter that made Jim and Reuel's reunion possible.

visits to Ann Arbor and left it with me. I took it home and found that I could not bring myself to listen to it for a couple of weeks. Finally, one evening, I popped it into a player and pushed the play button. The audio was surprisingly good. Jim started off talking to his girlfriend and asking her to give the tape to his parents after she listened to it. It was surprising to hear how he praised the care he was getting and how he played down his injuries. He tried to reassure everybody, saying that it would take more than an ol' booby trap to "take out the kid." He said that he would be coming home sooner than planned. He then went on to say that Vietnam was a nice place for a visit but that he would not want to stay for a year. He went on to describe how one of the North Vietnamese casualties on his ward was going a little crazy because he couldn't have anything to drink. He described how the guy pulled out his IV and tried to drink it and had to be tied down. He expressed his hope that everybody back home had a good Christmas. He said he was looking forward to getting back home. It was clear that he was short of breath and tired easily while trying to make the recording. He never mentioned that he had lost his legs.

INVINCIBLE

Following the reunion with Jim at the Dexter Bakery, the two of us had many more meetings, phone calls, letters and e-mail exchanges that allowed me to collect more and more details about Jim's life after Vietnam. There were some painful memories for Jim, but he endured and eventually shared it all with me. The word that best describes him is "invincible."

Jim was in his bed in the postoperative ward at the 27th Surgical Hospital at Chu Lai. Back in Flushing, Michigan, Jim Dehlin's father and stepmother received a telegram on December 24, 1970, notifying them of Jim's injuries. Jim's father, Charles Barrett Dehlin, who went by C.B., was a World War II Navy veteran. Jim had lost his mother, Beatrice Marie (Jahnke) Dehlin, to leukemia in 1957. Jim's father remarried to Lois Ann McCrady in 1958. Jim had five siblings—in birth order, Pat, Barry, Dick, Jim (born May 30, 1950), Kristin and David. The Christmas season of 1970 was not a season of celebration for the Dehlin family. Jim's folks got the audio tape that I had mailed to Jim's girlfriend.

Jim had been a standout at Flushing High School. He was six feet tall and captain of the football team, playing linebacker and offensive end. He also played basketball, and in 1967, his team won the Big Nine conference championship with a record of 22–2. They made it to the state quarterfinals where they lost to Lansing O'Rafferty. Jim was also the student council president when he graduated from Flushing High School in June 1968.

After graduating from high school, Jim went to Muskegon where he took a job in a paper plant. He then got in a car accident on a weekend visit back to Flushing. After recuperating, he took a job at the Chevy truck plant in Flint, Michigan. Jim had been out of high school less than a year when he joined the Army and was sworn in on February 27, 1969. It is not surprising that Jim has always been a patriot. He was born on Memorial Day weekend. He lived across the street from the cemetery where the Memorial Day program was held after the parade every year. His father and uncles had served during World War II. Jim felt that he had an obligation to answer his country's call. He was also attracted to the education benefits that would come with his service through the GI Bill. Like most men his age, having recently graduated from high school, there was no concern about mortality. He felt invincible. In his own words, "I was 10 feet tall and bulletproof on top of that, or young and dumb and full of shit." The only question posed by Jim's dad regarding his Army enlistment was, "Why didn't you join the Navy?" Regarding his enlistment, Jim wrote, "A friend of mine had gotten drafted and, along with another one of our running buddies, we went in together. My good friend, Frank, had dropped out of high school at 17 and joined the Marine Corps. Frank died on LZ (landing zone) Ross in a mortar attack in January of 1970."

Jim describes his military experience as follows: "Basic training at Ft. Knox in the winter was not fun. Our platoon had rampant upper respiratory infections going on, and we were sick! We lived in the old wooden World War II barracks and had to maintain them spotless of course. I was a squad leader, but that didn't get me out of KP or guard duty. The physical requirements were not that bad for me. I performed well in all aspects. I was six feet tall and about 200 pounds and able to hold my own. I applied for OCS [officer candidate school] while in basic and, after passing the background checks and sitting through an interview board, I was accepted. I still had AIT [advanced individual training] to go through, and I stayed right at Ft. Knox for Armor training. After Infantry OCS at Ft.

Second Lieutenant James Dehlin at Infantry Officer Candidate School, Fort Benning (courtesy Jim Dehlin).

Benning, I requested and received branch transfer to Armor. I was sent back to Ft. Knox for the Armor Officer Orientation course. Upon completion, I received orders to 5th Bn, 33rd Armor, at Ft. Knox, of course. I spent six months at the 5th of the 33rd, working in support of the Armor school and then got my orders to Vietnam."

Jim goes on to describe his shortened tour in Vietnam and return to the States. "I arrived in Vietnam in November of 1970."

"I was assigned to First Squadron, First Cavalry, based on Hawk Hill and assigned to the American or 23rd Infantry Division. There was a lot of bad press at the time because of Lt. Calley and his connection to the American Division. So all signage and stencils on our tracks were reprinted from American to 23rd Infantry Division. I served as a platoon leader in A troop. Our mission was to search for and engage suspected main force NVA [North Vietnamese Army] units that had been infiltrating down the Ho Chi Minh trail during the monsoon season. We would move into our AO [area of operations] and set up a defensive position (eight M113 tracks and two Sheridan tanks made up the circle). We

would then patrol the AO on foot, looking for signs of the NVA and local Viet Cong. Every village we went through had old men and old women, young women and children, but no young males. Hmmmmmmm. We had operations with Ruff Puffs [Regional and Popular Forces]. We didn't think much of the Ruff Puffs. They would vacuum up every piece of rice, every chicken, everything of value from these small villages. Not a very good way to win hearts and minds. They would also try to steal from us when laggard up together."

Jim Dehlin at Cam Ranh Bay in November 1970 (courtesy Jim Dehlin).

It was about noon local time on December 23, 1970, when Jim stepped on a booby trap. "I had a three-man sniper team deployed on high ground about 300 yards west of our Laager [night defensive position]. The sniper, radioman and M60 machine gunner came under attack from a force of NVA regulars who had been infiltrating our AO [area of operations] from Laos. We called in gunships from the 174th Assault Helicopter Company. The 174th consisted of gunships (AH 1 Cobras), the 'Sharks' and the Dolphins which was the lift platoon (UH1—Hueys). The Hueys could be gunships or slicks. Slicks were unarmed except for the door gunners and were used to transport troops, resupply, or medevac. When our sniper team called in that they were under attack, we mounted up two armored personnel carriers and headed across a rice paddy to relieve them. We got both tracks stuck in the rice paddy (not uncommon) and the slicks that dropped off the Blue Team came over and picked us up and flew us the short distance to where the Blue Team was assembled to assault up the hill. The Blue Team consisted of two squads of infantry that would accompany the gunships for insertion after the gun run. They would support ground forces or secure a downed helicopter or whatever the mission called for. The gunship pilots made a couple of passes after the sniper team popped smoke to show their position. One gunship pilot said that there were so many NVA that they were running into each other trying to reach cover. When we entered the heavy foliage to move up the hill, we saw the results of the gun run. Rockets had cleared openings in the bush, and there were blood trails. We also found an old man who had been wounded and then came across his wife in a trail watchers' hooch. Hiding inside the hooch were two NVA soldiers who we took as prisoners. When we reported that we had prisoners, we were advised that the higher ups wanted them flown back to our fire base for interrogation. As the rest of our forces continued up the hill, we started back to the helicopters with our prisoners. That was when I tripped the booby trap that changed my life in an instant.

"When the medic got to me, he started cutting off my T-shirt. I told him to just straighten out my legs. I had no idea about the wounds in my chest and abdomen. I looked down and saw that my legs were not where they were supposed to be. I was lifted out of the field by one of the slicks that brought the Blue Team in. They took me to the aid station on our fire base at Hawk Hill since it was the closest facility. When they put me on the helicopter, I had a moment of panic when I wondered if I was going to bleed to death. About that time we lifted off, and the rotor wash made me feel like the hand of God was sweeping over me. That is when He told me that I was not going to die, that I had more to do in this life.

I felt a calm come over me. When we got to Hawk Hill, the crew getting me off the helicopter and onto a stretcher slipped and almost bumped me off and onto the helicopter pad. It reminded me of a scene that I had seen in the *M*A*S*H* movie. I was stabilized and then put on another helicopter for the short hop to Chu Lai and the 27th Surgical Hospital. The medical staff at the 27th kept talking to me and asking me questions, trying to keep me with them. I just wanted them to knock me out and do surgery. I had no idea of the full extent of my injuries. Both of my legs had been so blown away that I had no blood supply below the knees. I had a compound fracture of my right arm, and shrapnel wounds in my neck, chest and abdomen. In the midst of all the action and the noise, I heard a calming voice asking me about my hometown. It was Dr. Reuel Long who was from Flint, Michigan, seven miles away from Flushing, where I grew up. His demeanor and honesty helped ease my mind somewhat. I asked him if they could save my legs, and he quietly told me that they would do everything that they could. When I came out of surgery, I was on a ventilator and felt like I was fighting for every breath. When they took the tube out of my trachea, I thought my lungs were coming out with the tube. That was pretty nasty stuff they used to coat that tube. I was still heavily medicated, but the pain when trying to cough was off the charts. I was in intensive care when I woke up and had an NVA regular in the bed next to me. The day before, we were trying to kill each other, and now we were close neighbors in the same hospital. When they told me that I had lost both legs below the knees, it was just confirmation of what I already knew but had not been willing to admit. I did sneak a hand down to do a recon on what else might be gone below the waist. Insert a little sigh of relief. Dr. Reuel Long came to visit me and brought along his cassette recorder. He said that I could record a message to send home to my family, and he would mail it for me if I was interested. I decided to give it a try, and he left the recorder with me after turning it on. I would record some and have to take a break, record some more and take a break. I was asleep when he came back to get the recorder and the tape to mail home for me.

"My squadron commander, Col. Sheldon Burnett came to see me along with his entourage. Col. Burnett was killed in action in a helicopter crash in March 1971, during Operation Lam Son 719. Col. Burnett's remains were not recovered until October 2004. He was buried in Arlington National Cemetery on April 13, 2005. Col. Burnett is on the Wall at panel W4, line 31.

"I spent seven days at the 27th Surgical Hospital. I cannot say enough about the doctors, nurses and techs that saved my life. We did not keep in contact, although I wish I could thank each and every one of them. The only person I saw again was Dr. Reuel Long, 45 years later, thanks to the little tape I saved that he sent home for me.

"When I was strong enough to travel, I was put on another helicopter for a trip to Da Nang and then on to the Army hospital at Camp Zama in Japan. I had to stay overnight in Da Nang before continuing on to Japan.

"Many years later, my sister-in-law asked me if I would have a chat with her neighbor who had been an Army nurse stationed at Da Nang. Chris Schneideer was the inspiration for the TV show, *China Beach*. We established that she was at Da Nang when I went through there, but our paths had not crossed. She needed someone to talk to because her PTSD was as real as that of any combat veteran. We struck an immediate bond, and I told her that her burden was much greater than mine because I only had to go through it once. She had to deal with it every day of her tour. Chris Schneider became one of my heroes that day. Like most who set foot in Vietnam, she was exposed to Agent Orange. Chris Schneider died of leukemia and is buried at Arlington National Cemetery.

"We touched down in Tokyo and were put on a bus. I couldn't see much on a stretcher but did notice that they were driving on the wrong side of the road. I was put in a ward with other wounded soldiers. During the first week, I was in and out of surgery to debride the ends of my stumps and to do the delayed closures of my many wounds. The day came when I was done with surgeries and had reached the repeated dressing change stage. For the first go around with dressing changes, I was given a shot of Demerol to ease the pain. Little did I know that I would be facing the dressing changes after that without something for the pain. I was in for a whole new world of pain. I had been on morphine and Demerol for a week, and coming down wasn't easy, but I wasn't the only one.

"I was on a ward of about 40 patients, amputees, burn victims, and horrific gunshot and shrapnel wounds. We had dressing changes twice a day. The nurses and aides would come in with a cart and start at one end of the ward and work their way down one side and up the other. The cries of pain started at the first bed and advanced toward me halfway down the first side. You knew your turn was coming because the screams got closer and closer until it was your turn. Take my word for it. Anticipation is a bitch. It's like when you were a kid and waiting for that spanking you were going to get when your dad got home, only much worse. When the cart and the crew got to me, I just wanted them to get busy and get it over with, and they did. Removal of the old dressings was the worst part because it tends to stick to all those exposed nerves. When they were done with me, they moved on to my neighbor.

I was exhausted, but the ordeal was not over. They had to complete my row and go up the other side, and I had to listen to each and every one of my wardmates' screams as they went through their own personal hell. We never blamed the medical crew for what we went through. They were all just doing their jobs as a joint effort to get us all healed, and we all knew it would be a painful process. During that painful period, I wanted every politician, every advisor, every person who had a part in the decision that involved all of us in Vietnam, to sit with me and watch what I was watching and hear what I had to hear during all those dressing changes. What if some of their kids were getting those dressing changes? Would they still have thought the price was worth it all? So much for wishing for something that was not going to happen. Back to reality. The dressing change hell was an everyday occurrence for a while, but it got better every day with less and less pain. I only cried once, just one night. Feeling sorry for yourself is natural I think, but how you deal with it is an individual choice. I must admit that I briefly railed at God asking, 'Why me Lord?' Then I did an inventory.

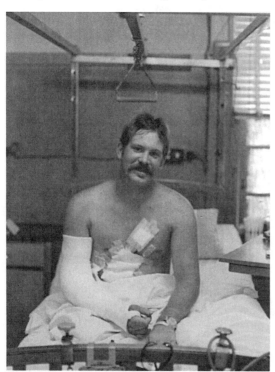

Pecker? Check. Two arms? Check. Eyesight? Check. About that time, I figured out that I was a hell of a lot better off than some of the other guys and told myself, 'QUIT YOUR CRYING.'"

"I met my friend, Andre, while I was in Japan. He was a helicopter pilot and had been shot down. He was ambulatory and would visit my ward to see if he could help in any way. Sometimes, just sitting down to talk to somebody was a big help. We actually ended up in the same hospital in the States, Valley Forge Army Hospital in

Jim Dehlin in his hospital bed at Camp Zama in Japan in January 1971 (courtesy Jim Dehlin).

Phoenixville, Pennsylvania. We have kept in contact and have remained friends for the last 50 years.

"I did learn from one of the cleaning ladies how to say good morning in Japanese, and I got to watch more sumo wrestling on TV than I really cared to watch. I did get to call home from Japan and talk to my family. That was emotional.

"Buying a good camera at a ridiculously low price was a goal I shared with many of the troops in Vietnam. I bought mine at the PX at Camp Zama, a Canon Ft QL single reflex. I've taken that camera everywhere and now have boxes and boxes of photos to go through in retirement.

"When my recovery reached the point that I could travel back to the States, I was assigned to Valley Forge Army Hospital in Pennsylvania since it was the closest to my home. I was fitted with a complete body cast and soon had a new appreciation for the word "uncomfortable." I left Camp Zama on January 21, 1971. I was bused to the airport and put on an Air Force C-141 Starlifter that was fitted with racks for our litters (what a name).

"En route to the States, we stopped to refuel in Anchorage, Alaska. During that time at Anchorage, the engines were shut down, and along with them, the heat went away. No heat in January in Alaska gets uncomfortable pretty fast. Fortunately, a group of Air Force wives brought us extra blankets, cookies and hot chocolate.

"We touched down at McGuire Air Force Base in New Jersey where we were then transported by bus to the Fort Dix Army Hospital for an overnight stay before continuing on to Valley Forge. I was put in a room with George who had lost a leg below the knee and had serious shrapnel wounds. He had been very vocal during the entire trip from Japan. After listening to him moan and groan for 18 hours, I finally had enough and told him 'George! Shut the fuck up!' Later on, at Valley Forge, he thanked me and told me that he needed that.

"Ward 4C/D at Valley Forge Army Hospital would be my home for the next year. I arrived by bus from Fort Dix along with George and a full load of other wounded veterans. At the time, I thought it ironic that we were part of the reduction in force and the winding down of the war in Vietnam. Our group of vets had a new war we were just starting.

"The first order of business when I arrived was to cut me out of the body cast that I had been packed into for the trip from Japan. I lost my modesty as the female nurses went to work, removing the cast, cleaning me up and re-dressing my stumps. I also got a new cast on my right arm, and my stumps were put into skin traction. That consisted of a cotton sock being glued to the upper part of my stumps with an open end that was tied in a knot. I was able to access my dressings and change them through the open end of the sock. Attached to the knot was a rope-and-pulley system on the end of the bed with a seven-pound weight that, over time, would pull the skin down to close over the wound on the end of my stumps. Whenever I was in bed, I would hook up.

"A few days after my arrival, my parents, Lois and C.B., my brother, Barry, and my girlfriend drove over from Michigan for a visit. I was sitting in bed when they arrived. They had driven 700 miles to see me, and it was great to see all of them. Barry was on his way to becoming a doctor and wanted to see my chest wounds. Saying that my scars were significant and ugly would simply be a huge understatement. My girlfriend thought the same thing, and she had to leave my room in order to visit the ladies' room where I think she tossed her cookies. Not a good sign, I thought.

"After the family visit, it was time for me to get to work on my recuperation. It started with something really simple ... get out of bed by myself, into a wheelchair, and go to the bathroom. Baby steps so to speak. Next was going to physical therapy to start the process of building up strength in my upper legs and abdomen. The physical therapists, nurses and doctors were all members of the military, and I cannot say enough about the level of care and compassion that they showed us. Taking care of their own. I was also fitted with plaster cast prosthetic legs to start the process of learning how to walk.

"I was nervous about putting weight on the ends of my stumps since they were not fully healed, but no guts, no glory. There were parallel bars that I could hold onto as I took those first few tentative steps. Over time, the pain eased when walking, and I started to get the feel of a normal gait. One step required shifting weight to one side, picking up the leg I wanted to move forward, and then using the muscles in my stump in order to shift the hinged lower leg forward. After pushing forward, the weight shift to that side is followed by the same process on the other leg. Practice, practice, practice, the only way to get to Carnegie Hall.

"About a month into my rehab regimen, my brother Dick, along with a couple of my high school friends, Craig and Mike, came into town for a visit. They stayed for a few days. During their visit, Jeannie C. Riley, the country music star, came to our ward for a visit and some photo ops. She was a beautiful woman and a real morale booster. After her visit, Dick came down to PT where I was walking on my pylons. He used my camera to take a couple of pictures before he was asked to leave. I guess they did not want those kinds of images out there. That same day, I was informed that I could go home on leave, since I was healthy enough to travel and had no surgeries scheduled. Dick and I both thought that they just wanted to get me and my visitors out of the place, so we made our way to the airport to catch a flight to Michigan. That's where I ran into my first barrier to life in a wheelchair. I needed to take a leak before getting on the plane, so I went to the men's room. This was 1971, and wheelchair access was still a thing of the future. The urinals were too high, and the stall doors were too narrow for wheelchair access. What to do? I bailed out of the wheelchair onto the floor and scooted my ass over that filthy floor to get to the toilet. Just a harbinger of things to come. I must say that accessibility has improved immensely over the years with awareness and legislation like the Americans with Disabilities Act. However, it was an uphill struggle for many years.

"We had a good flight and arrived safely in Flushing, Michigan, for my 30-day leave. I still needed skin traction for my stumps. My dad could build anything. He was a graduate of General Motors Institute. He was also a tool-and-die maker, and he ran the apprentice shop at Chevrolet Manufacturing in Flint, Michigan. He made two weights for me out of brass that weighed exactly seven pounds each."

"At that point, I had two options. Option 1: I could lay in bed all day with skin traction on my stumps. Option 2: I could get out and about all day and just do the skin traction at night. I chose option 2.

"I credit my brother Dick and my friend Mark with getting me out and about. They just were not going to let me lay in bed. We hit the bars. We visited friends. We got out in public! I was very self-conscious at first. There was a stigma associated with being physically disabled and in a wheelchair. One day we were in downtown Flint, and a woman with a young child came towards us on the sidewalk. When I saw her shielding her child's eyes so the child could not see me, it cut me

Weights for skin traction that Jim Dehlin's dad, C.B., made for Jim to use while he was at home (courtesy Jim Dehlin).

to the quick. It wasn't just a physical challenge that I was facing. There were mental challenges as well.

"When my leave ended, I retraced my steps (so to speak) back to Valley Forge. The Valley Forge General Hospital was built in 1942 near Phoenixville, Pennsylvania, and opened on Washington's birthday in 1943 to care for the wounded soldiers of World War II. Plans to close the hospital in 1950 were put on hold when the Korean War flared up. Covering 182 acres, Valley Forge was a 'city unto itself' with over 100 separate buildings, a chapel, movie theater, and golf course. It eventually became the largest military hospital in America. The buildings were interconnected with long corridors and had long ramps that we used to get up to the second floor in a wheelchair, where my ward was located. On the wall, next to the ramp, was a huge mural of Washington crossing the Delaware. That mural and the nearby Valley Forge National Historical Park were constant reminders of the sacrifice of the members of the Continental Army that wintered there in 1777–78.

"When I arrived back at Valley Forge after my convalescent leave, I had to navigate the long ramp to the second floor. I found that I didn't have the strength to push up the ramp, so I had to turn around and pull myself up backwards in the wheelchair. Over time, by building up my upper body muscles, it became an easy task to push the wheelchair up the ramp. Once mastery of the wheelchair was attained, I could pop a wheelie at the top and cruise down the ramp just like many of the others. When going downhill, mean old Mr. Gravity was our friend and made life easier. I was glad that no one was around to see my first, feeble attempt at the ramp, because my fellow amputees would have mocked me. It wouldn't have been mocking in a bad way, just in a way that would let you know that you were in the club. These things were just rites of passage to be in the club. The guys in the amputee ward were a close-knit group, and we drew together more with each passing day in our shared experiences. We would load up a bus and go to Philadelphia to see boxing matches or to watch the 76ers play basketball, or the Harlem Globetrotters put on a show. Downhill skiing trips were made for those brave enough to attempt it. One night, we watched a movie starring John Wayne entitled *In Harm's Way*. In the movie, he loses a leg in a naval battle. When the doctor comes to the bedside to give him the news, the ward erupted in cheering. Sick humor, I know, but in that moment, we all became John Wayne, or he became us.

"Back to the physical therapy, the dressing changes, and preparation for the stump revisions. Once the skin completely closed over the ends of my stumps, it was time for surgery. I had the left side done first by Dr. James Herndon. He was the best, and I considered myself fortunate that he would be working on me. A revision consisted of tying the tendons in my leg to the end of the femur and then closing up with a little cushion of tissue at the end to provide a better fit and comfort in the socket of a prosthetic leg. The surgery was successful, and I was allowed another convalescent leave when I healed up. I would not be so lucky on my next revision.

"By now, it was April 1971, and anti-war demonstrations and protests had risen to a fever pitch in the country. My leave would end towards the end of April, and a group called the Vietnam Veterans Against the War was planning a rally/protest in Washington D.C. the week of April 19–23. Dick and I decided that we would drive to D.C. to peacefully protest the war. This protest was named 'Dewey Canyon III' after two military incursions into Laos by U.S. and ARVN forces. The organizers of the protest referred to it as 'A limited incursion into the country of Congress.' Vietnam veterans from all over the country arrived with proof of their service, many in their jungle fatigues, and carrying the medals that they had been awarded for their honorable service. It wasn't a large group of veterans, approximately 1,000 veterans who wanted their voices and what they had experienced heard in the debate. In some quarters, we were described in less than favorable terms, 'bedraggled' comes to mind, along with 'long-haired hippies' and 'frauds.' The Nixon administration questioned our veteran status in an attempt to cast doubt on our testimony.

"We returned to the National Mall and, led by Gold Star Mothers, marched across the Lincoln Memorial Bridge to lay wreaths at the Tomb of the Unknown Soldier at Arlington National Cemetery. The gates were closed and locked, denying us entry. The Gold Star Mothers laid their wreaths at the locked gates and departed. We reformed and marched to the Capitol to lobby our congressional representatives and senators. My friend Bill and I were each in wheelchairs at the front of the column and received a bit of notoriety when that image of the two of us in wheelchairs hit the papers. Dick and I, along with other members of the Michigan contingent, were given a warm reception by our congressional representative, Don Riegle. The same could not be said for our meeting with Senator Robert Griffin of Michigan who responded to our calls for an end to the war by indicating that he was not going to do anything that would tie the administration's hands in its negotiations with the North Vietnamese. I met a reporter from the *Washington Star* named Mary McGrory who interviewed my brother and me. Mary wanted to know the who, the what, the where, the when and the why about everything. She was very dynamic and, as a longstanding member of the Washington Press Corp., she knew everybody. While we were speaking with her at the Capitol building, she would stop and greet some of the movers and shakers of the government as well as other well-known people. That is how I met Coretta Scott King.

"After lobbying at the Capitol, we regrouped on the Mall, where we camped in defiance of a Justice Department–ordered injunction against camping on the National Mall. Later that day, the District Court of Appeals lifted the injunction. The next day, April 20, 1971, Chief Justice of the Supreme Court Warren Burger reinstated the injunction, giving us until the next day at 4:30 p.m. to break camp and leave the National Mall. We took a vote, by each state contingent, and decided to stay. We were prepared to be arrested, but the Capitol Police defied orders to arrest us. On April 22, a large protest at the Supreme Court took place with the protestors demanding that the court rule on the constitutionality of the war. At that protest, 110 people were arrested for disturbing the peace. That same day, a Washington district court judge dissolved the injunction with a rebuke to the Justice Department lawyers for requesting the court order and injunction and then not enforcing it. We had rapport with the Capitol Police based on the court decisions and the respect we showed them, not to mention the fact that many of them were veterans themselves. I think it was mostly their own veteran status that led to their decision not to arrest us. The same day, John Kerry, acting as a VVAW spokesman, testified for two hours before the Senate Foreign Relations Committee. I told Dick at the time that it looked like he was using the protest as a springboard to a career in politics. On the final day, April 23, 1971, over 800 veterans lined up on the Capitol steps where we found that a fence had been constructed to prevent our approaching the building. Individually, each veteran stepped up to the microphone, gave his name and unit in Vietnam where he had served, some giving a short memorial to a fallen comrade, followed by throwing his medals over the fence and onto the Capitol steps. It was a very emotional, moving and controversial act. As we moved back towards the Mall, my friend Paul who was from Flint, Michigan, needed a ride on my wheelchair. He had been wounded in Vietnam and had leg injuries requiring braces and crutches. He was really out of gas. I got him up on the armrests of my wheelchair, and Dick pushed us. As we moved along the sidewalk, a family in a station wagon approached us on the road. The mother reached out the window as they passed us, and she flipped us off while yelling out a string of profanities that certainly was not appropriate language to be used in front of her children. They were probably used to it. That being said, sometimes the only appropriate response to such an outburst is 'Fuck you too!'

"Mary McGrory, who was on Richard Nixon's infamous enemies

list, was a political columnist for the *Washington Star*. She was an out-spoken critic of the war in Vietnam. She wrote a column about me that she titled, 'The Lieutenant Returns.' I had visited Washington, D.C., with a group of high school seniors from Flushing, Michigan, in 1968. During that visit, I had laid a wreath at the Tomb of the Unknown Soldier. Now, three years after that initial visit, after losing my legs to a booby trap while serving as a lieutenant in Vietnam, I had returned to Washington, D.C., to voice my objections to the war. So, her title was fitting.

"Dick and I left Washington, D.C., with mixed emotions. We felt that what we had participated in should make a difference, but we feared that it might not. When I arrived back at Valley Forge, my reputation had preceded me, and it was not a good thing. The rank and file in the ward had no problem with what I had done. The hospital administration was not happy with me, and I felt like a marked man. I went in for my second revision shortly after I got back. My right stump was shorter than the left and had suffered more damage. When the surgeon opened me up, he found a pocket of infection that immediately spread to the open tissue at the end of my stump. There was no other course of action but to start over. Dressing changes, cleaning and traction. Nothing to do but suck it up and get busy with what was, by now, a familiar program.

"I became closer to a few of my fellow amputees. A buddy named Jimmy had lost both legs above the knees from a land mine on May 4, 1970, another date that would live in infamy for Jimmy. He was from Chardon, Ohio, and had attended Kent State University before dropping out and getting drafted. He could never reconcile the fact that while he was providing covering fire for his squad with an M-79 grenade launcher, students at Kent State were being fired on by Ohio National Guardsmen resulting in four students being killed and nine more being wounded. Jimmy never recovered from all that had happened and committed suicide a couple of years after leaving Valley Forge. Another buddy from Oradell, New Jersey, was an academic. He dropped a class in graduate school but was still carrying a full load. It didn't matter to his draft board, and he was drafted anyway. In Vietnam, he was an advisor in MACV [Military Assistance Command Vietnam]. Tom stepped on a booby trap while on patrol with ARVN troops. He lost a leg below the knee. Tom was a very keen intellect, with listening skills and writing ability that served him well. After getting out of the hospital, I visited with him at his parents' home in New Jersey. Unfortunately, we have lost track of each other, but he is a man I would like to see again.

"Another buddy at Valley Forge was a guy named Eddie who was from New York City. He was a tall, lanky, redhead who had lost his leg at the hip when a round from an AK-47 ripped into him. If you wanted to learn how to roll a perfect joint, you went to school with the master—that was Eddie. He stopped by to see me in Michigan one time while on his way to California, and that was the last time I saw him.

"Then there was Major Fred Franks. He was a warrior in the truest sense of the word. A 1959 graduate of the United States Military Academy at West Point, Major Franks was the elder statesman and senior officer in the amputee ward. The mission statement at West Point is: 'To educate, train, and inspire the Corps of Cadets so that each graduate is a commissioned leader of character, committed to the values of Duty, Honor, Country, and prepared for a career of professional excellence and service to the Nation as an officer in the United States Army.' Fred Franks embodied the values instilled in him at West Point, and it explains his desire to stay in the Army after losing his left leg below the knee. He was injured during the invasion of Cambodia in May 1970. Major Franks was serving with the 11th Armored Cavalry Regiment when he was severely wounded by a hand grenade. His left foot and leg were mangled along with wounds to his back, arm and ear. He did not lose his leg right away. After several surgeries, he was left with two options while at Valley Forge. He could have surgery that would leave him something that looked like a foot but limited his mobility, or he could have a below-the-knee amputation and get fitted for a prosthesis. In January 1971, he decided to have the amputation. We all looked up to Major Franks at Valley Forge. At the time, we had no idea that we were in the presence of a great man who would go on to complete a stellar military career, retiring in 1994 as a four-star general. General Franks was the commanding general of VII Corps, and in 1991, during the First Gulf War, he led a coalition of nearly 150,000 troops that decimated the Iraqi Republican Guard. The famous 'Left Hook' attack caught the Iraqi army off guard and resulted in the largest tank battle in history. Superior training, tactics and great equipment led to the victory in 100 hours of combat.

"After the war, General Franks wrote a book with Tom Clancy entitled *Into the Storm: A Study in Command*. In the book, he tells his life story and the decisions he made that led to his historic leadership and victory. Just as important as his leadership role in combat, General Franks, along with other senior leaders in the military, helped to rebuild the Army after Vietnam. At Valley Forge, General Franks, then Major Franks, was aware of the shabby treatment returning veterans received. He recognized the disconnect between the public, senior leadership in the military and Vietnam veterans. The feeling of abandonment that many of the soldiers at Valley Forge felt lit a fire in General Franks that he described as 'The Hot Blue Flame.' In his own words General Franks described his passion:

> Though I was helpless to make up for the absence of senior leaders, as the months went by, I grew ever more determined to do something more for those soldiers than they were getting. I wanted to help, somehow, to make it clear to them that their lives—and their loss—had some meaning.
>
>   I wanted a fulfillment of their sacrifice. I wanted to make sure, if our country ever went to war again, if young men and women ever had to go answer Duty's call, it wouldn't end up this way.

"General Franks has held true to that resolve, and in retirement is the chairman of the board of the VII Corps Desert Storm Veterans Association, which assists veterans and next of kin of those who served in VII Corps during Desert Storm. General Fred Franks is one of my heroes.

"When my right stump finally healed and the infection had cleared, it was time for another surgery. Dr. Herndon was not available, so another surgeon did my right stump revision. The surgery went fine, but I woke up in recovery with severe, painful muscle spasms in the stump. I was given valium and morphine without relief from the painful spasms. I came out of the experience with a new truism in my life—Pain is Pure. This surgery was followed by another convalescent leave. I was starting to build frequent flyer miles before they were invented. When I left for my Vietnam deployment, I turned over my 1967 Camaro to my brother, Dick. He had left me his 1960 Chevy when he had left for his tour of duty. Well, Dick met me at the airport with my Camaro. He tossed me the keys and said, 'You're driving.' He had arranged for hand controls to be installed in my car. To add some realism, he also handed me a beer and a cigarette just to see if I could multitask. When my leave ended, I drove back to Valley Forge and had a new sense of freedom and independence. Back at Valley Forge, my stumps had shrunk. I had also done the physical therapy to build up the muscles necessary for navigating with permanent prosthetic legs. It was time to get busy! The limb shop was in Philadelphia. A trip into town was always an adventure. Casts of my stumps were made in order to form the upper sockets. The legs were made of a plastic resin that had the strength needed as well as the necessary light weight. It was relatively primitive by today's standards. The most advanced feature on a full leg prosthesis at that time was the hydraulic knee that assisted the forward movement. A very tight fit was required in order to hold the leg onto the stump by suction. It was quite a process to put them on and practice walking, doing stairs and just getting around. Fit adjustments were done in Philly, so there was quite a bit of back and forth to the limb shop. We watched each other's progress on the amputee ward and encouraged, cajoled, and ragged on each other. We were brothers in the best sense, and the support we provided to each other was, in my mind, the first outreach program. There was no formal mental health program. For those struggling with their new reality, something was needed. I went to Dr. Herndon and asked if we could get somebody to come into the ward to provide some counseling. After that, an Army psychologist would come in, and we would have group sessions. I'm not sure, to this day, if it did much good, but it was something.

"We did have VA counselors that we could meet with, counselors who explained the medical discharge process and the disabled veteran benefit program. Educational and vocational training options, along with aptitude testing were also provided. I heard, through the grapevine, that one of the counselors had told one of the guys that he could not do something because of his disability. After hearing that, I made up my mind that no one would ever tell me that I couldn't do something. One benefit that was available was the adaptive vehicle program. It was a one-time grant towards the purchase of a vehicle with adaptive equipment. Since my dad worked for GM, the employee discount along with the grant enabled me to purchase a new, 1971 12-passenger Chevy van, equipped with hand controls. I planned on traveling. I drove home to pick up my new van in November of 1971. With Thanksgiving coming up, I requested an extension of my leave in order to spend time with my family. My request was denied. I had spent the previous Thanksgiving out in the bush in Vietnam, and now I was not going to spend this Thanksgiving with my family either. I was not a happy camper as I headed back to Pennsylvania. Then something wonderful happened as I got on the entrance ramp to the Ohio Turnpike in Toledo. Lined up on the expressway ramp were college students hitchhiking home for the Thanksgiving break. I cleared that ramp completely as I filled all of the seats in my van. We quickly had a rolling party going. As we worked our way east, I would drop passengers, one by one, at their exits . The last tier of hikers left me just before Philadelphia. The Lord works in mysterious ways and brings us joy in unusual ways when we least expect it. It brings a smile to my face as I think back on my passengers and the stories they must have told about the guy in the van.

"In order to retire with a medical discharge, I had to appear before a medical board. I had to be medically evaluated and pronounced healthy. I had to be properly fitted with prostheses and demonstrate the ability to use them. In December 1971, I appeared before the board to be evaluated. I was discharged from Valley Forge with my final leave at home in Michigan, having been officially medically retired from the Army on February 8, 1972. My military career was over.

"My girlfriend eventually told me that she did not think we had a future together. The six-foot guy with two good legs that she had fallen in love with was now very different physically. The sight of my ugly scars, not to mention my missing legs, overwhelmed her. She was a very sensitive girl, an artist, and would eventually become an accomplished painter.

"When I returned home to Flushing, Michigan, in December 1971, I found a *Flint Journal* advertisement for a mixed breed puppy that indicated the puppy was 'Free to a good home.' It was a female, Lab/Shepherd mix. I took the puppy, and it was the best dog I ever had. In January 1972, my friend Mark and I rented a farmhouse just outside of Flushing, Michigan. Then in March 1972, I embarked on a road trip out west with my brother, Dick, Snappy Sam and two dogs. The summer of 1972 was a life-changing period of time for me. It involved another road trip west, this time with one Carol Meiklejohn and two other friends, Susie and Jeff. I had known Carol Meiklejohn for years. She had moved to Flushing, Michigan, from Lockport, New York, in 1964, when her dad, George, was transferred from Harrison Radiator to the Buick plant in Flint. She had dated my brother, Dick, for a while but was unattached when we decided to take the trip west. We fell in love on that trip, and the rest is history.

"In August 1972, I decided to go to Spain with a friend of mine, Joe. While in Spain, I developed some medical problems that required surgery. I went to the Torrejon Air Force Base hospital where I underwent repair of a midline abdominal hernia at the site where I had been opened in Vietnam to remove shrapnel. Then in October 1972, I bought a new 1972 Volkswagen Camper Van with hand controls and a 4-speed transmission. A couple of months later, Carol Meiklejohn and my friend, Mark, came to Spain to join me."

"Then Carol and I traveled to Samos, Greece, where we rented an old boathouse on the beach in the fishing village of Avlakia. We returned to Spain in August 1973. Then in December 1973, we decided to return to the good old U.S.A. I drove my VW Van from Madrid to Antwerp and put it on a boat destined for New Jersey. I then took a train back to Madrid. We spent Christmas of 1973 with the family in Flushing, Michigan.

"In January 1974, Carol and I headed to Fort Myers, Florida, to meet up with a couple of friends, Ed and Sandi. They had a 28-foot sailboat, and the four of us sailed to the Dry Tortugas, which was 70 miles west of Key West. From there we sailed to Key West, Marathon Key,

Jim Dehlin and Carol Meiklejohn with their Volkswagen camper van (courtesy Jim Dehlin).

Key Largo and then to Fort Lauderdale. In March 1974, I headed west again, to New Orleans, Texas, and Arizona. I stopped to visit Lee, a friend in Flagstaff. I joined the International Wheelchair Pilots Association in Phoenix. I really wanted to learn how to fly and was searching for a flight school. I was inspired by my old friend, Andre, who told me about a *Today Show* segment he had seen. The segment was all about a B-52 pilot who was paraplegic after a crash. The paralyzed pilot was learning to fly using hand controls at a facility in Richmond, Virginia. I could go for that.

"I next headed north towards British Columbia, stopping in Salt Lake to visit with Bob and Anna, the couple I had met in Samos. During the summer of 1974, my travels took me south along the coast to California. I gradually worked my way back to Flushing, Michigan, for a visit with the family. Then it was off to Richmond to check out that flight school I had heard about. In March 1975, I moved to Richmond and enrolled in a ground school class at a local community college and began flight training. I rented half of a duplex on Britannia Avenue and started an electronics course by mail. I received my private pilot's license in July 1975.

"In August 1975, I bought a small corner lot on a land contract. It was located on the corner of Broadrock and Britannia Avenue in South Richmond. I partnered with my neighbor, Jeff, and we started a worm farm. On November 20, 1975, I lost my sister, Kristin Louise. She perished in an apartment fire. I was living about a mile from the VA hospital in Richmond and decided to go into training to get fitted with a new set of legs. In 1976, Carol Meiklejohn and I were married at the courthouse in Richmond. On November 5, 1976, our bicentennial baby, Jesse Meikle Dehlin, was born at Chippenham Hospital in Richmond. The hospital was located on Jahnke Road. Jahnke was my mother's maiden name. Seemed like an appropriate location for our firstborn to enter the world."

"The worm business did not work out, and Carol and I and baby Jesse moved back to Michigan. My wanderlust persisted, and I started another trip in the spring of 1978 with Carol and Jesse. We packed up the VW Van again. Krishna, the family dog, made the trip west with us too. Our first stop was in British Columbia to see our friends, Jim and Barb and their two kids. Our real destination was Alaska. The Alaska highway had not yet been paved all the way. Some of it was not in great shape, but we made the long haul with no problems. I used Willow, Alaska, as home base. From Willow, I would travel down to Homer on the Kenai Peninsula, north to Fairbanks and all the way to Circle City and the mountain called Mt. McKinley, now known as Denali, 'The Great One.' I met Hank, the owner of Willow Air Service. Hank flew a Dehavilland DHC2 Beaver on floats off of

Jim and Carol with baby Jesse (courtesy Jim Dehlin).

Willow Lake. Jesse got his first airplane ride when Hank flew Jesse and me out to a remote river for some salmon fishing. I did some two-day trips with Hank up into the Talkeetna Mountains to relocate Hank's gold claim. In August, Hank started flying hunting parties out to the bush, and I would help him pump gas into the Beaver during the turn-arounds. As fall approached, we were preparing to head back to Michigan. Then Hank offered me a job that would allow me to stay at his lodge and do the weather reporting for that region of the state of Alaska. Carol really didn't like being so far away from the family, so I declined the offer and we headed back to Michigan in September, just as the aspens started turning color. As we continued south and then across Canada, into Minnesota and then the Upper Peninsula, the fall colors were peaking the entire way. The best color tour we ever had.

"In 1978, we rented a house on Higgins Lake and fell in love with the area. We decided to look for property where we could build a house using the VA adaptive housing grant that is part of the benefit for 100 percent service-connected disabled veterans. In January 1979, I enrolled in the Airframe and Power Plant Mechanic Program at Kirtland Community College. The aviation program was located at the Grayling Army Air Field in Grayling, Michigan. I had joined the Army with the intention of going to school on the GI Bill. At the time I didn't think that the price for that benefit would be my legs, but now I was going to make use of the benefit.

"I really wanted to own my own airplane. I figured that I would have to be able to do the maintenance myself in order to afford one. The two-year program was pretty intense and governed closely by the Federal Aviation Administration. It was five days a week, 6½ hours per day. It consisted of 2½ hours of lecture and 4 hours of lab each day. It was during this time that I met Dennis, a guy known simply as 'Doc,' at Kirtland College. He had been a helicopter pilot in Vietnam and had logged over 1,500 combat hours in UH-1 'Hueys' and Cobra gunships. We have been friends ever since that meeting. Doc and I were the original outreach program. I also met Mark who had been a grunt with the 1st Cavalry Division in Vietnam. Mark and I became lifelong friends. Mark migrated to Willow, Alaska, after A & P school, becoming a bush pilot and big game guide, hunter, trapper and mechanic. Mark was truly 'a renaissance man.'"

"During the summer of 1979, I took courses for an associate degree in Applied Sciences, Aviation Maintenance Technology at the main campus of Kirtland Community College. The courses were English Composition, American History and a business class, six credits in all, which was considered a full load by the VA during the summer. From the fall of 1979 to December 1980, I completed the A & P school and graduated with an associate's degree in Applied Science—Aviation Maintenance Technology and received the Outstanding Student A & P Award. During the summer, Jesse, Carol and I lived in a tent on a lot that we had purchased to build a house. I planned to build a house with the help of a grant from the VA for a wheelchair-adapted house.

"During the winter of 1980–81, I rented a small, two-bedroom house where we could live while the construction was completed on our new house. We affectionately referred to our little rental as 'the corn crib.' It only had wood heat, so I bought a Timberline airtight wood stove to keep us warm during the winter. We moved into our new house in May 1981, and we took the wood stove with us. That wood stove is still there to this day. On January 17, 1981, we were blessed with the birth of our daughter, Kristin Marie Dehlin, in Traverse City, Michigan. Yes, I cried tears of joy.

"In April 1981, I was hired by George, the head of the aviation program at Kirtland, to fill in as a part-time lab instructor. I worked as a lab instructor from April to the end of May when the semester ended. Then, during the summer of 1981, I was hired as a mechanic at the Houghton Lake Airport. In August that summer I was invited back to KCC to fill a position as an adjunct lab assistant. I took the position even though it ended up being a pay cut since I lost my Social Security disability payments. George, who hired me at KCC, had been a Coast Guard Senior Chief. He had been born in West Virginia and had joined the Coast Guard right after high school. He had started out as a lighthouse keeper, but then decided he wanted to get into aviation. After going through mechanic training, George rose through the ranks, serving all over the country from North Carolina to Oregon, Kodiac, Alaska, Elizabeth City, New Jersey, and Traverse City, Michigan. He learned to fly along the way and eventually became an instructor pilot. George met his wife, MaryLu, in Traverse City, Michigan. Upon retirement, they moved back to Michigan, landing in Roscommon, with George hiring into Kirtland as a maintenance instructor, eventually becoming the director of the program. George became my mentor as a mechanic, pilot and instructor and one of my best friends. He was one of the most influential people in my life.

"In 1982, I started back to school to get a bachelor's degree in Technical Education at Ferris State College. All the classes were offered at the old Maritime Academy building in Traverse City. My boss, George, one other instructor and myself would travel every Thursday evening from Grayling to Traverse City for all the undergraduate classes. From 1982 to 1986, I worked at Kirtland while going to school. I plowed snow

The Jim Dehlin family—Carol, Jesse, Jim, Kristin (courtesy Jim Dehlin).

Jim Dehlin's birthday celebration with Jesse and Kristin, May 30, 1982 (courtesy Jim Dehlin).

in the winter. During the summer, I worked as a mechanic at the Houghton Lake Airport."

"I was living the dream in 1984. I bought my first airplane, a 1972 Piper Cherokee PA 28–140. I was also named the Maintenance Technician of the Year by the Federal Aviation Administration Flight Standards District Office in Grand Rapids, Michigan. I had been nominated by my old boss, George, at Kirtland. In May 1986 I received my BA in Technical Education and started working on my master's degree in Occupational Education. In May 1989, I received my master's degree in Occupational Education from Ferris and then went on to school for Designated Mechanic Authorization in Oklahoma City. Then I hired in at Northern Michigan University in Marquette, Michigan, as an assistant professor. I hired on with two other instructors to start the aviation maintenance program. I then sold my airplane to my friend, Bob, who was the program director of the auto service program at Kirtland.

"In 1992, I was elected to the board of the Aviation Technician Education Council. ATEC is the organization that represents FAA Part 147 aviation maintenance programs. Two board meetings a year and an annual conference brought together industry representatives and educators to address issues affecting the industry. ATEC partnered with the University Aviation Association, and together, they would man a booth at the Oshkosh annual fly-in, promoting aviation careers, both pilots and mechanics. I served as a board member, vice president and finally as president of ATEC.

"For anyone who has never heard it said, I give you a simple fact, 'If you can't stand prosperity, buy an airplane.' In 1996, I traveled to Ohio with my friend, Bob, who had bought my airplane. We made the trip to look at a Piper Comanche. That one did not work out. Then we saw another one advertised in Trade-A-Plane that looked interesting. I ended up buying a 1958 Piper Comanche PA 24–180. I rented hangar space at the Marquette County Airport. Every fall and spring, I would have a cookout with the aviation students and give them rides in my airplane."

"In 1996, I underwent rotator cuff surgery to repair damage sustained while skiing. I had joined a team in the Thursday night Bud racing league. I had learned how to ski at Park City, Utah, after an ATEC conference in Salt Lake City. My wife, Carol, arranged for a lesson for me. When it was determined that I could use a monoski, with outriggers, she bought me a Yeti monoski. Both of our kids were skiing at Marquette Mountain, and this was a way to get me out of the bar and onto the hill. It worked!"

Jim Dehlin flying his Piper Comanche with daughter, Kristin, in the copi-lot seat (courtesy Jim Dehlin).

"In May 1999, I was named Kirtland Community College Outstanding Alumnus. I have also done my part to support the medical profession. I had my gallbladder removed in 2000. In 2001, a herniated disc in my neck required surgery and a fusion with hardware at C 4–5 and C 5–6. My dad, C.B. Dehlin, passed away, and my youngest brother, David,

Jim Dehlin (center) with Bill Carter and Barry Dehlin (courtesy Jim Dehlin).

died in his sleep in 2001. I was diagnosed with rheumatoid arthritis in 2001."

"Happier times would come in 2005, when my grandson, Nicholas James Dehlin, was born on September 14. I retired from Northern Michigan University in 2006, on long-term disability because of the rheumatoid arthritis. I had been in a manual wheelchair for 35 years, but the arthritis was making the manual chair difficult to use. I had sustained significant loss of strength in my hands and wrists and reduced range of motion in my shoulders. I really needed an electric wheelchair. I started working with the VA Prosthetics Department at the Iron Mountain VA

Jim Dehlin accepting donated Navy jet for the Northern Michigan University aviation program. Also pictured is the pilot, U.S. Naval Reserve Commander Erick Gerdes (courtesy Jim Dehlin).

Hospital and was authorized to use an IBOT electric chair, a quantum leap in technology from most other personal mobility devices. It was capable of four-wheel drive, elevation, two-wheel drive and stair climbing. I went through IBOT training at the Madison (Wisconsin) Regional VA Medical Center. I had to write a letter to a VA Board in Washington, D.C., describing how the chair would be used and how it would improve the quality of my life. I was the first veteran in the Upper Midwest to receive an IBOT.

"Carol and I had kept a piece of property in the Higgins Lake area, and in 2007, we decided to build a house there to be closer to our kids, grandson Nick and the family in Flushing. My dream had been to live in Marquette on Lake Superior, and I had been able to make that dream come true. Now it was time for a new dream, and time to make it happen. I contracted with Ripplecraft Log Homes in Mio, Michigan, for a log home package and got busy with the site prep. I promoted myself to general—as in general contractor—and started the process with a construction loan at a local bank (you can't hide good credit). With money in hand, I brought in my friend, Nick, the excavator, to clear the site and dig the basement. A well went in by F & F Well Drilling, 120 feet with static water level at 60 feet. Best drinking water in the world. Toby was my concrete man and laid up the basement walls. J.D. built the deck, and the logs arrived in late September. Ripplecraft laid the logs, and then my friend, Tom, came in with his crew and did the rough in, closing in the roof and windows. My brother, Dick, came down from Alaska, and my friend, Brent, came down from Marquette. Along with Carol's brother, Jimmy Meiklejohn, we finished the electrical rough-in and then did the insulation after the electrical, structural and mechanical inspections were completed. My hunting partner and friend, Billy, did the plumbing rough-in and later the finish plumbing. In December, Billy was diagnosed with ALS (Lou Gehrig's disease). By now, it was February 2008, and really cold. Billy had put a forced-air furnace in the basement, and I had a gas fireplace insert in the great room. The day the furnace cycled upon reaching a steady 60 degrees, we had a celebration—as the song goes, 'Whiskey for my men, beer for my horses.' It took the rest of the year to finish the house. Carol had been in Marquette prepping our house there for sale. In May, she came down full time, and we worked as a team on trim work and the kitchen. I had bought a set of Makita cordless drills for her birthday—best present ever! My friend, Bill, did the tile work in the bathrooms and the foyer and laid the maple wood floor. No carpet. Wheelchairs and carpet don't get along. In December 2008, all inspections were completed, and we received a certificate of occupancy. From 2009 to the present, we have been living the dream in retirement. We travel to Midland and other venues across the state to watch our grandson play hockey. We travel to see our daughter, Kristin, in Grand Rapids, where she works as an electro-diagnostic technician in the neurology department at Spectrum Hospital. My friend, Bob, and his wife, Cathy, live in Arkansas and they visit every summer. Bob and I drive over to Airventure in Oshkosh, Wisconsin, and camp for a few days. Bob has always liked my Comanche. When I lost my FAA medical certificate, I told him that I was going to sell my plane. He went to Cathy and told her that he had fallen in love with another airplane. After selling the Cherokee, he bought my Comanche."

"In 2012, I was honored by being named the Stormy Kromer Living Legend. In 2013, I was named to the Flushing High School Outstanding Alumnus Hall of Fame.

"I have continued to keep my hand in aviation by doing maintenance and annual inspections for a select group of friends. I am a member of the local Experimental Aviation Association chapter and work out of a small grass strip in Houghton Lake. I was diagnosed with renal cell carcinoma in 2016 and had my left kidney removed in May 2017. Dr. Reuel Long came to the University of Michigan hospital after that

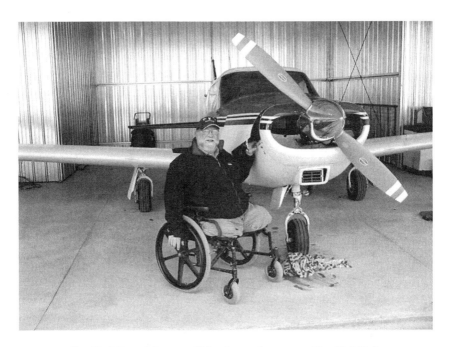

Jim Dehlin with one of his planes (courtesy Jim Dehlin).

surgery for a visit, 47 years after the first time he came to see me in Vietnam.

"While living in Marquette, I would speak at the local schools, including classes at Northern about my experiences in the military and Vietnam in particular. On one trip to Minnesota, I stayed with my cousin whose son was a senior in high school. He asked if I would come to his school and speak to the class. It was not an easy task to dredge up the memories so carefully stored away. At the same time, it was cathartic. My family physician in Marquette had a young son who interviewed me for a class project. He asked me a very insightful question: 'If you could go back and change it, would you?' I'm from the 'don't saw sawdust' school and had never really thought about that. I promptly told him that I would not change a thing. If you change one thing, it changes everything else. I would not be the man that I have become. I wouldn't have my wife and family. I would not consider changing any of it for an instant. I wake up every day and thank God for every single day that I have lived past December 23, 1970. Every day is a bonus! Most of all, I am thankful for my wife, Carol, without whom I would have nothing."

In 2017, a film entitled *The Vietnam War* was produced by Ken

Jim Dehlin with his grandson, Nicholas (courtesy Jim Dehlin).

Burns and Lynn Novick. There were a number of segments dealing with different periods of the war. Each segment leads with an introduction which shows film of, among other things, the demonstrations against the Vietnam War in Washington, D.C., in the spring of 1971. In that little introduction that prefaces each segment, one can see two Vietnam veterans in wheelchairs at the front of the group of veterans who were protesting the continuation of the war. The wheelchair on the left of the screen held a veteran with below-the-knee amputations. The occupant of the wheelchair on the right of the screen had bilateral above-the-knee amputations. That wheelchair on the right of the screen was occupied by Jim Dehlin.

At the John F. Kennedy gravesite, there are inscriptions taken from his inaugural address.

Jim Dehlin with his dog (courtesy Jim Dehlin).

Jim and Carol Dehlin (courtesy Jim Dehlin).

One portion reads:

> Let every nation know
> Whether it wishes us well or ill
> That we shall pay any price—bear any burden
> Meet any hardship—support any friend
> Oppose any foe to assure the survival
> And the success of liberty

Just to be clear, the "we" who would pay the price and bear the burdens and hardships for the commitment Kennedy made to involve our country in Vietnam are those whose names are on that black, granite wall in Washington, D.C., along with their loved ones and all the thousands of others who were mutilated and scarred and would have too many of their nights disrupted by that war for the rest of their lives.

CLOSING THOUGHTS

While sitting with my laptop computer in December 2018, I clicked on the Facebook site for the Fire Base Mary Ann 1971 survivors and looked at the reunion pictures. I wondered which of them I had treated at Chu Lai. They all looked like old men now. Then I reminded myself that they were all 8 to 10 years younger than me. I began reflecting on the Vietnam era and how it had all happened. I clicked on Google Earth and zoomed in on areas in Vietnam where I had served. I was not surprised to see no remnants of the hospital facilities at Chu Lai. The old airfield at Chu Lai which was located between the two medical facilities was now an international airport. Turning to the Da Nang area, I could see that there were no remnants of the hospital facilities. I could see the road along the beach. The fishing village at the base of Monkey Mountain seemed to still be in place with no dramatic commercial development. The housing showed improvement. Numerous fishing boats could be seen in the bay. Oddly, the site where the hospital was located appeared to be open and undeveloped. It was easy to find Marble Mountain. The internet revealed that tourism was pretty active in the area and all along the coast. In the central highlands, Pleiku showed a lot of commercial development. I found myself thinking about how much trade now existed between the United States and Vietnam. I had noticed that the shrimp being sold at Meijer, Kroger, Sam's Club and Costco all came from Vietnam, and a lot of shirts and other clothing I had seen at a number of stores was made in Vietnam. After all the death and destruction, we are trading partners on friendly terms.

The Vietnamese were under French colonial rule for more than 100 years, and they did not want to be under the control of any foreign power. They wanted to be free. We overthrew the colonial rule of Great Britain, but our leaders failed to appreciate the desire of the Vietnamese to be free. Ho Chi Minh admired our Thomas Jefferson and quoted him. When Ho Chi Minh declared the independence of Vietnam in

September 1945, he began his statement with language taken directly from our own Declaration of Independence: "All men are created equal. They are endowed by their creator with certain inalienable rights, among them are life, liberty and the pursuit of happiness." He publicly embraced our founding principles and had every reason to expect our support. After all, our declaration said, "all men," not just men in America. When we had the opportunity to support the Vietnamese with their desire to be free, especially after World War II, President Truman chose to support the French. Then our leaders chose to get more and more involved in Vietnam as the French departed from the scene. We supported the corrupt leaders in South Vietnam in the name of stopping the spread of communism. The Vietnamese only turned to the communists to help them secure their freedom because our leaders had failed them. Our leaders supported the French who were denying the Vietnamese their freedom, and then we stepped in to take the place of the French as the enemy of the Vietnamese people.

Yes, the involvement of the United States in Vietnam was a profound mistake. We had presidents who were not honest with the American public and more interested in securing their own power than preventing the death and destruction going on in Vietnam and neighboring countries. Mistakes must be recognized and become a learning experience. All presidents must be held accountable for any and all commitments of United States blood and treasure abroad by a politically neutral, aggressive free press. That is why we have a free press, to question the powerful and temper their power by shining a bright light on their conduct and decisions. Unfortunately, the press has failed our country, abandoning their protected role in favor of political partisanship with an agenda to drive. There has also been a dramatic failure in our public education system, kindergarten through college, and an agenda that favors indoctrination over education. A failure to teach history and examine our mistakes puts us at high risk of repeating such mistakes. Considering the foreign entanglements in which our country has been engaged since the Vietnam era, there is little or no evidence of a learning curve.

The evolution that has taken place with both political parties has undermined the security of the republic. In his inaugural address on January 20, 1961, John Kennedy said, "Ask not what your country can do for you, ask what you can do for your country." The message of far too many politicians today is, "Vote for me, and I will give you more from the government trough." Both parties have enlarged government, increased the debt and made promises for the express purpose of maintaining their power. It has been said many times that when half the people in the country are voting themselves benefits at the government trough, the days of the republic are numbered. Too many in the voting public have turned Kennedy's admonishment on its head, asking the politicians what the country can do for them. Meanwhile, Jim Dehlin and I will make the most of our remaining bonus time, satisfied with having answered the call to contribute and serve the country and hopeful for an awakening that will ensure that our republic will endure. Both of us look to the future, secure in the promise of the gospel of Christ, with an attitude so well expressed in a familiar hymn, "When Christ shall come, with shout of acclamation, and take me home, what joy shall fill my heart."

Addendum

The M-16 Debacle: The Untold Story

The Vietnam War ushered in the M-16 as the replacement weapon for the M-14. The new weapon turned out to be a major frustration for our troops in the field. In the automatic mode, under rapid fire, the weapon would jam with a spent shell staying in the weapon. Troops found themselves in major fire fights with a weapon that was useful only as a club, not good when the enemy was armed with the excellently performing AK-47. American troops began writing home to family and friends, as well as to politicians and the gun manufacturer, about the lack of reliability of the weapon. There were many accounts of dead American troops being found after a battle, dead in the field with a jammed weapon lying next to their lifeless bodies. A review of the literature, including declassified military documents, reveals the prevailing causes that were put forward as the basis for the jamming problem. The dirty jungle conditions resulting in a dirty weapon that was not properly and routinely cleaned was blamed. The failure of the manufacturer to chrome the inside of the barrel was blamed. The grooving inside the barrel was blamed. The ammunition was blamed. Cleaning was emphasized to address the problem, and there was a change in the ammunition which somewhat mitigated the problem but did not address the basic cause. In the declassified report of the Army's review panel on the M-16 problems, it is stated that the failure to extract was the most serious malfunction experienced by U.S. forces in Vietnam. The report indicates that the failure to extract was due to poor cleaning, worn extractors and extractor springs and corroded and pitted chambers and was the reason for the decision to chrome the chamber. Such explanations could be accepted by the public as unforeseen problems that had to be addressed when recognized. However, there would have been hell to pay and outrage against the government if there was something else to blame and a weapon with design flaws had been provided to our troops that cost many of them their lives. In fact, a clean, new weapon that had never been out in the field, in the dirty jungle, could be fired in the automatic mode and would jam, and this was known by the government. When I went through basic training, I was familiarized with the M-14 only and had no exposure to the M-16. When Jim Dehlin went through basic training at Fort Knox in 1969, he qualified on the rifle range with the M-14. During his infantry OCS at Fort Benning, he and his fellow candidates carried an M-14 every day, everywhere they went. Jim says that when he and his classmates qualified with the M-16, they appreciated the light weight as compared to the M-14. Jim recalled that during the training on the M-16, he and his classmates were instructed to limit automatic fire to three-round bursts. Thinking back on those instructions, Jim said, "That's fine in theory and makes sense as far as accuracy goes. However, when bullets are flying, troops are going to respond in kind. Move the select over to 'Rock and Roll' and let it rip." The military clearly knew that they had a defective weapon that could not be used in full automatic mode without the risk of jamming unless only short bursts were fired. They instructed troops to only fire three-round bursts in full automatic mode but never warned of the risk of jamming if longer bursts were fired.

My friendship with Dan Sebastian, whom I accompanied to the Mayo Clinic for his pheochromocytoma surgery, resulted in discussions which shed new light on the M-16 jamming problems. Dan was a metallurgist and spring expert when he witnessed an evaluation of the M-16 in 1970. Dan described his history with me and the circumstances that brought him to a room in Connecticut in 1970 where a secret meeting was being held by individuals with security clearances to evaluate the M-16 and propose a solution for the jamming problem. The cause of the jamming problem was pointed out by one of Dan's colleagues, and that cause appears nowhere in military documents or in the literature. A solution was offered, but it was not adopted. Dan in his own words:

"In the mid–1980s, I was the general manager of a spring manufacturing plant in Ann Arbor, Michigan. Arriving home one evening, my wife and daughter excitedly informed me that they had a great deal to tell me about, a deal that we just could not turn down. They had discovered that they could rent a horse for $50 a month and ride it all they wanted. I said OK. It was only $50. Not much of a financial commitment. Well, we were soon going to horse shows almost every weekend, horse shows where a lot of other mothers and daughters were competing, and I trailed along like any good dad.

"One particular weekend, a friend of my wife informed her that she was dragging her husband along and suggested that the two husbands might get together and share horse stories. That weekend changed my life forever. I met Dr. Reuel Long. We could not have been more different. He was the chief of staff of a community hospital and lived in the world of medicine. I was an engineer-turned-manager, trying to turn around the company's flagship operation in the automotive world. Our wives introduced us at the fairgrounds and, almost immediately, vanished with our daughters and their horses, leaving this unlikely pair to find a way to make it through the day on their own. We had nothing in common, but that proved to be the catalyst that would form the basis of a 35-year friendship. Neither of us had to be concerned with being what people expected of us in our daily work world, and a bond of friendship rapidly developed. Reuel did not have to talk about medicine, hospital affairs or deal with issues of doctors or hospital administrators. I was free from dealing with demanding customers, employee issues, union leaders or company officers, each with their own set of issues. We were free to concentrate on what really mattered, family and friends and fishing. Reuel became the brother I never had growing up with two sisters, which allowed me to share things that you would only share with a brother. One day, as we were talking about our travels through the turbulent '60s and '70s, I shared with Reuel the collision of the worlds of engineering and science with Washington politics that I had been privy to at the beginning of my career.

"The year was 1969, and I had a solid prospect for a job at Associated Spring, working at their research center where I could be a metallurgist and make a real difference. Associated Spring was founded in 1847 in Bristol, Connecticut, and became the largest spring manufacturer in North America in the 1920s. The engineers at Associated Spring secured numerous patents and authored many articles which had confirmed its position as the industry leader by the 1920s. In the 1960s and '70s, Associated Spring's research and development center was considered the industry leader. I only had two obstacles to my pursuit of a job with Associated Spring, an order from the draft board to report for a pre-induction physical and a few more metallurgy courses at Lehigh. The first was going to be the most challenging.

"Early one morning, I reported to my local draft board on Main Street in Bristol, Connecticut. A large bus was waiting for us. It turned out that about half the guys arriving for the bus ride were my high school classmates who, like me, had a four-year deferment that was expiring. We all boarded the bus with a class reunion atmosphere for our ride to New Haven. On arrival, the bus was immediately boarded by a Marine recruiter. He was about 5'6", a real ramrod with a chest full of

ribbons. He began his loud pitch, 'You are all about to pass your physical. You will all pass and then go to Vietnam. I am here to offer you a
chance to volunteer for the Marines. As a volunteer, you will not have
to have the lower than pond scum designation of draftee.' Well, he was
quickly greeted with a chorus of booing as he left the bus. We all then
left the bus and began the process, which was like a sketch from *Saturday Night Live*, the telling of which would make a good two-beer story
for some other time. The old drill sergeant was almost right. Nearly
everyone passed. Those who did not pass were given orders as to when
they should return. Needless to say, the trip home was far less festive.

"When I got back home, I went to the draft board office and asked
to talk with whomever was in charge. I explained that I only needed a
six-month extension to finish my degree. The woman to whom I was trying to make my case immediately said, "No." I urged her to reconsider
and argued that, with my degree, I would be much more valuable to the
country since there was a shortage of metallurgical engineers in the military, and we were needed for the development of new systems. She then
indicated that she would check into the "fantastic story" that I had told
her. Several weeks later, I received a card with a six-month extension.

"During the extension period, I did complete my degree. More
importantly, President Nixon implemented the draft lottery, and I got
a number so high that the Russians would have had to be at the gates of
Denver before they got to my number. I had gotten beyond the two hur-
dles that were impeding the start of my career. I had earned my bachelor's degree in Metallurgical Engineering from Lehigh University. I also
held an associate's degree in Mechanical Engineering from Waterbury
State Technical Institute which I had earned prior to attending Lehigh.
I had multiple job offers, but I was attracted to one particular prospect.
I had an academic understanding of static and dynamic physics as well
as extensive knowledge of the fundamentals of steel metallurgy. Now it
was time to put it all to work in the real world where they made things
that stood up to the stress of everyday usage. The place I was attracted
to was an excellent place to learn. The company had assembled a team
of spring industry experts, all with strong academic backgrounds tem-
pered by years of experience in the factory. I reported for an interview
with the director of research at the research and development center of
the largest spring manufacturer in the country, Associated Spring Company, in Bristol, Connecticut. The interview was lengthy and covered a
lot of topics. Perry, the director, had a distinguished career as an engineer, which included time with the U.S. Army as the coordinator with
Colt Firearms during the Second World War that produced the M-1 rifle
that helped win the war. As the interview was about to conclude, Perry

looked over at me and asked about the pin on my lapel. I responded with a smile, indicating that the pin was an eagle, a pin that I had earned when becoming an Eagle Scout. With a broad smile, Perry looked at me and said, "I was an Eagle Scout too. You have the job." In true military fashion, I was assigned two mentors, an experienced metallurgist and Joe, the chief engineer for the company. Joe had only about a year to go before retirement. He was one of the most remarkable engineers I had ever met. He had graduated from Yale many years earlier with a degree in English literature. When he graduated from Yale, he really had no more interest in pursuing more college education and could not afford any more. Like so many young people today, Joe had a degree that did not provide him with any employment opportunities. That was no impediment for Joe. He talked his way into a job in sales at Associated Spring in Bristol, Connecticut. He quickly discovered that sales was not his calling. He noticed that the engineers seemed to make pretty good money, so he persuaded the chief engineer to give him a chance. Well, Joe took to engineering like a duck to water. He was an avid reader. He acquired textbooks and articles on spring design. He taught himself physics, static and dynamic, as well as calculus. He then plunged head long into his work, trying to get involved in every problem that came along. I asked him how he did it, and he replied, "With a lot of time in the library and the motivation of providing for my family." He was truly the one in a million that could have accomplished all that he did. One of the first things Joe drilled into me was the concept that a spring was the ultimate demonstration of Newton's First Law of Motion: For every action, there is an equal and opposite reaction. When you apply a load to a spring, it transfers the load down the spring until it reaches the end, then pushes back with the same but opposite force. It is like throwing a rock into a pond. The wave moves to the shore, then stops when the shore blocks it (equal but opposite) and sends it back. The wave in a spring is almost undetectable at low speeds but can affect its performance at very high speeds, a dynamic issue. There were many other lessons to come. I think Joe liked working with me because I was eager to learn and apply all the lessons to how different materials would react. Joe was a great teacher.

"One day I noticed Perry and Joe in what looked like a very animated conversation. Soon after that, Joe appeared in my office and asked if I would accompany him and Perry to the corporate library for a meeting. This was very unusual, as we never had meetings in the library because it was buried in the center of the research center with no windows. There were several people in the room when we arrived. Perry introduced Joe and me to the others. One gentleman was a former colleague of Perry's from his days at Colt. The other gentlemen were engineers from a government arsenal that I recognized as the name of the arsenal that had been dragged through the mud as the supplier of "faulty ammunition" that had caused so many M-16 weapons to misfire during the Tet offensive in Vietnam. One of the men from the arsenal asked if I had a security clearance. Perry said that I did not have a security clearance but that both he and Joe could assure them that I was OK. After a few minutes of discussion, they decided to let me stay. The door was closed and locked. A movie projector was produced, and we were shown film in slow motion of an M-16, with the recoil spring exposed, being fired at different speeds. At high cycling speeds, the spring would leave its secure position and not allow the spent cartridge to be expelled, preventing the insertion of the next cartridge. It is like a series of tsunami waves hitting the shore and being pushed back. The wave action gets so frequent and builds up to the point that the shore is overwhelmed. The waves are not pushed back by the shore, and the shore is overwhelmed with flooding. The high-speed photography was impressive. At high cycling speeds, the waves began to come so fast that the first wave had not completed its cycle when the next one came. The cause of the jamming was obvious. It was clear to the Associated Spring people why there was a jamming problem. Spring engineers refer to this problem as surging. At low speeds, the wave action of the spring allows for the compressed spring to react and expand and push back. At very high speeds, the waves are coming rapidly, one on top of the other, overwhelming the ability of the spring to push back and eject the spent cartridge. I was astounded at what I had seen. Any competent spring engineer could calculate what speeds would produce this phenomenon. Needless to say, old Joe had taught me how to do it and why it was necessary. Quality control people would describe this as the root cause for the weapon's malfunction. All the other things like unclean weapon, ammunition charge or failure to chrome the barrel were, at best, contributing factors. The spring design was the fundamental root cause of the jamming problem for the M-16.

"The arsenal people seemed surprised at what they heard from our people as to the cause of the jamming. They asked Joe if he could solve the problem. Joe answered with an emphatic, "Yes!" He told them that he needed just a few days. He made some prototype springs that were designed to minimize the surging problem. The solution was pretty simple: If the spring was made out of braided wire like the cables on a suspension bridge instead of a single strand, it greatly reduced the chances of surging at high speeds. The braided wire, with strands rubbing against each other, frustrates the surging phenomenon at high cycling speeds. Joe shared with me the design and how to calculate the spring parameters. He then told me that he had actually used the same solution on a problem that had occurred during the Second World War.

"We were not aware of who all was involved in the decision-making process regarding our proposed solution, but we never heard back. The arsenal engineers, clearly, suspected a problem with the spring. Why else would they have prepared an M-16 so that the spring could be observed, with high-speed photography, unseating with rapid cycling? Were there liability concerns or concerns about a public backlash against the government if what we had determined to be the cause of the problem had been made public? Whatever the reason or reasons, the findings at our meeting got buried, everything else got blamed for the problem and emphasis was placed on chroming the inside of the barrel, cleaning and changing the ammunition to mitigate the problem.

"The military after-action report never recognized the root cause of the problem. A panel of military brass, college academics, and Pentagon bureaucrats never addressed the real issue. Did they ever talk to the spring experts after it was determined that the spring design was the problem? Not to our knowledge. The ways of Washington have never changed. Young men and women can die as long as you do not embarrass bureaucrats, generals, politicians or lobbyists. If you google the spring in the AK-47, you will find that they used a design similar to the one Joe proposed for the M-16, a braided wire spring. At the end of the meeting, I was told that what I had witnessed was classified, and I could not tell anyone about what I had witnessed. Fifty years have passed since that meeting, and Reuel shared an early draft of his book with me. After reading it and the stories of real heroes like Jim and Reuel, I decided to share my story and my frustrations."

IN SUMMARY: The military did indeed send our troops into battle in Vietnam with a defective weapon. The weapon that was fired and jammed during the evaluation that Dan attended was clean, with no worn parts and no pitted barrel. When spring and metallurgical experts at the Associated Spring Company viewed the slow-motion photography of the M-16 firing in automatic mode and jamming, they determined that the problem was in the design of the extractor spring which was a single strand of coiled wire which would function fine with anything other than the rapid cycling that occurred in the full automatic mode.

However, in the rapid cycling mode, such a spring displayed a phenomenon, known as surging, that would not allow for ejection of a spent cartridge and would cause the weapon to jam. It was explained that this action by a single strand spring could be remedied with a braided wire spring that would minimize surging. Such a spring would be more costly to produce than the single strand spring. The government officials never embraced the braided spring solution. Maybe it was the cost. Maybe it was because they didn't dare let the word get out that such a

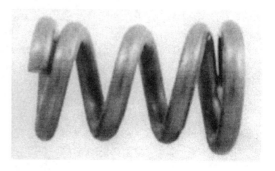

The M-16 single strand ejector spring.

defective weapon had been provided to our troops and had cost so many of them their lives, all over a defective spring design. Instead, cleaning was emphasized, the barrel was chromed on the inside, and the ammunition load was changed. They danced all around the basic problem when they simply needed to modify the weapon with a braided spring. The enemy had the very reliable AK-47. When I searched the internet for photos of the extractor spring used in the AK-47, I found a photo, and it was a braided spring.

The M-4 carbine which has replaced the M-16 has also had some issues with jamming. When I checked the internet for the design of the extractor spring used in the M-4 carbine, I found that it was also a single strand spring. The military-industrial complex failed our troops in Vietnam. They sent our troops into battle with a defective weapon. Then, when the solution was presented to them, for whatever reason, it was not adopted. Many of the names on the black, granite wall in Washington, D.C., would not be there except for the failure of the military to provide a fully functional weapon that functioned without fail at all rates of cycling. So many would not make it to a medical unit. They were slaughtered by an enemy that was armed with a weapon that was equipped with a braided extractor spring that did not cause jamming. What a shame.

The braided wire AK-47 ejector spring.

INDEX

AK-47 115, 192, 213, 219, 220
All in the Family 63
Apollo 11 14
Apollo 13 19, 20

"The Bear" 54, 58
Berry Plan 10
Black Cloud 55
Blizzard of 1978 145, 146
Brent 9, 63, 111, 164
Burns and Novick 207

Calley, William 32, 80, 180
Camp Bullis 23
chaplain 56, 79
Collins, John Norman 14
Cuban Missile Crisis 35

DeBakey, Dr. Michael 129
Detroit riots 9
Detroit Tigers 13
Dewey Canyon III protests 189
Diem Ngo Dinh 37
Dr. S 136, 137, 149

Flint Police Department 35
Fonda, Jane 129
Franks, Gen. Fred 192, 103

Gaylord, Michigan 13
Genesee County Medical Society 10
Geer, Col. Thomas 59, 87, 89
Gene 94, 95, 96
Gray, Richard Joseph 100
"Gross Charlie" 54
Gus 56, 94

Herb 36
Ho Chi Minh 17, 209, 210
Holden Red Stamps 33
Hyde Park 30

Kennedy, Pres. John F. 37, 207, 208
Kent State 20, 191
Kerry, John 190
King, Martin Luther, Jr. 9

LeDuan 17
LeGree, Sgt. William 33
"The Lion" 55, 67
Lolich, Mickey 13

M 16 1, 31, 213–214, 218–220
Mansfield, Sen. Mike 103
McGrory, Mary 189, 190, 191
McKinley Junior High School 11, 142
McLaren General Hospital 10, 15, 17, 18, 19, 21, 136, 147
Mendenhall, Colonel 24
My Li 32

Nixon, Pres. Richard 20, 66, 71, 100, 189, 190, 216

obligated volunteer 10
Oswald, Lee Harvey 37

Pentagon Papers 103
Puerto Rican Nationalists 33

"The Rabbit" 55, 57, 89

Saint Joseph Mercy Hospital, Flint 15, 16, 18, 21
science professor 10
Seaboard World Airways 41
Suchon, Clarence Myron 78
surging 218

TET Offensive 9, 218

"The Wizard" 54